# Endorsements for *The Smart Stepfamily* by Ron Deal

"This book offers clear advice on how to solve the common challenges faced by all who enter a second marriage with children. I highly recommended the first edition, and I am even more excited about this new edition."

—from the foreword by Gary Chapman, PhD,
author of *The Five Love Languages*

"Ron Deal has given the church and stepfamilies a real gem. . . . He compassionately and competently describes the spiritual and relational challenges facing stepfamilies. Ron provides practical and wise instruction for successfully navigating the stepfamily journey. *The Smart Stepfamily* is the best book available for stepfamilies that I've seen. . . . Buy it, read it, and share it with a friend."

—Dr. Dennis Rainey, president, FamilyLife®,
and author of *Stepping Up*

"*The Smart Stepfamily* has become THE go-to book for anyone interested in the difficult task of blending a family. We've pointed countless couples to this outstanding resource. And this revised and updated edition is better than ever!"

—Drs. Les and Leslie Parrott, founders
of MarriageMentoring.com, and authors of
*Saving Your Second Marriage Before It Starts*

"Ron Deal has, by far, the best material available on stepfamilies. The insights and suggestions he shares work. Every stepfamily will benefit from reading this book."

—H. Norman Wright, licensed marriage, family, and child therapist,
founder of Christian Marriage Enrichment, and author

"I love this book! It adds an important dimension to the understanding of stepfamilies and reads as if sitting down with wise friends. Written on the 'information is power' premise, *The Smart Stepfamily* weaves together a review of biblical materials, current psychological and sociological research, best practices, practical insights, and anecdotal stories to educate and support stepfamilies and the clergy who serve them."

—Dr. Margorie Engel, former president and CEO,
Stepfamily Association of America

"I have long recommended Ron Deal's work as the very best for stepfamilies. If you are looking for a clear, hands-on resource to strengthen your family from a deeply Christian perspective, you've come to the right place."

—Scott M. Stanley, PhD, research professor, University
of Denver, and coauthor of *A Lasting Promise*

"When people come up to me at a parenting seminar and are looking for a great resource on stepparenting, I give them two words: Ron Deal. I believe Ron Deal's insight is the very best in America on this subject. This book is practical, positive, and brings hope. *The Smart Stepfamily* is my 'go to' resource for this important subject."

—Jim Burns, PhD, president, HomeWord, and author of
*Confident Parenting* and *Creating an Intimate Marriage*

"Ron Deal is the 'go-to-guy' for stepfamilies. His revision of *The Smart Stepfamily* is practical, insightful, biblical, and just plain fabulous!! Today's stepfamily is hurting, and Ron reveals how to overcome the complexities and create a marriage that can go the distance. With the vast number of stepfamilies, this resource should be in the hands of every pastor, church leader, and marriage ministry."

—Laura Petherbridge, author, international speaker,
and founder of Sisterhood of Stepmoms

"Ron Deal's new edition of *The Smart Stepfamily* is a must-have resource for remarried couples who are just starting out or who have been on the stepfamily journey for decades. Ron's personal experience of loss since the first edition has intensified his compassion for the challenges of remarried couples.

"The combination of updated research, practical advice, and related stories provides excellent direction for stepfamilies and remarried couples. The hazards in the trenches of stepfamily life can be conquered through redemption and forgiveness. Honestly, the resources, research, and encouragement bear witness to our personal experience of blending a family into a new hopeful legacy!"

—Gil and Brenda Stuart, authors and
codirectors, Restored and Remarried

"This book is *vital* for all stepfamilies and for the professionals and clergy who serve them. It's the first book I recommend when someone asks about resources for stepfamilies. Yes, it's partly because all the information and the practices suggested are empirically sound; but mostly it's because Ron shares his wealth of knowledge and experience with an open, loving, and generous heart. You will be comforted, uplifted, and empowered."

—Dr. Francesca Adler-Baeder, professor of human development
and family studies, director of the National Stepfamily
Resource Center, Auburn University, Alabama

THE
**SMART**
STEPFAMILY

## Books by Ron L. Deal

# THE
# SMART
# STEPFAMILY

**7** Steps to a Healthy Family

# RON L. DEAL

BETHANY HOUSE PUBLISHERS
*a division of Baker Publishing Group*
Minneapolis, Minnesota

© 2002, 2014 by Ron L. Deal

Published by Bethany House Publishers
11400 Hampshire Avenue South
Bloomington, Minnesota 55438
www.bethanyhouse.com

Bethany House Publishers is a division of
Baker Publishing Group, Grand Rapids, Michigan

Printed in the United States of America

This edition published 2014

Library of Congress Cataloging-in-Publication Data
Deal, Ron L.
    The smart stepfamily : seven steps to a healthy family / Ron L. Deal ; foreword by Gary Chapman. — Revised and expanded edition.
        pages cm
    Includes bibliographical references.
    Summary: "Stepfamily expert addresses key concerns and practical issues facing every stepfamily"— Provided by publisher.
    ISBN 978-0-7642-1206-2 (pbk. : alk. paper)
    1. Stepfamilies. 2. Remarried people—Family relationships. 3. Stepparents. 4. Parenting. 5. Stepfamilies—Psychological aspects. I. Title.
HQ759.92.D4 2014
306.8747—dc23                                                                2014003656

Cover design by Eric Walljasper

15   16   17   18   19   20   21       8   7   6   5   4   3   2

To my wife and best friend, Nan
Three diamonds
All my love, for all my life

# Contents

# Foreword

Not all stepfamilies are alike. Some have young children; others, teenagers or young adults. Some are the result of divorce, while others come after the death of a spouse. However, there is one thing every stepfamily has in common: family members have a history that involved at least one other parent and spouse. Memories of the past may be pleasant or painful, but those memories do influence attitudes and emotions.

The high divorce rate in first marriages indicates that building a loving, supportive, caring marital relationship is not easy. However, those who succeed find marriage to be very satisfying. The fact that the divorce rate is higher for second marriages indicates that building a second marriage is even more difficult. Those who succeed find it worth the effort.

For those who have been widowed, the first marriage may have been a wonderful relationship or one with many struggles. If the relationship was fulfilling, they anticipate the second marriage will be fully as good as the first. But without help, many of them may be disappointed.

Almost every week someone says to me, "Have you written anything on blended families?" (sometimes they say stepfamilies). My answer is always the same: "No, but I know someone who has." I then recommend *The Smart Stepfamily* by Ron Deal. I recommend this book with confidence because I know the ideas that Ron shares are practical. The first edition of the book made a vital contribution to the field of marriage and family ministry. Ron was one of the first to identify the challenges of stepfamilies and to offer a road to success. Many pastors and counselors use *The Smart Stepfamily* in their premarital counseling for couples who are getting married for the second or third time. Parent educators use it in helping those parents who are bringing children into a new family setting.

*The Smart Stepfamily* has awakened the church to the need of stepfamily ministry. I remember the couple who said to me a year after I had recommended the book, "Thanks for sharing with us Ron Deal's book on stepfamilies. It has been a lifesaver for us." I will continue to highly recommend this book to all couples who are involved in bringing two families together.

This new edition is packed with even more practical tools to strengthen stepfamilies. It also includes information for couples who are dating and contemplating creating a stepfamily. The research in the book has been updated and new guidance is given on money management and estate planning, which are often areas of conflict in stepfamilies. Ron discusses the pros and cons of adoption. You will also find realistic ways to approach stepsibling relationships, parent alienation syndrome, and adult stepfamilies.

One of the reasons this book is so helpful to couples is that Ron does not write from an ivory tower. For twenty years he has invested his life in helping couples create healthy relationships. As a counselor, he has taken couples where they are and led them to where they wanted to be when they got married. No one enters a second marriage with the desire to repeat the failures of the first. And yet, without help, many of them do.

Not everyone can find a counselor who is equipped to deal with the common struggles of stepfamilies. However, when you read *The Smart Stepfamily* you will find yourself sitting in the office of a counselor with great experience.

No two stepfamilies are alike, but this book offers clear advice on how to solve the common challenges faced by all who enter a second marriage with children. I highly recommended the first edition, and I am even more excited about this new edition.

—Gary Chapman, PhD, author of *The Five Love Languages*

# Preface to the Revised Edition

A lot has happened since 1997, when I first started writing this book (which was first published in 2002). More specifically, a lot has happened with families and with me personally; together these changes necessitated in my mind the need for a revised and expanded edition of this book. More on these changes in a moment.

A few things, however, have not changed. For one, the core principles of this book—which work, by the way. Thousands have written me through the years expressing their appreciation for the key steps outlined in this book. Consider this post from Lisa:

> I read *The Smart Stepfamily* four years ago when I remarried. It was such a help and truly helped me to STAY married! You helped me realize how difficult stepfamily bonding would be and you were right! My first marriage of twenty-one years ended quite suddenly. When I remarried, my three daughters were seventeen, nineteen, and twenty-one. My stepson was nineteen, and his dad, my now husband, had been single for fifteen years before we married. One year after we married, my stepson came to live with us for two years. Then my youngest daughter moved in! Your wise advice helped me to be extremely patient, and slowly all the relationships are stabilizing.

Lisa, like many people, experienced multiple transitions and dynamics in her family that she couldn't control, but the principles she learned in this book prepared her to cope.

I could also tell you of others who have benefitted from this book. For example, I could tell you about a widow and widower who married later in life and found marriage and stepparenting far more difficult than they had anticipated, but who now have a healthy, growing family.

I could tell you about a couple with a complicated history, including multiple divorces, seven children, four grandchildren, substantial financial assets, and a new child born to the marriage, that is strong and loving each other through challenges with ex-spouses and cancer.

I could tell you about dating couples who decided to give more time to dating before jumping into marriage only to write me a few years into the marriage and thank me for helping to ease their transition to becoming a family. Apparently their patience paid off.

I could tell you about dating couples who decided not to marry at all—and thanked me for helping them to "dodge a bullet."

And I could tell you about a dedicated thirty-year-old Christian who shouted cuss words at her father when he told her he was getting remarried, but who five years later was showering words of love and affirmation on her stepmom on a national radio broadcast. They were all helped by this book—and I believe you will be too, if you apply the concepts to your family with wisdom and prayer.

But while the core principles of the first edition of this book have not changed (I think you'll love the new material added to this revised edition), some things have. From a cultural perspective, stepfamilies, for example, have become even more prevalent in American society and in cultures around the world than they were twelve years ago. One study found that in America today, 40 percent of married couples with children are stepcouples (a term I will use throughout the book to refer to couples in which one or both of them had a child from a previous relationship before they married).[1] The specific statistics vary by race (55 percent of African American, 39 percent of white, and 36 percent of Hispanic married couples with kids are stepcouples), but the conclusion is the same—stepfamilies are part of the norm in our culture, comprising a huge people group that must be considered part of mainstream American life.

This increase in stepfamilies has also been witnessed in countries around the world. When I first released this book, I had no idea it would be purchased in places like Australia, Great Britain, South Africa, Canada, Singapore, New Zealand, etc., or that I would be interviewed by reporters and radio broadcasters throughout the world. I suppose, though, I should have anticipated that the number of stepfamilies around the world would increase, and with it, the demand for practical help.

Many other social changes have occurred as well:

- The most common societal term for stepfamilies has shifted from stepfamily to blended family (although in Europe and Australia the most commonly searched term is still *stepfamily* or a derivative, such as *stepparent*).
- Blended families and cohabiting stepcouples (87 percent of cohabiting couples with children are stepcouples)[2] are a common premise for TV shows and movies.
- There is a national Stepfamily Day (September 16).
- Stepfamily ministry has slowly become a recognized area of marriage and family ministry.

I should mention here that the original edition of this book concluded with a chapter on stepfamily ministry and the church. My editor asked me why a book for stepcouples needed a chapter on ministry. I defended the strategy by saying, "You must understand that couples in stepfamilies are the ones starting small groups and teaching ministries, not the pastors. It's grassroots at this point. We have to empower couples to do this or it won't get done." That was true at the time. However, I'm pleased to say that the tide has shifted; now it is pastors who primarily ask for training, resources, or conference events in their churches. Though I still want to encourage couples to ignite ministry groups in their communities, we opted in this edition of the book to delete the chapter on stepfamily ministry (in part to make room for more content on stepfamily living). However, you can access that and other free bonus material at SmartStepfamilies.com/view/learn.

There has also been an increase in stepfamily research; we simply know more about stepfamilies than we used to. Specifically, we know more about what makes stepfamilies work and how they can overcome their challenges. I will offer these new insights throughout this edition.

There have been a lot of changes in my life as well that have changed my writing, speaking, and insight into stepfamily living (anyone who tells you that the personal lives of authors doesn't impact their writing is sorely misguided). In brief, a family tragedy has changed me and has opened my eyes to what the first volume of this book failed to offer.

I'll share more details throughout this book, but in 2009, my middle son, Connor, died at the age of twelve. His body was attacked by MRSA, a staph infection that no one saw coming. His journey from first symptom to death lasted just ten days. My family's journey through grief will last until we meet him again in eternity. I've shared various aspects of this experience in other books, *The Smart Stepdad* and *Dating and the Single Parent* specifically, and I've talked about my loss in conferences throughout the country. When I looked back at the first edition of this book, I realized I needed to say more about the impact of grief. Loss is a universal experience among both children and adults in stepfamilies. Losing a child is in some ways far different from losing a spouse to death or for a child losing their family to divorce, but in other ways, it is very similar. Throughout this revised edition, I will share with you my insights and lessons learned as they pertain to loss, your family, parenting, and trusting again.*

For over a decade this book has, to my delight, offered practical help to families around the world. A few things have changed over that time; a few things haven't. One more that hasn't changed is my desire to bring a blessing to your home. I pray that something you read offers hope, promise, and practical help for your life.

---

**The following Bonus Material and Deleted Chapters
from the first edition are available free online:**

- Smart Questions, Smart Answers—Topics include difficult ex-spouses, the needs of children, co-parenting strategies, stepparenting, military stepfamilies, dealing with family conflict, stepgrandparenting, and more.
- Ministering to Stepfamilies—I estimate that traditional marriage ministry and parent training are about half of what stepfamily couples need. Learn what your congregation can do to prevent redivorce and break the generational cycle of divorce.

This and more is available at SmartStepfamilies.com/view/learn.

---

\* To learn more about the nonprofit we have created in Connor's memory and to hear his beautiful voice, visit ConnorsSong.com.

# Acknowledgments

*for the Revised and Expanded Edition*

The dedication of Bethany House Publishers to enriching the lives of stepfamilies is amazing. When I wrote the first edition of this book, I had no idea that Bethany House and I would go on to publish many more books together or that they would come to me a decade after this book was first released and inquire about a revised and expanded edition. They have taken many risks on behalf of blended families and are to be commended. It has been a wonderful partnership. To everyone at Bethany House, I say thank you. Specifically, I should mention Ellen Chalifoux, Carra Carr, Brett Benson, Tim Peterson, Julie Smith, Steve Oates, and Jim Parrish. What a team!

To my agent, Chip MacGregor, again I say, "You're the best." Two parts coach, one part counselor, three parts strategist, and best-part friend.

Nan, none of this would happen without your support. Thanks for tolerating my five a.m. writing schedule. And thank you for giving your blessing for me to share our sacred sorrow about Connor with others.

A very special word of appreciation goes to all the families who have shared their lives and stories with me through the years. You have taught me much about the stepfamily journey and in turn have been a blessing to others.

And finally, to the One who gives me eternal hope and life and purpose, I have very little to give but my praise. It's all yours.

# Acknowledgments

*for the First Edition*

Like any healthy stepfamily, this book has taken a long time to develop. And like any healthy stepfamily, this book is the result of a careful integration of people, ideas, backgrounds, and relationships. I am grateful to so many who have offered their encouragement and talent along the way—this book could not have been created without your help.

Special appreciation goes to Ashleigh Short Givens and David and Robbie Hutchins for their early reviews of the manuscript and technical writing input. You helped this project get noticed and ultimately published—thank you. Also, a special thank-you goes to Rebecca Warnick for her administrative support and to the Southwest Church of Christ elders for their encouragement. Your vision for a family ministry that extends beyond the Jonesboro community has resulted in a ministry whose borders, by God's grace, are expanding daily. I couldn't have done this without your blessing.

Others whose friendship and professionalism have made this journey possible include H. Norman Wright, Steve Laube and the Bethany House team, Dr. Margorie Engel and the Stepfamily Association of America's board of directors and institute faculty, and the researchers and clinicians whose work is referenced throughout this book. I must especially acknowledge the work and influence of Dr. Emily Visher, whose life has come to an end, but whose inspiration and research will live on. This book stands on the shoulders of her scholarly research, shared writing with her husband,

John, and personal stepfamily experience. Yet equally impacting was her encouragement of me as a young writer and teacher. I am exceedingly grateful for her influence and wisdom. Also, to the original Southwest Step-by-Step education group, I say thanks. You boldly supported each other and shared your stories with me so that I might help others. You have blessed my life; I hope you have been blessed in return.

To my dearest friends and spiritual partners, Randy and Judy Lewis, Gregg and Elisa Barden, Shawn and Arlene Mayes, and Jeff and Misty Floyd—your encouragement and faith have challenged me to be used by God through this book and seminar ministry. Let's give him the glory!

# Introduction

Have you ever tried to put together a 3-D jigsaw puzzle without instructions and without a picture on the box to show you what the final product should look like? Try adding a blindfold. Sounds impossible, doesn't it? In fact, it may not even sound fun to try. Attempt to combine members of two (or more) different households and you'll encounter similar frustrations.

Putting together or *integrating* a stepfamily is one of the most difficult tasks for any family in America today. Integration involves combining two unique family histories and styles, various personalities and preferences, differing traditions, relational pasts and loyalties. Yet most people make the decision to bring two families together without consulting any guidelines or instructions or taking the time to develop a shared image of what the final jigsaw puzzle will look like (e.g., how the stepfamily will feel, operate, and conduct itself). Blinded with a well-intentioned ignorance, couples march down the aisle a second or third time only to discover that the building process is much more difficult than they anticipated, especially in the beginning.

But here's the good news that thousands of couples and families have learned from reading this book: Take your blindfold off and learn what a healthy blended family is and does, and the odds of your success increase dramatically. When you know how to be a smart stepfamily, integration, or the merging of your two families, is accelerated and the rewards to both children and adults increase dramatically.

---

**Adult Stepfamilies**

Later-life couples with adult children, or what we might call adult stepfamilies, often mistakenly assume that because their children are out of the home the family won't have difficulty integrating. They quickly realize that they have just as many adjustments and challenges as stepfamilies with younger children. The specific stressors will vary, but the emotional demands are similar.

---

## Working Smarter, Not Harder

The purpose of this book is to give you a healthy picture of a successful stepfamily. And believe it or not, it can be done *if* you work smarter, not harder. Working smarter essentially means understanding the dynamics of stepfamily life and development and making intentional decisions about how you will grow together emotionally, psychologically, and spiritually.

In the book *The Smart Stepmom*, Laura Petherbridge and I tell the story of a never-married forty-something woman who became a stepmother when she married a man with three teenage daughters. The first couple of years she and her husband struggled with parenting issues; no matter what the subject, they seemed to end up on different sides. Then one day something dawned on the stepmom. She put it this way, "I just figured out that I live in a stepfamily, but my husband doesn't." What she meant was that her husband was a married man with three daughters and didn't see his relationship with his wife or kids as competing, nor did he feel like he was choosing sides if he shared a daughter's perspective with his wife. However, the experience of the home for the stepmom was very different. She constantly felt on pins and needles trying to gain favor with the girls and status as a parent figure, and she felt jealous of her husband's attempts to get her to see things from the kids' point of view.

That insight not only made her smarter, it caused her to stop working harder. For example, she let go of the feeling that she had to get her husband to see everything from her perspective (something that caused her to argue with him to no end). This gave birth to a strange peace within her even when her husband seemed not to understand her plight as a stepmom. How could he understand? His experience of the family was going to be different. Didn't this mean she was going to be isolated in her experience?

Ironically, no. Once she relaxed from trying to change her husband's mind all the time, she noticed that he had been prioritizing her all along. Each smart step resulted in another smart step that gradually, but powerfully, shifted the family toward health. Not every aspect of the family became comfortable, but many things improved significantly.

If you are currently married and perhaps finding that your three-dimensional puzzle is resting on a fragile foundation, read this book with an eye for what you can change. Once you've developed concrete ideas for putting the pieces of your family together, begin working the plan cautiously but with much determination. You'll be amazed at God's power to heal your heartaches and turn your unstable or crumbling puzzle into an edifice that is safe, beautiful, and built on a firm foundation.

If you are currently single, divorced, or widowed and are considering marriage, and if one or both of you have children, you've turned to the right source. There are many hidden challenges in stepfamily life, and you need to be as prepared as you possibly can be. Taking off your blindfold and seeing clearly the journey ahead is the best choice you can make. Indeed, your decision to form a stepfamily by marriage needs to be an informed choice; otherwise you may regret the decision once the challenges hit you head-on. Smart stepfamilies can bring great joy and fulfillment to the lives of children and adults. But please understand that a great deal of work and determination are required to develop a healthy stepfamily. You cannot afford to go into marriage armed only with "better than last time" intentions. The process demands that you know and understand more than that. This book will tell you what you need to know.

Please know that this book has grown out of the belief that the home is the primary context in which we learn and experience the character of love. It is my firm belief that stepfamilies, just as biological families, can be homes of love. Compared to biological families, a few challenges will be different and some will be the same. But love can be what holds the jigsaw pieces of the smart stepfamily together, resulting not in a bunch of broken, disconnected pieces, but a home.

I am more optimistic than ever about the redemptive power of healthy stepfamilies. I'll talk about this further in chapter 1, but you should know right now that God wants to work through your current marriage, parenting, and family relationships to redeem your story of loss, sadness, heartbreak, and brokenness, to offer healing, and to turn your home into a haven of safety that blesses your children. How life is now and how you got here may not have been how you would have written the script, but given that you're in the middle of the story already, God wants to author a redemptive narrative to the remaining chapters. Your family story is still being written and the best is yet to come.

Now, speaking of a story, let me give you some perspective on the typical stepfamily story . . . from beginning to end, or should I say, from Egypt to the Promised Land.

The people of Israel groaned because of their slavery and cried out for help. Their cry for rescue from slavery came up to God. And God heard their groaning, and God remembered his covenant with Abraham, with Isaac, and with Jacob. God saw the people of Israel—and God knew. [He was concerned about them.]

Exodus 2:23–25

# PART ONE

# Headed for the Promised Land!

Can you imagine what freedom must have been like to the Israelites? For some four hundred years they had been oppressed by the Egyptians, held in bondage against their will, and forced to live as slaves. For years the Lord had heard their cries, and now the time had finally come for freedom. It's hard to imagine the joy, relief, and utter exuberance the Israelites must have felt. They were going home! But where, exactly, was home?

Moses, a rather unsung hero at the time, through God's power had become their leader. A pillar of cloud by day and a pillar of fire by night made it obvious that God was leading his people to the Promised Land. Yet the joy and celebration of being set free was soon quenched when the Israelites found themselves hemmed in by the Red Sea on one side and an angry Pharaoh—who had changed his mind about letting them go—and his army on the other. In their terror the Israelites cried out,

> Is it because there are no graves in Egypt that you have taken us away to die in the wilderness? What have you done to us in bringing us out of Egypt? Is not this what we said to you in Egypt: "Leave us alone that we may serve

the Egyptians"? For it would have been better for us to serve the Egyptians than to die in the wilderness.

Exodus 14:11–12

Did you catch that? Isn't it amazing how quickly, when under duress, the Israelites changed their tune? Just a few days before they had seen the mighty hand of God work on their behalf. Just a few days had passed since miracles had taken place to free them, and yet their joy and celebration turned to self-pity in a heartbeat. *Certainly we are going to die because of our horrible leader, Moses,* they thought. "What have you done to us?" they accused. And then you'll see, in my opinion, the most fascinating aspect of their response: "It would have been better for us to serve the Egyptians." This suggests they were *longing for the circumstances of slavery and oppression over freedom.* Freedom from slavery was what the Israelites pleaded for and yet oppression and bondage actually became attractive to them as soon as the journey became difficult. Their trust was gone, their self-pity took over, and they longed for safety. The security of slavery was often more inviting than the insecurity of traveling an unmarked road to an unknown destination. They just hadn't learned how to trust God to give purpose and provision in unfamiliar territory.

Many stepfamilies walk a similar path.

# Through Wilderness Wanderings

"Is it because there are no graves in Egypt that you have taken us away to die in the wilderness? What have you done to us in bringing us out of Egypt? Is not this what we said to you in Egypt: 'Leave us alone that we may serve the Egyptians'? For it would have been better for us to serve the Egyptians than to die in the wilderness."

And Moses said to the people, "Fear not, stand firm, and see the salvation of the Lord, which he will work for you today."

Exodus 14:11–13

Disillusionment is nearly a universal experience for the adults in stepfamilies, and it often occurs within a couple of years. Believing that remarriage will release them from the bondage of divorce, loss, loneliness, and painful emotions, couples load up their children and possessions and launch into the wilderness toward the Promised Land of marriage and family life. The wedding seems to mark a release from oppression. *At last,* they think, *I am loved and important again. I am free from the confines of single-parent living and my children will have the benefit of a two-parent family. This is going to be great!*

But just as with the Israelites, what often occurs for couples in step-families is a shift from celebration and positive expectation to self-pity. The realities and challenges of stepfamily living overwhelm unrealistic fantasies, and disillusionment sets in.

Remarriage or a stepfamily marriage for most adults seems to be their second (or third) chance on life. Already life hasn't worked out the way they planned, and to some degree or another life has been painful. But things are looking up—they've fallen in love again and the dream of a normal family life has returned. A new journey of hope has begun.

The journey, however, almost always takes some unexpected turns. For example, your spouse's dedication to his or her children was noble before the wedding, but now seems to be a challenge to your marriage; a teenager living in one of the other homes decides to live with you; parenting styles differ more than you expected, and conflict erupts frequently. The trip is filled with uncertainty, and couples realize they feel lost much of the time. Like the Israelites, people sometimes think, "Is this marriage going to die, too?" "Who is to blame for bringing me out to the wilderness?" "I feel trapped—maybe it would have been better to stay in Egypt." Meanwhile, the daily grind of stepfamily life continues and progress is slow. It seems like being lost in the wilderness.

Let me pause for a moment and make a quick prediction. Those of you who were feeling disillusioned before you picked up this book are now thinking, "Oh my, has Ron been peeking in our windows? How did he know I felt this way?" On the other hand, those of you who haven't yet reached a place where you feel caught between Pharaoh and his army and the Red Sea—usually dating or recently remarried couples—are thinking, "What is Ron trying to do, scare us to death?"

Let me assure you, I'm not trying to be a pessimist or a killjoy. I am trying to be realistic. I have spent more than twenty years as a stepfamily therapist, coach, educator, and researcher, and I've heard the stories enough to know what is normal. There are some stepfamilies whose journey from Egypt to the Promised Land is quick and painless, but for the vast majority, the journey takes much longer than anticipated. Because I care about your family, I promise to shoot straight with you—more important, I promise to guide you through the wilderness. But you do need to acknowledge that feeling lost in the wilderness is par for the course.

Let me share a different situation that is similar in creating disillusionment. Since the death of my son (the Preface provides some background to his death), I have a whole new set of life issues and circumstances that make me feel lost much of the time. How do I grieve well? How do I help my wife and other two sons grieve? How do I parent my sons—when should compassion for their sadness moderate my expectations and when does sympathy get in the way of instruction and discipline? When will this generalized depression about life go away, and how do I function as a father, husband, and employee in the meantime? Will life ever feel normal again? Do I always tell every new person I meet about Connor, and what do I do when they quickly skip over or flat-out ignore the largest piece of my life story? What do I have to do to feel normal in a crowd of people, instead of odd and like an outsider?

> ## Hold on to Hope
>
> Because "Hope deferred makes the heart sick, but a desire fulfilled is a tree of life" (Proverbs 13:12), make sure to hold on to hope. A common emotional experience for couples is first anticipation and excitement, then disillusionment and fear, then struggle and discouragement, then satisfaction and safety. Allow hope to see you through each season.

It's my guess that you, too, have a set of unanswered questions like this. There is a new normal in my life and yours—and much of it is unwelcomed. Much of it is not within our control and we have to find our way through. There's no going back. With God's help, we will find our way through the wilderness. As I implied, finding our way starts in part by acknowledging common stepfamily struggles and feelings in the journey.

## Don't Look Now; We're Being Pursued!

Just as the Israelites found themselves caught between the Red Sea and Pharaoh's army, so stepcouples frequently find themselves caught between the future and the past. Behind them, debilitating pain and loss from the days of bondage (divorce or death of a spouse) are quickly pursuing. In the present, feelings of anger, resentment, rejection, and guilt siphon energy from people's emotional tanks, while losses too numerous to count (especially for children) make for cautious emotional investments with new stepfamily members. In short, the pain of the past makes for a tremendous fear of the future. Consider these statements from the Thomas family:

BIOLOGICAL MOTHER, MEGAN: *"I'm afraid it's not going to work, and we'll get divorced. And then three times I've failed. I'm afraid Frank [her new husband] is going to get aggravated with his stepchildren—my kids—and he's going to walk because as he's already said, 'There's only so much I can take.' I'm afraid my kids are going to turn against me because they didn't want Frank as their stepfather. It would just be another failure."*

OLDER SON, JOHN (AGE SEVENTEEN): *"I'm afraid of getting close to anyone. I'm not very trusting. With all I've had to live through, I keep waiting for it to happen all over again—the constant blaming and getting stuck in the middle. And I won't let it ever happen again."*

MIDDLE DAUGHTER, SUSAN (AGE FIFTEEN): *"I ain't afraid of nothing. I'm not scared of anything. I mean, if you broke up, it wouldn't be the first time. I might be a little worried where we'd go or something like that. But as far as you breaking up, I mean, two times gets you ready for it to happen at any moment."*

YOUNGER SON, RANDY (AGE FOURTEEN): *"I try to get closer sometimes but then the fear happens and I hide out from doing things with Frank and keep farther apart from him than I should be. . . . I want to get close, but not too close, for fear of something that might happen in the future."*

STEPFATHER, FRANK: [regarding his marriage] *"I'm afraid to be in another relationship where I'm nobody and have no say about what's going on in the house.* [Regarding the stepchildren] *I'm afraid that if we don't change things right away, they're going to grow up and we'll never have a relationship. They'll just be stepkids who come and visit at holidays. I don't want it to be that way."*

It's easy to hear that the pain of their past is driving their fears of the future, which, in turn, is leading them to be guarded and untrusting in the present. If these heartaches and losses are not successfully resolved for this family (and yours), the result will be a tired, disillusioned couple unable to draw close to each other, let alone meet the emotional needs of their children. Painful emotions from the past must be resolved in order for you and your children to move on.

---

**Are These Fears Typical?**

Not all family members have this much fear. Kids, for example, can some-times be very excited about the new family, but they can be confused about it at the same time. Adult fears seem to escalate when dilemmas generate feelings of uncertainty. Fears are common; don't panic when facing them. Recognize them and the actions they lead you to take (these actions are often problematic). Focus on understanding fears and preventing them from determining your actions. Fearful responses are often experienced by others as unloving ones.

---

## Facing a Sea of Opposition

Blended families face a Sea of Opposition. Common uncharted waters include:

- achieving marital intimacy after being hurt
- parenting and stepparenting roles and rules
- questions of spiritual integrity and church involvement
- how to integrate the members of a stepfamily over time
- dealing with ex-spouses and co-parenting issues
- helping children emotionally and spiritually
- handling sexual pressures between stepsiblings
- issues of money management and financial autonomy

Be careful not to let these common issues change the direction of your heart. It's not uncommon for persons to start wondering, much like the Israelites did, if maybe they should return to the bondage of Egypt, that is, divorce or single-parent living. Sure, it was miserable and unfulfilling, but at least they knew what they had. Disillusionment gives birth to grumbling, complaining, and conflict. Emotions run high and problems escalate. Here is a common story: The stepparent, who from an outsider's position can more clearly see and feel the disharmony in the home, often voices this disillusionment first. The biological parent, who is still blinded by their strong relationship with their children, frequently discounts the stepparent's request for change. Slowly but surely, this builds distance and blame in the couple's relationship. To make matters worse, this often comes at a time when they are trying to figure out how to manage their family and really can't afford to be out of touch.

The temptation to return to Egypt continues: "What have I done? Maybe I should have stayed single. Maybe God has abandoned me." Wrong! While I doubt that the God of the universe will reveal a path to you with a cloud or pillar of fire as he did the Israelites, he has most certainly not abandoned you and will provide strength and direction for your journey, even when the path seems dismal.

If there is one message that stepfamilies need to hear, it's this: *There is a stepfamily Promised Land of marital intimacy, interpersonal connectedness, and spiritual redemption! God has not abandoned you. If you will listen, trust, and continue walking by faith, you will hear him confirming your journey, offering guidance and healing, and providing a path on dry ground. But you must trust him.* Don't be like most remarried couples who end their journey in divorce within the first three years; they quit before ever crossing the Sea of Opposition or finding the rewards on the other side. God beckons you to remain persistent and see your family through to the Promised Land. There is a reward to be gained. But you must hold God's hand and walk through your Sea of Opposition.

## Is the Journey Difficult for All Stepfamilies?

Stepfamilies vary greatly in composition and complexity. While it isn't always true, generally speaking the greater the complexity, the greater the family stress. For example, some stepfamilies have children from just one spouse and involve only one household. This usually occurs after the death of a parent and a remarriage to a stepparent without children. (This is not to imply that the death of a parent makes stepfamily living easy; it is just less complex.) Other stepfamilies are much more multifaceted with "yours, mine, and ours" children, two or more ex-spouses, plenty of stepparents and stepgrandparents, and visitation schedules to multiple households.

Not all stepfamilies have a difficult journey, but most will experience unexpected challenges. Some will face a great many barriers. It is important to remember that the number of barriers you face reflects neither on you nor on whether or not you should have married. When encountering opposition, some people convince themselves that it wasn't a good idea to marry in the first place. Then they begin looking for a way out.

When stepfamily life gets tough, remain dedicated to your commitment. A man once drove six hours to talk with me about his stepchildren and marriage. He hoped that once I heard him describe the Sea of Oppositions he was facing, I would give him "permission" to leave the marriage. I did not (and he was terribly annoyed). What I did do was agree with him that the marriage, in its present condition, was not healthy, nor was God honored by an angry, resentful relationship. I suggested that with guided help he could choose to work on his marriage and remain open to how the God of the impossible might provide a path through the Sea of Opposition. Furthermore, avoiding divorce by simply tolerating a miserable marriage, I suggested, does not honor God. Commitment requires that you strive for a better life together, even when you don't feel like putting forth your best effort or have convinced yourself the marriage should never have happened. Ironically, people who make the effort often discover the safe marriage they had given up on.

## A Quick Word to Dating Couples

To those of you who are perhaps engaged or considering remarriage, I am so glad you are reading this book now. I can't tell you how many couples attending my stepfamily seminars have said, "Why didn't anyone ever tell us these things before we married? We could have saved ourselves a lot of grief if we would have only known." May I suggest you learn from their experience? Keep reading with these intentions:

- Use this book to enlighten yourself to the possible struggles you may face in your stepfamily journey.
- Equip yourself and your relationship with practical strategies to meet the challenges.
- Use the stories and information here to help you make an informed decision about marriage.

Remarriage and stepfamily life can be filled with many blessings, but the journey probably won't start out that way. You'll have to work diligently to reach the Promised Land. To that end, have you truly considered the costs? Do you know what the costs are? This book will help you identify them. I've also written an entire book walking single parents and those dating them through the process of meeting someone, dating well, making decisions about marriage, and planning for stepfamily living—all with an awareness of the children throughout the process. I highly recommend you take the time to read *Dating and the Single Parent* so that you manage your dating and marital decisions with wisdom.

In addition, I recommend that you find a group of stepfamilies or a stepfamily couple in your church or community and ask them some questions:

- What do they wish they had known before they remarried?
- What are their three greatest challenges?
- How could they have better prepared themselves for stepfamily living?
- What painful emotions from the past did they not resolve well prior to remarriage?
- What blessings have they experienced at this point in their journey?

The lure of marriage is tremendous. *Finally,* you think, *someone to take care of me. I feel so good when I'm with them.* But stepfamily life is so much more than just your couple relationship; it also includes children, loss, and a variety of family complexities. In biological families, the couple's relationship (i.e., the marriage) provides the foundation to the family from day one. In stepfamilies, the parent-child bonds predate the couple's relationship, often making the marriage the weakest relationship in the home

### The Wrong Time to Date

Parenting responsibilities should impact the timing of dating. For example, I discourage dating if one child is struggling with emotional issues (anger or defiance, depression or anxiety) or is displaying prodigal behavior. These children need a focused, available parent, not one dividing their time. Plus, kids don't need to add to their concerns feeling unimportant or in competition with a parent's new love. Help your child through a difficult season, and then open yourself to romance. This order will also make the child's acceptance of a new stepfamily more likely should dating lead to marriage.

and vulnerable to family stress. Being in love with someone who "makes me feel good again" is just the beginning of what it takes to survive. In *Dating and the Single Parent,* I put it this way: "Coupleness" does not necessarily lead to "familyness." They are two separate processes; falling in love with a person does not necessarily mean you can be a family. So please, do yourself and your children a favor—find out everything you can about stepfamily living, and count the cost before deciding to marry. If after much prayer and dating you do marry, give it everything you've got, and trust God to lead you through.

> **Kids Talk**
>
> "I wish she would recognize her own impulsivity and emotional roller coaster. She does and says things without recognizing that to some extent our whole family is dating this guy." —Rachel, twenty-two years old[1]

## The God Who Heals

Shortly after escaping from Pharaoh's army, the Israelites journeyed through the Desert of Shur. For three days they traveled, and the only water they found was bitter and not fit for consumption. Again the people complained, and again God provided for his people. God had Moses throw a piece of wood into the unpalatable water, turning it sweet. God then refers to himself as Jehovah-Rophe, the "LORD who heals you" (Exodus 15:26 NIRV). In so doing, God declares a promise. If his people will listen to his voice and do what is right in his eyes, he will heal—he will make the bitter waters of their life sweet again.

I believe God is waiting for a chance to heal your past hurts and to eliminate all that pursues you. But that's not all he offers. He will provide strength to keep your commitments, and he will provide wisdom to overcome the obstacles that lie ahead. He wants you to be successful. But you can't rely on yourself. Depend on him and he will clear a path.

## Food for the Journey

Water was not all that God provided for the Israelites. He also caused manna and quail to rain down upon the people. Similarly, I suggest two

### Getting Smart Has Benefits

"We sing the praises of your seminar to everyone. God totally answered our prayer. It was five years of hard trials and not knowing what to do with our family and why certain members acted the way they did. God painted a clear picture through your conference. It has been eight months since the seminar and God has changed us so much. My family is awesome. The children are different because of it and so are we."
—David and Tracy

types of food to help nourish your journey: practical information and support from fellow travelers. This book will provide the practical stepfamily information. After laying down some key stepping-stones for the stepfamily journey, I will discuss common challenges to the stepfamily and provide practical guidance.

But don't stop there. I highly recommend you find another couple or a group of couples and meet together on a regular basis to study and encourage one another. Discussion questions for individual dating and married couples are included at the end of each chapter in this book, but just the two of you talking is not the same as meeting with a group of couples. I have been involved in support and therapy groups for a number of years, and stepfamily groups are among the most dynamic I've seen. The common stories that are shared and the pressures and crises that are experienced together create an incredible bond among group members. My small-group material, *The Smart Stepfamily Small Group Resource DVD* and accompanying *Participant's Guide*, is an educational resource you'll want to consider. Watching the teaching video and discussing the group questions will help you process the information in this book, internalize it, and apply it in your home. For more on leading an educational group or stepfamily ministry, see SmartStepfamilies.com/view/learn.

### Is It All Worth It?

Tim was remarried, and after three years he was just beginning to understand how difficult the journey was going to be. His life experience had shown him that the stepfamily journey can be tough, and now he was hearing me confirm that in a live seminar. During one of the breaks, this conscientious thirty-eight-year-old man asked an honest question: "I'm beginning to think the payoff can't be worth all this hard work. It feels like

I'm married to my wife, and she's still married to her kids. That makes it very hard for me to work at liking and accepting them. If you don't know what you'll have in a few years, is it worth the effort?"

He spoke for many people who silently wonder if they're heading down a dead-end street. My answer is no, you're not. A smart stepfamily *is* worth the effort. The Israelites discovered the Promised Land to be everything they dreamed. Not all stepfamilies have all their expectations realized, but with hard work and commitment, the rewards are worth striving for.

## Promised Land Rewards

Theresa, reflecting on her family's journey through the wilderness, contributed these thoughts to my website recently (SmartStepfamilies.com), and she is right on target:

> The change from being a single divorced family to a stepfamily has been very challenging . . . don't expect a miracle overnight. . . . God is always faithful in every situation and with Him as the central part of all your decisions you can make it through. It is a day-to-day process, and only putting your faith and trust in God will make things better. Having a stepfamily is very rewarding and it is worth working on!

At the heart of the stepfamily journey is the search for family identity. Knowing how to relate to one another, what to expect from yourself and the roles of others in the family—even how to introduce each other in public—are basic questions stepfamilies ask themselves repeatedly throughout their journey. And as stressful as this journey of family identity formation is, there are some rewards along the way, including:

- high-quality marital relationships
- a new marital heritage to celebrate
- a healthy family means healthier kids
- cooperation between homes results in well-disciplined children
- respect and care between stepparents and stepchildren
- multigenerational blessings in later-life stepfamilies

- experiencing love, extending grace
- redemption of your family story

### High-Quality Marital Relationships

Research of couples in stepfamilies—conducted by internationally recognized marriage and family researcher Dr. David Olson, president of Life Innovations, and me—confirms that couples in stepfamilies can create high-quality marital relationships. In our book *The Smart Stepfamily Marriage,* we detail the qualities of high-quality stepfamily marriages and reveal how couples can deepen their intimacy and gain relationship strength. Qualities like effective communication, the ability to resolve conflict well, a relational style that is flexible and adaptable, enjoying leisure activities together, and couple spirituality prove to be very predictive of a high-quality marital relationship.

In other words, couples can create mutually satisfying, intimate, God-honoring marriages within stepfamilies. Undoubtedly there are a number of unique barriers to overcome (see chapter 5), but remarriages can be healthy relationships. Furthermore, I've observed that couples who endure the adversity of the journey frequently have a bond that is powerful enough to withstand anything. There is strength and a sense of victory after surviving what for some is a difficult journey.

How long does it take for couples to find an increase of satisfaction? E. Mavis Hetherington reports in her highly scientific book *For Better or For Worse: Divorce Reconsidered*[2] that it takes most couples five to seven years to get through the tensions of stepfamily life to the point that their stress level declines to match that of a husband and wife in a first marriage. Furthermore, surviving the tumultuous early years common to stepfamily living seems to give couples a staying power that keeps them going . . . and growing. There is a honeymoon for couples in stepfamilies, but keep in mind, it comes at the end of the journey and not at the beginning.

### A New Marital Heritage to Celebrate

A strong stepfamily marriage is critical for the relational development of the children. Stepfamily children, especially those who have lived through a parental divorce, need to witness and learn from a healthy marital relationship. This counteracts the negative and destructive patterns of interaction they witnessed in their parent's previous marriage (and since the divorce). Instead of arguments filled with yelling and personal agendas, they watch two people who maintain a win-win attitude negotiate the best solution for their family. Instead of a distant relationship between two people living parallel lives, they witness two people giving time and attention to their relationship. Instead of an unbalanced relationship, where one spouse is constantly chasing an ever-distancing, never-available spouse, children see a husband and wife who continually seek to sacrifice for the other out of love. On the other hand, if children witness repeated marital breakups, the net effect is a weakening of the child's sense of permanency to marriage and an increased lack of trust in the people they love.[3]

It's worth mentioning that many children do not welcome their parent's remarriage, especially in the beginning. They may even be antagonistic toward the stepparent's efforts to join the family. This is normal, as children hold on to the dream that their biological parents will remarry. Despite the children's resistance, a strong stepfamily couple will have positive benefits for them over time. The key is to remember that during the early integration years, children may resent the stepparent's presence in the home. Maintain a long-term perspective and live as if a healthy marriage is just what the kids desire. Someday they may come to appreciate, even celebrate, your marital commitment.

Some time ago a woman sent me an anniversary card she received from her stepdaughter. Debbie had kept the card because it meant so much to her. It made her realize just how much her stepdaughter was watching and learning from her marriage. Nearly a decade into her remarriage, Debbie received the card, which read, "Glad to see you two still haven't lost the magic. Happy anniversary, Mom and Dad!" The handwritten note inside the card was even more encouraging: "Happy Anniversary! I just wanted to thank you for the wonderful Christian example of how a marriage should work. The way you solve conflict with humor is fun to watch. When the time comes for the Lord to bless me with a mate, I hope I am as lucky as the two of you are! I love you both, Kara."

Now, that's what I call a Promised Land reward!

## A Healthy Family Means Healthier Kids

In 1998 James Bray published research culminating the first ten-year longitudinal study of stepfamilies in America. His research revealed that a loving, well-functioning stepfamily over time can negate many of the detrimental psychological impacts of divorce on children. While not all of the negative effects can be reversed, it is certainly a message of hope for parents and children. It seems that with time, healthy stepfamilies can have benefits that counteract the negative costs of divorce.

Bray says, "A strong, stable stepfamily is as capable of nurturing healthy development as a nuclear family. It can imbue values, affirm limits and boundaries, and provide a structure in which rules for living a moral and productive life are made, transmitted, tested, rebelled against, and ultimately affirmed."[4] The key here is a "strong, stable stepfamily" which, of course, takes time and effort, but brings many blessings to children.

Recent research, for example, suggests that a healthy stepfamily can help to diminish behavioral problems in children that arise after parental divorce. Parental divorce occurring when children are in preschool (age five or younger) predicts an increase in behavioral problems throughout preschool and even into mid-childhood (ages six to ten). However, the transition into a married blended family before children reach age ten appears to have a calming effect on child behavioral issues. What's more, a child's residual negative behavior seems to be more related to the original divorce than the new stepfamily.[5]

But there's even more good news. The benefits to children from healthy stepfamilies carry over to their adult years and positively impact their marital choices. It appears they have a lower divorce rate (compared to other children of divorce), and the quality of their own marriages more closely mirrors the stepfamily's healthy marriage than the poor-quality marriage that ended in divorce.[6] In other words, a strong step-couple begins to undo the generational cycle of divorce—in just one generation! This is great news for parents, their children, and society at large.

> **Stopping the Cycle of Divorce**
>
> A high-quality stepfamily marriage provides a positive role model for children and may mitigate the effects of observing a low-quality parental marriage that ended in divorce.

42

## Cooperation Between Homes Results in Well-Disciplined Children

When children grow up in a stable stepfamily home, they benefit tremendously. When co-parents (birth parents, separated by divorce) cooperate, the benefits are even more profound. It doesn't happen often, but some co-parents, like Jason and Leigh, have learned not to let their marital differences and past conflicts keep them from cooperating when it comes to the discipline of their children. For a long time Samuel (age nine) and Wesley (age six) told Jason, their dad, one story and Leigh, their mom, another to get out of school responsibilities. When Jason and Leigh realized what the kids were doing, they buckled down on the boys with the school's help. When Samuel and Wesley figured out that they couldn't play one parent off the other, their misbehavior at school diminished significantly. Gaining this level of cooperation is not easy for most, but seeing the rewards in well-disciplined children makes it worth the effort. I will spend concerted time in chapter 6 discussing how co-parents can cooperate for their children's well-being.

## Respect and Care Between Stepparents and Stepchildren

Over time, stepparents and stepchildren can develop a tremendous bond with one another. The pace of this developing relationship varies (see chapter 7), and some will never be more than respectful friends (especially if the children are adults at the time of the marriage). But for most, a basic sense of mutual respect and care for one another is genuinely attained. Others will develop a deep, loving, and trusting bond that is very special.

## Multi-Generational Blessings in Later-Life Stepfamilies

Many couples marrying later in life mistakenly assume that because their children are adults, their transition to a stable intergenerational stepfamily will be smooth. As with younger stepfamilies, later-life marriages bring many emotional transitions for adult stepchildren. Initial fears that grandchildren will not be prioritized, feelings of abandonment, renewed grief over a changing family heritage, and concerns with family inheritances and finances are common. However, these negative emotions can eventually give way to feelings of bondedness and connection, and multi-generational blessings.

A later-life couple, Bob and Vicki, and I were being interviewed for the national broadcast *FamilyLife Today®*, when host Dennis Rainey asked Bob's adult daughter, Katie, to tell her stepmother how she felt about her. Between you and me, I gasped when Dennis asked her to share because none of us knew what she was going to say. What I did know was that there had been some struggles the first few years. Would Katie have anything positive to say? I held my breath just a little as she started to respond.

> I guess Vicki already knows this because we do have such a close relationship, but right after she and Dad got married, I went through some personal stuff and she was there for me in a motherly and friend way. She talks to me like a mother, she calls me out like a mother, she loves me like a mother, and she is one of my best friends. The way that she loves my children warms my heart. . . . The things that she does behind the scenes—if you knew this woman—she's always thinking of someone else. And I just love her.[7]

I was so relieved—and so inspired that this family was experiencing multi-generational rewards. Later-life stepfamilies, like younger stepfamilies, sometimes struggle to find their fit. But the rewards are worth the effort.

### Experiencing Love, Extending Grace

Learning to love again after being hurt is a fearful, risky endeavor—very risky. Extending grace is part of that risk. Without it we cannot give and receive love. God taught us this. Romans 8:12–24 reminds us that God through Christ's sacrifice has adopted believers as his children. Despite our sinfulness, his grace casts out of us a spirit of fear and replaces it with a spirit of hope. He chose to love us; he chose to extend grace to us. In so doing, he made it possible for us to experience love and grace in deeply profound ways.

I have seen this process replicated many times in stepfamilies, for example, in adults who extend to ex-spouses the grace that God has given them and stepparents who choose to love stepchildren who are cold and aloof. Imitating God's love and grace can bring about profound changes to relationships. The warmth of one heart eventually softens the anger of the other. I've watched children once empty due to the abandonment of their mother or father begin to bloom under the loving care of a stepparent. I've been inspired when a non-custodial mother speaks well of her children's stepmother and insists that they respect her. Despite personal fear and risk, people in stepfamilies are choosing love and extending grace.

### Redemption of Your Family Story

Is there a part of your personal life story or family story that you wish you could change? At this point does the tragedy in your story seem to define you? And what of the choices you made in the past that you now regret—those can't be changed; they haunt you. What can you do about the legacy of shame they have created?

In his insightful book *A Grace Revealed: How God Redeems the Story of Your Life*, author Jerry Sittser suggests that each of us is living a story. As Christians our story is being caught up into God's story (even if we're not aware of it), specifically, the story of his redemption of those who call upon his grace. It doesn't really matter that you can't change the past. What matters is that God is changing the trajectory of it. For example, the worthless, nonsensical parts of life can find purpose, and our tragedies can become service to others (remember Joseph, sold by his brothers into slavery, became the one who saved the Hebrew nation and his family from famine).

Nan and I have most certainly experienced this. Just four years after the loss of our son, our journey to find his legacy resulted in the completion of a giant Lego-like art center in Ghana, West Africa, that provides therapeutic support and healing through creative expression to rescued child slaves. It's an amazing story (stunning even still to me) that includes the collective energy of five former designers and two carpenters from ABC's *Extreme Makeover: Home Edition*, hundreds of volunteers and donors, and the healing care of two parents, Pam and Randy Cope, who themselves lost a child and in his memory established the Touch A Life Foundation. The Copes reached out to us after our son died just as they reach out to trafficked children and rescued us from drowning in our sadness.

The Connor Creative Art Center is helping to redeem the stories of children from tragic circumstances—and at the same time it's redeeming our family story. Does this beauty from our ashes bury our ashes? Absolutely not. I tell people all the time I will live with my suffering every day for the rest of my life. But that's not all I have. Right beside my pain is my faith; it doesn't cancel my pain, but it does inform it. My faith calms my pain, provides perspective to it, and reminds it that this life is not all there is.

Because God is redeeming all things, he will make Connor—and me—new someday and then I'll see him again. Where would I be if I weren't allowing God to wrap my story up into his bigger story of redemption? I'll tell you: telling a sad story of loss without any hope.

And what of your story? Does the story you tell of your past include any perspective of a redemptive present? What if remarriage and this new family is the present-day portion of God's redemptive work in your life? When you seek to demonstrate the fruits of the Spirit, you partner with God's activity to move your family story out of the past and into a redemptive present. And here's the amazing outcome of the far-reaching power of God's redemption—when God works all things for the good of those who love him (Romans 8:28) it doesn't change the past, but it does change the story we tell about the past. When light is directed on the dark, it casts the dark in a new light. It changes our understanding of it, our interpretation, the meaning we give it, our role in the story, the outcome we see for our lives, even how we live in the present in light of the past. The past is, therefore, redeemed.

Your family story, even the part that is embedded in the past, is not over. You are in process—God's redeeming process. When you walk with him in faith, your story, even the worst parts of it, is caught up into what he is doing to redeem all things to him. There are more chapters to your family story yet to be written, some in this generation and some in the generations to come. Walk in faith and watch in awe how God authors a new legacy.

## Noticing What God Has Done

During the journey to the Promised Land, the Israelites experienced many periods of doubt; perhaps you have too. I hope, when they stopped to look back at how far they had come, they could see the hand of God and how many times he had acted on their behalf. Perhaps you haven't looked back recently. Perhaps the barriers that stand in front of you now are fueling doubt and pessimism. Take a few minutes to notice what God has done to help you navigate your journey so far. In what ways has his Word provided insight for decisions and encouragement? How has trusting in his truths about marital fidelity, kindness toward your enemies, and having a servant's heart helped you and your family to overcome obstacles along the way? Make a list of his faithfulness and thank him for it.

Ritu Ghatourey said, "You must never forget who was there for you when no one else was." Noticing what God has done for us sometimes includes realizing that the very family members with whom we struggle are also the ones who have been there when others weren't. Seeing one another as a gift—yes, sometimes a frustrating gift—moves your heart in the direction of gratitude. When that gratitude is experienced by family members, their heart can't help but be softened a little, and they move closer to you—and everyone together moves a little closer toward God.

Is there a Promised Land for stepfamilies who don't quit, who faithfully follow their Lord, and who learn all they can about navigating the journey? Absolutely. And it's well worth the effort!

### Questions for Discussion

To help you apply what you are learning, each chapter concludes with questions for parents and children, pre-stepfamily dating or engaged couples, and all couples (appropriate for all couples, whether dating or married). I suggest you work through the questions on your own before discussing them with your kids, dating partner, or spouse. Not all of the questions are appropriate for children or stepchildren, so before talking with them, consider their ages and your overall relationship with them.

Recommended resources for further discussion:

- *Life in a Blender* by Ron L. Deal—this booklet for children ages ten and up brings perspective and practical guidance to children in stepfamilies. The accompanying *Parent Discussion Guide* helps you engage your children in insightful conversation about what they've read. Available at FamilyLife.com.
- *The Smart Stepfamily DVD Small-Group Resource* by Ron L. Deal— an eight-week video curriculum for small groups or personal study. Available online and in bookstores.

■ FOR PARENT-CHILD DISCUSSION (Discretion based on the age of the child and the quality of adult-child relationships is advised.)

1. Begin by briefly telling your child the story of God's rescue of the Israelites from the hand of Pharaoh (their age will dictate how much detail you share). Then say, "Our family is kind of like that story.

We are traveling together as a new family, and some days it's difficult to know where we are going or how to get there. Other days we are doing well. But every day we have to trust God to lead us through the wilderness."

2. What part of this story can you relate to?

3. What joys (or rewards) have you already experienced?

4. What questions do you have for me about our family and our journey?

### ▪ For All Couples

1. What aspects of your past did you hope marriage would "cure"?

2. Which of the following emotions have you felt in the past? Which still haunt you from time to time? Anger. Bitterness. Depression. Sadness. Longing. Hurt. Resentment. Guilt. Fear. Pain. Rejection.

3. In what ways have you experienced disillusionment in your step-relationships and at what point did you realize things weren't working out as you had expected? How have you adjusted your expectations?

4. In what ways was your remarriage another loss for your children? How can you be sensitive to that loss without being guilt-ridden (or easily manipulated because you feel guilty)?

5. Look again at the list of uncharted waters (under Facing a Sea of Opposition) early in this chapter. Which of these represent areas of growth for you or your stepfamily? What areas do you consider to be the priority growth areas right now?

6. In what ways have you or your stepfamily members experienced God's leading or his healing hand? Be sure to share with your stepfamily how you see him at work in your lives.

7. What Scriptures have been helpful or inspiring to you recently? If you haven't been reading your Bible much lately, how can you begin to do so again?

8. Share a time with your spouse when you weren't sure the work was worth the effort. If that time is now, what do you need to help you stay determined? If you trusted God to bring you through, what would you be doing differently than you are now to work in that direction?

9. Which, if any, of the Promised Land Payoffs have you experienced to some degree already?

- High-quality marital relationships
- A new marital heritage to celebrate
- A healthy family means healthier kids
- Cooperation between homes results in well-disciplined children
- Respect and care between stepparents and stepchildren
- Multi-generational blessings in later-life stepfamilies
- Experiencing love, extending grace
- Redemption of your family story

10. To give and receive support for your journey, I recommend that you create or join a stepfamily small group. Is one available in your church? If not, go to Familylife.com/blended to search for a ministry in your area or find resources to start your own group.

### ■ CASE STUDY IN STEPFAMILY FEARS

Read again the fears from the Thomas family at the beginning of this chapter, and then answer the following questions.

1. Which fears of the biological and/or stepparent can you relate to and why?
2. What are you doing to prevent these fears from becoming a reality?
3. Think through your previous losses and painful family experiences (either family of origin or first marriage). How do your current fears connect with those experiences? How have they sensitized you to avoiding more pain in current relationships?
4. If you weren't hamstrung by the past, how would you be different in the present?
5. Consider the fears mentioned by the children. Which might your children also feel?

### ■ FOR PRE-STEPFAMILY COUPLES

1. In what ways do you feel intimidated and frightened after reading this chapter?
2. What challenges are you beginning to see that you had not thought about before?

3. Think of a stepfamily couple that you can interview. Ask them the following questions. If possible, start attending a stepfamily support group to help you make a more informed decision about marriage.

- What do you wish you had known before you married?
- What are your three greatest challenges?
- How could you have better prepared yourselves for stepfamily living?
- What painful emotions from the past did you not resolve prior to marriage?
- How long have you been traveling this journey?
- What blessings have you experienced and at what price?

# Key Stepping-Stones

It's been a real struggle trying to be a stepmother to my husband's son. We butt heads quite often, and my husband doesn't know how to help. Usually he and I start arguing about his son, but before long we're arguing with each other. It's been three years, and I just thought things would be so much better by now.

Without question, this stepmother is struggling. I receive numerous emails such as this, and most of them come from good-hearted people who are discouraged with their journey. The Promised Land can seem so far away when daily problems continually drain your energy. The real question is, can you trust God and persevere in your journey while trying to understand what obstacles stand in the way and what solutions will help you overcome them?

Let me pause for a moment and clearly say that I don't ask this question flippantly. I realize spiritual advisors and ministers often hand out the easy "Just trust God" solution and then walk away. Since my son's death, I really understand how incredibly difficult trusting God can be when the cost of your circumstances is extremely high. Two weeks after his brother died, my youngest son, Brennan, then age ten, opened Connor's CaringBridge website (created when Connor was in the hospital so people could receive updates and share prayers). He pointed to the counter on the screen and said, "Look, Dad. We had over 35,000 people praying for Connor. Why did God let him die?" With my eyes filled with tears I said all I could come up with: "I don't know, buddy. I'll have to get back to you on that one." In hindsight, I've realized that in part Brennan was asking, "Can we trust that God is good even when he allows life to stink?" It's a very good question.

I had read the book of Job before Connor died, but after his death I realized that I had never *really* read the book of Job. I have read it dozens of times since and committed some parts to memory as a way of coping with my son's death. One aspect of his story that has sustained me is how Job's faith was transformed through his tragedy. Not immediately, I assure you, but only after a long argument with God. For thirty-five chapters, Job argues, petitions, and takes on God regarding the loss of his family, wealth—essentially his life. Believing that God is punishing him for some evil he knows he has not done, Job accuses God of injustice. In his suffering, essentially for thirty-five chapters Job postures that God cannot be trusted to bless good people.

Then God speaks (see Job 38). Unfortunately for Job (and me) he doesn't explain the behind-the-scenes circumstances and Satan's involvement, nor does he tell Job why he allowed the death of his ten children. Wasn't there some cosmic purpose that God could share with Job that would somehow settle his suffering? Instead, when he speaks, God reminds Job that he alone is God, the creator of the universe and everything in it, with power and intellect beyond anything Job can understand. God doesn't defend himself, he just defines himself.

And somehow, in this response, Job's faith is transformed. How do I know? In chapter 42, Job makes an interesting remark after listening to God: "I had heard of you by the hearing of the ear, but now my eye sees you; therefore I despise myself, and repent in dust and ashes" (Job 42:5–6).

The man whom God himself at the beginning of the story said was blameless and upright (see Job 1:8) was now indicating that his faith had grown significantly; something had matured his faith. Suffering had invited Job to "see" God in a way he never had before. For months after my son's death, I asked everyone I knew what they thought Job now saw. Finally, after many disappointing conversations, Jimmy Adcox, a trusted ministry friend of mine, suggested that what Job learned was that he could trust God with the things that in this life he would never have the privilege of understanding. Apparently Job had trusted God to be good, but didn't know he could trust him with the unknown circumstances of life that brought great sadness and suffering.

I cannot change my past sufferings; neither can you. I cannot predict the unknown of the future; neither can you. But we can trust that God is good in both our pasts and ours futures, even if we don't understand the circumstances.

## Stepping-Stones: Step Here, Not There

There are a few land mines to avoid while journeying through the wilderness. In part, trusting God with the unknown means trusting that when he says, "Step here, not there," doing so will bring blessing to your home. Essentially, stepping-stones are important attitudes and perspectives that will enable you to endure the wilderness and cross your Sea of Opposition. Each one overtly says, "Step here," meaning do or act this way. But there's always an implied, "Don't step there, that's a land mine" message as well—that is, avoid doing this or acting like that. The "Step here" message is provided below; I invite you to determine the "Don't step there" message yourself.

As you read these key qualities, celebrate the ways you have already begun living them and imagine ways you need to improve.

### Spiritual Integrity and Christlikeness

This stepping-stone goes straight to the heart of any successful family. It occurs when family members voluntarily put themselves under the lordship of Jesus Christ and make an internal, personal commitment to follow him and accept his gracious forgiveness of the sin that separates us from God. Living in faithful response to this grace will ripple into every aspect of your home. For example, when we understand how much we have been forgiven, we can extend forgiveness to those who have deeply hurt us. Furthermore, just as Christ was not swayed from acting fairly toward those who falsely accused him, stepparents who seek to imitate Christ can find ways of rising above their stepchildren's manipulative ploys and

If your spiritual life is currently off course, who could you reach out to for support or guidance? Take one step today toward a local church or pastor that may be able to help.

not "pay back evil with evil" (see Romans 12:17–21 NIRV). Christ's spiritual integrity (doing what is right despite how you feel about it) is a model for how you are to treat one another. When his integrity becomes yours, a transformation will begin in your home that defies the odds.

Christlikeness involves a personal commitment to holy living. There are, of course, thousands of Scripture texts that help us understand living as Christ did. Let's sample just a few. Read the following and apply them specifically to the relationships within your stepfamily. Ask yourself how you might put them into practice with your spouse, ex-spouse, children, and stepchildren.

Put to death therefore what is earthly in you: sexual immorality, impurity, passion, evil desire, and covetousness, which is idolatry. On account of these the wrath of God is coming. In these you too once walked, when you were living in them. But now you must put them all away: anger, wrath, malice, slander, and obscene talk from your mouth. Do not lie to one another, seeing that you have put off the old self with its practices and have put on the new self, which is being renewed in knowledge after the image of its creator.

Colossians 3:5–10

Put on then, as God's chosen ones, holy and beloved, compassionate hearts, kindness, humility, meekness, and patience, bearing with one another and, if one has a complaint against another, forgiving each other; as the Lord has forgiven you, so you also must forgive. And above all these put on love, which binds everything together in perfect harmony.

Colossians 3:12–14

Love is patient and kind; love does not envy or boast; it is not arrogant or rude. It does not insist on its own way; it is not irritable or resentful; it does not rejoice at wrongdoing, but rejoices with the truth. Love bears all things, believes all things, hopes all things, endures all things. Love never ends.

1 Corinthians 13:4–8

Finally, my brothers and sisters, always think about what is true. Think about what is noble, right and pure. Think about what is lovely and worthy of respect. If anything is excellent or worthy of praise, think about those kinds of things. Do what you have learned or received or heard from me. Follow my example. The God who gives peace will be with you.

Philippians 4:8–9 (NIRV)

But the fruit the Holy Spirit produces is love, joy and peace. It is being patient, kind and good. It is being faithful and gentle and having control of oneself.

Galatians 5:22–23 (NIRV)

Let no corrupting talk come out of your mouths, but only such as is good for building up, as fits the occasion, that it may give grace to those who hear.

Ephesians 4:29

The application of these texts can be profound for your family. For instance, you might find it much more difficult to argue with your ex-spouse if you "don't keep a record of wrongs." Compassion can help you to be sensitive to your spouse who feels caught between love for you and love for his or her children. Gentleness with stepchildren who have made it perfectly clear they don't want you around is very difficult but may eventually win them over. Finding and focusing on what is "praiseworthy"—instead of rehashing what is upsetting—helps create energy for problem solving and gives you hope for the future. And finally, not letting your children hear "unwholesome talk" about the other household is a gift, just as "building up" your children's stepparent is a gift you'd like the other home to do for you.

Let me say another brief word about this last example and the wisdom of Scripture. Negative comments about your children's other stepparent (an ex-spouse's new spouse) often flow out of frustration or hurt but sometimes are an attempt to keep your children loyal to you. Parents don't realize they already have their children's loyalties; a stepparent will not replace a biological parent in a child's heart. Negative comments are simply unnecessary. If you are successful in getting your children to become uncooperative and disrespectful toward the stepparent, stress is created in the other home, which, ironically, is then carried back into your home by the children. In other words, unwholesome talk about the other home is an effective form of self-sabotage! God's way really does work best.

### Listening

The second stepping-stone involves one of the hardest skills in relationships—listening. If stepfamily members are not willing to hear one another, they can't know how to love and honor one another. Listening is a process by which persons set aside their own agendas long enough to tune in to someone else. This allows you to see another perspective and gain insight into that family member's feelings, desires, and goals. In contrast, an unwillingness to listen and value the perspective of another can make them feel invalidated and unimportant.

Outsiders in stepfamilies are those who are not biologically related to other stepfamily members; insiders are biologically related and have a shared family history together. Sometimes an outsider (e.g., stepparent) is told they shouldn't have a say in a situation because they "just don't understand" the history or the circumstances. The insider parent (biological parent) feels justified not listening to the outsider stepparent and so, then, do the children. Such invalidation usually brings about resentment in the stepparent and usually prevents them from moving from an outsider to an insider. This should not be. Even though opinions will differ, everyone in a stepfamily has the need to be heard.

When conflict erupts, the biblical admonition to "be quick to listen . . . and slow to get angry" is of tremendous value (James 1:19 NLT). During conflict, most persons want so badly to be heard that they talk over others or are devising their next comment when they're supposed to be listening. Proverbs 18:13 (NIRV) reminds us, "To answer before listening is foolish and shameful." It takes great discipline, but people who can apply the principle of *listening first to understand the other before trying to be understood* will find their conflicts de-escalating and more productive.

> **Best Practices: Parenting Teenagers**
>
> Listening to teens is particularly important when rules are changing or unwanted transitions in the family are taking place. Adolescents need to know they are being heard and that their opinions are being considered. Especially when their thoughts are not changing your mind or the circumstances, take the time to hear and show them you understand their feelings.

56

## *Understanding*

Listening is the skill that makes understanding possible. It can be difficult to fully understand someone else's perspective, but standing in another's shoes in order to see the world from that person's point of view is a good first step. This is an important process in stepfamilies because, for example, each individual has traveled a different journey into the stepfamily. Imagine yourself standing in New York's Grand Central Station, the largest train station (by number of platforms) in the world, with forty-four platforms and sixty-seven tracks, watching people arrive on different trains. As they exit the train, you realize that though they started in many different places, they are now all arriving in one location.

So it is with your family. Perhaps some children in your home, for example, after the death of a parent journeyed on a train through the valley of the shadow of death. Their loss is distinctively permanent and their daily longing for that parent is never satisfied. But because their parents had a strong marriage, they are used to responding to united parents. Other children in your home, however, arrived on a different train: the divorce train. They are used to angry, divided parents who perhaps belittle each other. These children must travel back and forth between two homes and navigate the tension of doing so. This difference in history brings to your living room—Grand Central Station—very different children with different expectations, hurts, and fears.

To make matters more challenging, the adults have also traveled on different trains from each other and the children. The result? Biological parents and stepparents experience the stepfamily differently from each other and from the children.

To put yourself in the shoes of the other persons in your family is a tremendous act of courage, but it is absolutely necessary in order to understand their experience of you. You may find, for example, that a stepdaughter's resentment of you is not so farfetched given how she has been hurt by others in the past. Or you may discover that your husband's style of discipline is understandable (even if you don't want to replicate it) once you understand what he experienced in his first marriage and family of origin.

Try putting yourself in the shoes of each person and wonder what it must be like to be them. Ask yourself:

- What losses has he or she experienced? (Make a list of the losses your children have experienced, and you'll be humbled by what they have been forced to give up.)
- How do the other members of our stepfamily treat this person? How do I treat him or her?
- What is it like for each child to live in the other home?
- What challenges does he or she face in trying to belong?
- What responsibilities, roles, relationships, etc., does he or she have that I don't have to deal with?
- What is his or her favorite part of this family?
- What part does he or she care for the least?

Ask each family member to share the answers to some of these questions with you. Listen intently and strive to understand how these aspects impact his or her daily life with you. Such understanding will help you develop empathy and perhaps compassion for each member of your family, which in turn helps you relate more effectively.

### Perseverance

Life is filled with trials, tribulations, and challenges. It is the norm for all types of families (biological, single-parent, and stepfamily). This is especially true at the beginning of the stepfamily journey; in fact, uncertainty, disillusionment, and discouragement commonly characterize the first few years. The stepping-stone of perseverance can carry you through.

I'm talking about being determined and sticking with your marriage and family when the going gets tough. Henry Blackaby in *Experiencing God*[1] talks about the "crisis of belief" that Christians experience when God's will becomes evident. When God speaks his desire for us, whether through Scripture or circumstance, we face a crisis of belief. Will my belief lead to action and take me wherever God has directed—even if I personally don't want to go there—or will my belief remain simply words?

This willingness to surrender to what God directs or allows in our life is challenging when the life circumstance is a little inconvenient, but it is extremely unsettling when the cost is very high. Loss is one of those circumstances that gives birth to a crisis of belief for most of us. Whether it is the loss of a child, a marriage through divorce, a spouse by death, financial ruin, or lost dreams about a new family, we often find ourselves, like Job, having to examine our assumptions about God, our ability to control our circumstances—even the foundations of our faith. Many people drift from God and the fellowship of his people when loss happens; not understanding or feeling disappointed with God leads to withdrawing. Others run to God in blind trust, hoping to find strength to endure. What about you? Which direction have you gone in the past? In which direction are you headed now?

I have a great deal of admiration for people who face the discouragements and disappointments of stepfamily living with raw determination and resolve. Because determination in this situation is sacrificial, it is not a convenience. It is a crisis of belief. In effect, determination says, "Trusting God to be faithful as the Lord of Possibilities, I will be faithful and persevere in my marital responsibilities even if this marriage and family is not what I want it to be."[2] Perseverance, then, while at times is quite costly, paves the way for hope to become reality.

## Commitment

Determination, when combined with the decision to persevere, results in a strong commitment to building your stepfamily. The bedrock of this commitment is dedication to your spouse and your vow to love, honor, and cherish each other for a lifetime. But sometimes we need to be reminded that marital vows are not multiple choice. The preacher probably didn't let you choose: "I'll take richer, for better, and in health—but leave off poorer, for worse, and in sickness." No, you committed yourself to all of them. As life teaches you what that commitment means, keep your dedication to your partner and your vows high.

Commitment means remaining dedicated to the vows you expressed (or will express) on your wedding day. Every day of your life you will make a decision whether or not you will live up to those words. If you choose not to, your stepfamily will not survive.

## Patience

Stepfamily integration hardly ever happens as quickly as adults want it to. Stepfamily

> ### Growing Us Up
>
> There's nothing like marriage to teach us just how selfish we are. Marriage is where God grows us up.

researcher James Bray discovered that stepfamilies generally don't begin to think or act like a family until the end of the second or third year.[3] Furthermore, Patricia Papernow, author of the book *Becoming a Stepfamily,* discovered that it takes the average stepfamily around five to seven years to integrate sufficiently to experience intimacy and authenticity in steprelationships. Fast-paced families can accomplish this in four years, if the children are young and the adults are intentional about bringing their family together. Slow families, according to Papernow, can take nine or more years.[4] In my experience, very few adults come into their stepfamily believing it will take anywhere near this long. They assume—and want—a quick, painless blending process. I have often wondered if they had known the journey would take so long, would they have signed on in the first place?

Why does it take so long for stepfamilies to integrate? One reason is that the stepfamily is filled with complex dynamics. For example, family therapists have long recognized that divorce doesn't really end family life; it just reorganizes it. In effect, it spreads the family out over multiple households, and relational dynamics that preceded the divorce continue even though the family's living arrangements have been restructured. New stepfamily relationships become part of the larger expanded family. I've talked with an ex-husband, for example, who was stunned to find out that when his ex-wife's new mother-in-law had a crisis, it impacted his home. Children were emotionally affected, and it forced his ex-wife to change her visitation schedule, which, of course, dramatically altered his life and plans.

> **When does the family integration period begin? Before or after the wedding?**
>
> See more on this topic in the Smart Questions, Smart Answers bonus material, available at SmartStepfamilies.com/view/learn.

Stepfamilies need to realize that all the people sharing a relationship (by blood or marriage) with their children and stepchildren are part of their "expanded" family. Start counting, and the total number of people can be exasperating! From a mathematical perspective, the number of possible interactions in a stepfamily containing children who move back and forth between two homes, and who have stepparents who have biological children of their own, can be thousands of times greater than a biological

## Are Some Stepfamilies Easier to Integrate?

Yes. The less complex a stepfamily is, the easier it is, in general, to combine family members. For example, integration is less complicated when only one adult brings children to the marriage, when children are younger, and when the stepparent is a man (stepdad) and the children are boys. Stepfamilies following the death of a parent are not necessarily easier; they are less complicated because there's not another home, but still emotionally challenging in their own way.

family's possible interactions. That's why family therapists and stepfamily educators Emily and John Visher point out that stepfamilies don't have a family tree, they have a family forest! This complex forest simply takes time to integrate—and time requires patience.

A conference participant once asked me what he could have done differently to build a relationship with his stepdaughter. He described how he took his new twelve-year-old stepdaughter out shopping and to get ice cream whenever possible. He asked her what activities she liked doing and then made sure they did them together. In his words, "I tried and tried, but she never warmed up to me, so I gave up." A bit bewildered (he had done a lot of things right), I asked for more information. He had become this girl's second stepfather after her mother divorced a second husband. The girl's biological father was uninvolved in her life, leaving a deep wound in her heart. Her first stepfather was aloof, distant, and critical. I suggested to the gentleman that, because of them, he had two strikes against him when he married her mother. But the real clincher came when I asked how long he attempted to win his stepdaughter's heart. *Three months.* He gave up after only three months. You see, he simply didn't take into consideration all that this girl had been through and how long it takes for steprelationships to develop. His intentions were good. His actions were on target. He just wasn't patient enough.

### Flexibility

Have you ever tried to force a square peg into a round hole? Because the stepfamily is different from a biological family, you need to learn flexibility. The rituals, expectations, and assumptions our society trains us to have about family life become our square pegs that, when forced into the round stepfamily hole, just don't fit. Becoming stepfamily smart starts with understanding the nature of your round peg and how it differs from the biological square peg. Said another way, you need stepfamily answers to stepfamily questions, not biological family answers to stepfamily questions.

What would happen if while riding a bicycle you made a 90-degree right-hand turn by turning the handlebars the same way you would a car steering wheel? You'd flip right over the handlebars and face-plant on the ground! The bicycle is a different vehicle than a car and requires different movements to steer it correctly. If you try to steer your stepfamily the exact same way you would a biological family, you're bound to flip over a time or two. Almost immediately some rituals, styles of parenting, and expectations will work just as they do in biological families, and others will eventually work well once the family has bonded together. Other ways of relating, however, will always be different, requiring flexible handling.

> Stepmoms are women who do a lot of mothering, but frequently don't get to be the mom.[5]

One important example is the differing role of stepmoms and stepdads. Imagine a biological mother who has three children. Together they have survived the loss of their first family and made it successfully through a few single-parent years. Mom's role is one of emotional caretaker, disciplinarian, authority, encourager, and teacher; she is also the emotional hub of the family—connected to everyone, their schedules, and their inner thoughts and experiences. But what she may discover upon becoming a stepmom is that her stepchildren don't want or need her to be those things for them. To them she is an outsider, not the insider emotional hub of their family or personal life. So what is her role? She is still Mom to her children (insider), but she's confused about her role with her stepchildren (outsider). If she doesn't learn flexibility she will try to force a mom-like role with her stepchildren, which will likely lead to less cooperation and acceptance from them. We'll talk more about stepparenting in a later chapter, but for a deeper dive into the roles of stepmoms and stepdads in particular, read my books *The Smart Stepmom* (with Laura Petherbridge) and *The Smart Stepdad*.

## *Humor*

In the midst of a chaotic moment, humor is definitely the best medicine for stepfamilies. Humor brings a perspective that helps you to step back from the crisis or circumstance and see it in a whole new light. In fact, you might even enjoy a good laugh.

I often reference two cartoons that make this point clear. The first pictures a man reading a piece of mail to his wife. "It's bad news, Anne," he says. "The traffic judge assigned to our case is my first wife." Clearly, unless he has an incredibly grace-filled relationship with his ex-wife, this couple is in trouble. Is it funny? Not really. But finding the ability to chuckle just a little might relieve their hearts from excessive worry and anxiety. The second cartoon pictures two young children standing in the front yard. The little girl is pointing at the boy, reminding him, "No, your dad cannot beat up my dad because your dad is now *my* dad, remember?"

Incidentally, that cartoon took on new meaning when I applied it to Jesus—the most famous stepchild who ever lived. Think about it: He wasn't raised by his natural father. Was Joseph his stepdad? Yes, it is a unique circumstance, but you still can't avoid the fact that the Creator of the universe entrusted his Son to be raised by a man who was not his biological father. Picture Jesus as an eight-year-old talking to his stepsiblings: "Oh no, believe me, your dad cannot beat up my Dad!"

Learning to laugh at yourself and your circumstances is not about denying problems or responsibilities. It is about not taking yourself or life too seriously so you can gain perspective on your circumstances.

## Share Your Travelogue: A Tool for Developing Compassion and Understanding

How many of the key stepping-stones does your family possess now? Just where is your stepfamily in this journey to the Promised Land? Are you just beginning, toward the end, or somewhere in the middle? I'm sure you have definite ideas, but your children may view it differently. As I mentioned earlier, there are similarities in how persons experience their family life, but the differences in stepfamilies can be profound because each person in the stepfamily has traveled a different path to where they are now.

Patricia Papernow has developed the travelogue as an effective tool that helps stepfamilies listen and understand one another.[6] The technique is based on the notion that if people in your family went to a foreign country for a month, upon their return you would probably ask them for a travelogue, that is, the story of their journey. You'd ask where they ate, what food they liked, what famous sites they saw, what was most exciting or disappointing, and so on. You'd want to know what the journey was like for them. Showing interest in each family member's biological, single-parent, and stepfamily journey affirms the person's experience and can teach you what it is like to be him or her.

At a family meeting, ask each person to share his or her travelogue, a personal account of their stepfamily journey. Remember, the task is to maintain enough curiosity ("tell me more") and empathy ("that must be tough") in the face of differences and disappointments so that each person is able to share joys, pains, heartaches, and experiences without fear of retaliation or rejection. As people share, everyone must maintain a nondefensive attitude. Focus on listening, not defending yourself. If one or more family members cannot listen openly, you might consider breaking into smaller groups, perhaps even one-on-one, to walk through the exercise with more emotional safety. The purpose of the travelogue is to listen and understand one another better, and to invite family members to hear the desires of each other's hearts. This also facilitates bonding and compassion for one another. When done with respect and openness, family members move toward one another.

To begin, say something like, "You know, everyone in our family has traveled a long way to get to where we are. And even though we're in the same family, we've probably traveled different paths to get here. Maybe we could share what it's been like so far. Starting with your first family and the single-parent years, let's all take turns and talk about what this journey has been like until now. The rest of us will listen just as if we're listening to someone who's been to a foreign land. We'll ask questions and try to imagine what it must have been like for whoever is talking."[7]

Once you've opened the door to honesty and understanding by sharing your travelogue, keep the conversation going by giving the children a chance to share. Once someone starts telling their travelogue, don't stop or interrupt them. Follow their lead. Here are some questions that might help:

---

**Managing the Emotion**

Sharing your travelogue includes talking about the loss of the first family; this will undoubtedly bring some sadness to the experience. Don't skip over this to prevent tears, but given the group setting, let each person share as much or as little as they choose. Also, if divorced, parents should share very little about their emotional pain and avoid casting blame toward the ex-spouse in front of the children.

---

- After death: What is one really good memory of your deceased parent? Share one way your life changed after they died.
- After divorce: What was the good and bad of your parents' divorce (our divorce) for you? How did your life change after that?
- What have you lost that hasn't been regained?
- What do you think has changed for others?
- During the single-parent years, what was good or okay for you? What was painful? How was life different for you?
- As much as you can remember, what were your daily schedule and responsibilities when we were a single-parent family?
- Share a first impression of your future stepparent/stepchildren.
- When we were dating, what did you grow to look forward to? What concerned you?
- How did life with your mom/dad/children change once the remarriage occurred?
- What hopes or dreams did you have for this stepfamily that have already been fulfilled? Which ones haven't come about yet?
- What painful emotions have you been feeling lately?
- What fears do you have about this stepfamily or yourself?
- With older children and teens, describe insider and outsider positions in the family. First, ask everyone to share with whom they are an insider or outsider and how it feels in that position. Then discuss what it would be like to be in the other's (insider/outsider) shoes.
- Discuss the common myth of instant love (see chapter 4) and share how you envision love developing between stepfamily members.
- End your travelogue meeting in prayer.

The travelogue exercise can be repeated in your home over time. Family meetings are the perfect time to ask questions and be updated on everyone's travels. Biological parents might also find one-on-one time with each child to discuss their current travelogue.

## Keep Stepping

The journey to the Promised Land is not always an easy one, but then again, few significant endeavors in life are easy. In this chapter I've suggested that maintaining key attitudes and qualities—*stepping-stones*—will advance your journey in the Lord.

- *Spiritual integrity* demands that you allow Jesus to be Lord over your heart and home.
- *Listening* and *understanding* help family members develop compassion and empathy for one another.
- *Perseverance* will help you stay the course when the going gets tough.
- *Commitment* expresses itself in dedication to fulfilling your marital vows.
- *Patience* means enjoying your stepfamily as it is, instead of pushing everyone to arrive at the Promised Land on your schedule.
- *Flexibility* includes changing your assumptions of how things should be and opening yourself to creative solutions to common problems.
- *Humor*—the gift that focuses on the lighter side of dark moments.

I have sought in this chapter to give you hope on your journey. In the next section we will examine seven smart steps that nearly all stepfamilies must take to reach the Promised Land. The dynamics of stepfamily life can be challenging, but they are not impossible. Keep stepping.

### Questions for Discussion

◼ FOR PARENT-CHILD DISCUSSION (Discretion based on the age of the child and the quality of adult-child relationships is advised.)

1. Let the travelogue section at the end of the chapter serve as your parent-child discussion guide for this chapter.

■ FOR ALL COUPLES

1. Have you had any informal travelogue talks? What did you learn?

2. Discuss the pros and cons of having everyone present for the travelogue discussion versus only biological parents and children.

3. What is one of your chief frustrations or complaints about your stepfamily right now?

4. On a scale of 1 to 10 (with 10 being the highest), rate your personal level of spiritual integrity. How are you doing trusting God with things that you will never understand in this life? What spiritual challenges stand in front of you and how are you addressing them?

5. Describe a time when you tried to force your will on God. What was the outcome?

6. Choose one of the Scripture passages in the spiritual integrity section in the chapter and share how applying that verse will help your stepfamily's growth.

7. If you were to ask your children and your spouse whether they felt you were a good listener, what would they say? In what ways does defensiveness keep you from listening well?

8. Identify the person you have the most conflict with or the child to whom you are the least bonded. Share what you think it would be like to be that member of your stepfamily. Consider his or her losses, sense of belonging, fears, responsibilities, and hurts.

9. Read James 1:2–4. If the testing of our faith produces perseverance (which in turn helps us mature), how has the testing of your stepfamily helped you grow as an individual?

10. List three things you could do this week to express your dedication (commitment) to your spouse.

11. In what ways have you been impatient with the status of your stepfamily bonds? How have you tried to force or pressure people to love one another?

12. In what ways is your stepfamily different than a biological family? Share some of the flexible solutions you've already discovered that have helped.

13. Share a humorous occasion or story from your stepfamily's life. If you can't think of one immediately, try to step back from your circumstances in order to see the humorous side.

### ■ For Pre-Stepfamily Couples

1. Feel free to begin having travelogue discussions as a couple and with your children. Keep in mind that before the wedding most children cannot adequately anticipate all they will feel. Be sure to ask them again later. How might you go about having travelogue discussions now?

2. Which of the stepping-stones characterize your relationships now?

Therefore, since we are surrounded by so great a cloud of witnesses, let us also lay aside every weight, and sin which clings so closely, and let us run with endurance the race that is set before us, looking to Jesus, the founder and perfecter of our faith, who for the joy that was set before him endured the cross, despising the shame, and is seated at the right hand of the throne of God.

Hebrews 12:1–2

# PART TWO

# Seven Steps in the Journey

A n old Chinese proverb states that a journey of a thousand miles begins with just one step. While the stepfamily journey involves many challenges, there are a few major steps that must be handled well. This section of the book provides the nuts and bolts to integrating a stepfamily.

Each chapter discusses a key step in the integration process. It's likely that you won't take each of these steps just once. You'll probably find yourself navigating them again and again as children grow and as relationships in your and the other household change. These seven steps create a dance that must be danced repeatedly before harmony is achieved on the dance floor of life.

# Smart Step One: STEP Up!

*Discover a redemptive God who loves, forgives,
and provides strength and direction for the journey*

For while we were still weak, at the right time Christ died for the ungodly. For one will scarcely die for a righteous person—though perhaps for a good person one would dare even to die—but God shows his love for us in that while we were still sinners, Christ died for us. Since, therefore, we have now been justified by his blood, much more shall we be saved by him from the wrath of God. For if while we were enemies we were reconciled to God by the death of his Son, much more, now that we are reconciled, shall we be saved by his life. More than that, we also rejoice in God through our Lord Jesus Christ, through whom we have now received reconciliation.

Romans 5:6–11

Another translation of the above verses suggests that being reconciled to God is to be made friends with God. Can you imagine God calling you his friend? Given his holiness and our, well, ungodliness, it's a tough concept to grasp, especially if guilt or shame feelings from your past choices and behavior make you feel unworthy of his grace and mercy, let alone his friendship. So, how do you embrace his grace? And what should you do if attending church makes you feel unworthy or second-class because your family isn't the ideal the pastor talks about? What if you fear God's judgment for your past?

## The Rally Cry Response

I believe God has called me to educate and equip stepfamilies for healthy living. Furthermore, I consider it part of this calling to shout a rally cry to church leaders, inviting them to better minister to stepfamilies in their communities (see SmartStepfamilies.com/view/educate). However, the rally cry response has been met with some opposition by those who are concerned that stepfamily ministry somehow condones or encourages divorce and a merry-go-round attitude about marriage. In addition, there is hesitation from a few who wonder if ministering to the remarried is the equivalent of abandoning God's design for marriage. Let me clearly state that I want to uphold and teach God's ideal that one man and one woman be married till death do them part (and in my experience every mature divorced and remarried person agrees that God's ideal is best). In no way should we compromise God's plan for the foundation of our homes. My

### When a Spouse Is Deceased

If divorce is not part of your past, this chapter still pertains to you. Read and be reminded of God's redeeming work in the lives of countless reorganized families.

desire to educate and equip stepfamilies, then, is not about condoning a past. It is, rather, an effort to help stepfamilies walk hand in hand with their Lord in the present.

You see, the problems and pressures of stepfamily life are a distraction from what really matters—making Jesus the Lord of your life and sharing your faith with the children under your care. Satan knows that one of the greatest influences on your life is your family, and if he can mess it up, he will likely get you as well (and the next four generations to come!). But if you dedicate your family to God, you're well on your way to finding the strength and answers you need to make your family successful. Satan would much rather see you distracted, discouraged, and defeated!

And that's exactly where many stepfamilies end up—feeling that they don't belong in church and believing they aren't good enough for God's grace. What contributes to that? First, let's examine a stepfamily's relationship to the church.

### Spiritually Marginalized From God's "Hospital" Church

- "Thanks for recognizing that we're not the church's dirty little problem."
- "I never thought I could go back to church again."
- "Once the divorce happened, the majority of the church members had nothing to do with any of us, including my children. I was working at a bank, and one of the deacons refused to stand in my line because I was a divorced person. . . . When you go through a divorce, you need your family and [church] friends' support. I received no support from the church; instead, I was treated like a second-class citizen."

Second-class citizens. That well sums up how many stepfamilies are made to feel. They don't reflect God's ideal family constellation, so they just aren't quite good enough. One friend of mine shared how their small group at church taught her to fear judgment from others. She and her husband were newly married and had recently joined a new Bible study. One day after the study, a group member's child ran up to them and asked if they had any kids. Because they were a newly married stepcouple they hadn't come across that question yet. "We didn't know what to say at that point," she shared with me, "so I answered yes just as my husband answered no. Everyone looked at us oddly, so we had to share our family story with the group. They weren't sure what to say. We felt uncomfortable and weird." What an awkward moment that must have been for them.

She continued the story. "A few months later, I was having lunch with the wives in the Bible study group. I brought my stepdaughter with me to play with the other kids. The next week my friend told me that her daughter asked why my stepdaughter called me by my first name. My friend told me she side-stepped the question because she didn't want to 'expose her daughter to divorce.' She acted like I would understand. Shame, embarrassment, and guilt washed over me immediately; I suddenly felt so much pressure to try to be a 'normal family' and hide our brokenness. Words like *ex-wife, stepkids, stepfamily, stepmom, custody, divorce* . . . all freaked out my friends. I quickly learned that there are few people who don't judge us. I kept my struggles to myself and didn't share my feelings with my new group of friends. It has taken about eight years to find other stepmom friends with whom I could find support and comfort." Notice how isolated this stepmom became and how quickly she and her husband learned to hide their past. Now they walk the tightrope of engaging the church for fellowship, but not engaging to the point of being vulnerable and open about their past.

If that example is troubling, this one is downright defeating. One couple was studying with a preacher who was trying to help them come back to the Lord after a number of years away. When the preacher discovered they were divorced and remarried, he closed his Bible, looked at them, and said, "I'm sorry. Your background and past might infect everyone else, so we can't have you in our church." He then turned and left their home.

Can you imagine? A man claiming to proclaim the grace of God told them they were so sick they needed to be quarantined from the hospital! I thought hospitals were for the sick, for those who need healing. I guess I missed the part of the Bible that says only perfect people belong in church. I should add that God wasn't finished with this couple. After hearing this preacher's condemnation, they visited the church where I served as family life minister. After much prayer and repentance, this couple resurrected their relationship with Christ, and we eventually put them to work leading our stepfamily support group.

But the message divorced and remarried persons sometimes receive from the church is only half the problem. Stepfamily adults can become spiritually marginalized due to their own sense of guilt and unworthiness.

### Spiritual Shame

"I am not sure if I am accepted by God because of my remarriage. I am almost afraid to read the Bible, because I'm not sure what I may find."

"I have tried to get my life back on track, but as a divorcée, that stigma and my own guilt combined to make me feel like an outsider. That outsider feeling made me not want to give up my sinful life. Satan would step in and say, 'Why should you commit to this church? They look at you weird; they know you are divorced. If they do not care about you, why should you care about them or be committed to their God?' So before I could develop any ties to a local church, I would lose interest in getting my life straight. I would quickly return to my life of sin—lost, frustrated, and now even more embarrassed."

Sometimes feeling unworthy of God's love is self-imposed. Yes, sometimes it's an excuse to avoid responsibility, and sometimes it flows from a legalistic theology that believes we have to earn our salvation. But no matter its origin, the impact is the same: People keep their distance from God and his church.

"Okay, Ron," people have interjected before, "just how does God feel about me and my stepfamily situation? I mean, if we could ask him, what would he say?" My guess is he feels about you the same way he felt about the imperfect families of the Bible. Let me illustrate.

## The Family of Promise

Nan and I waited a number of years before having children. Once we began making plans to conceive a child, I began praying for God's insight and wisdom into how I should be as a father. Furthermore, I began searching the Scriptures to find a healthy, faithful family that could serve as a model for me. My training in marriage and family therapy had primarily focused on the dynamics of change with dysfunctional families, so I needed to see more of what a functional family looked like. Besides, I wanted to see how faith and family dynamics would integrate to make a "perfect combination." So I began to survey the families of the Old Testament.

Murder is not new to us in America. Besides the violence in the streets, murder is not uncommon in our schools, suburban neighborhoods, and even within homes. Yet the first incident of family homicide came from Adam and Eve's family. Cain was so jealous of his brother's favor in God's eyes that with premeditation he lured him to an isolated place and killed him (Genesis 4:1–8). Not a good start for the first family, huh?

And then there's Noah and his sons, Shem, Ham, and Japheth (Genesis 9:20–27). We're all aware of their incredible faithful journey on the ark, but are you aware of what happened later? Noah got drunk one night, leaving himself naked and exposed to his son Ham. His brothers respect-fully covered their father's nakedness, but the damage had already been done. Noah cursed Ham for the shame he experienced (wasn't Noah partly responsible?); he later blessed the other two brothers. In effect, Noah set the brothers against each other, and a pattern of jealousy and competition was handed to the next generation.

My search then led me to the "family of promise." Abraham is well known for his faithful walk with God and for God's promise to make him into a great nation. Eventually the seed of Abraham would bring the Messiah, the Savior, Jesus Christ himself. As I surveyed biblical families I remember thinking, *Adam and Noah's families were disappointments, but surely I'll find a good model family here.*

In Genesis 12:13–20 Abram coerced his wife, Sarai, to lie to the Egyptians in order to save his life. "Say you are my sister," he told her. Because Sarai was a beautiful woman, Abram feared that Pharaoh would have him killed in order to have Sarai for himself. Wives, if your husband refused to own you in public and was willing to put you in jeopardy in order to save his own skin, how would you feel? Furthermore, what if he gave you to another man, knowing he would take you to be his wife and have intercourse with you—now how would you feel? What if he did it *twice*?!

Believe it or not, Abraham (God had changed his and his wife's names) again said—this time to Abimelech—that Sarah was his sister. (See Genesis 20.) He feared Abimelech, the king of Gerar, would have him killed, so he handed her over to become Abimelech's wife. In case you're wondering, this is not what men's ministries have in mind for husbands! Abraham was a man of great faith. But he was far from the perfect husband.

But the pattern of selfish husbandry doesn't stop there. Isaac, Abraham's son, who probably wasn't even born when his father disowned his mother, told the same lie about his wife, Rebekah. He too feared for his life, so he told the king of the Philistines that Rebekah was his sister (Genesis 26:1–11). Abraham and Isaac's lies were eventually found out, but not before a great many people were hurt by the deception.

In chapter 5 we'll examine further the expanded family dynamics of Abraham's home. For now let's remember that while Sarah was barren, she suggested Abraham take her maidservant, Hagar, to be a second wife so they could conceive a child through her (Genesis 16). Once Hagar conceived, jealousy and competition become the name of the game between Sarah and Hagar. Anger, bitterness, and favoritism are the result. (I called this home an "expanded family" because there were multiple wives and competition for how the children would be treated by the biological father, Abraham. Some are calling the stepfamily of modern America an "expanded family.") Even though the family composition is different, the dynamics of Abraham, Sarah, and Hagar's home mirror some of the dynamics of today's stepfamily. We'll examine those dynamics more in the chapter on marriage. Suffice it to say for now that Abraham's expanded home was full of anger, jealousy, competition, bitterness, and loyalty conflicts—all of which were handed down to the next generation.

In Genesis 27 we read how Abraham's daughter-in-law Rebekah conspired with her favored son, Jacob, to deceive her husband, Isaac. If it worked, Jacob would receive a critically important blessing meant for his older brother, Esau. Jacob had already cheated his brother out of his birthright, but he wanted more. He wanted a special position; whoever received the blessing would be served by the other brother and his descendants. Rebekah and Jacob's plan worked, and a divided house became even more divided as Esau set out to avenge his loss and kill Jacob. Talk about sibling rivalry! But that's not the whole story for the "family of promise."

Jacob then passed on the family pattern of favoritism to his son Joseph, who was his favorite. Jacob even gave him a special robe to signify his love. Joseph's brothers, however, didn't appreciate Joseph's favored status, so they devised a plan to kill him. Only at the last minute did they stop short of murder and decide instead to sell him into slavery (which would have ultimately led to his being killed, since slaves were used until they had nothing left to give and then killed). Can you imagine? And you thought the kids in your house were unruly.

My attempt to find the model biblical family was not successful. Indeed, within a few generations of Abraham there were family power struggles, failures to become properly individuated from parents, family secrets, exploitive and coercive relationships, marital game-playing that led to triangulation, parent-child alliances, vindictiveness, anger, and sibling rivalries. But that's not all.

The family pathology within the family of promise continued to mushroom through the family of David. Even though the Bible does refer to him as a "man after God's own heart," David's behavior included premeditated murder to cover an affair, an out-of-wedlock pregnancy, and a son who replicates his father's disgrace by raping his half-sister. Later another of David's sons would avenge his sister's humiliation by hunting down and murdering the brother who raped her.

Are you feeling any better about your stepfamily situation?

So much for the family of promise being a family to emulate. And the other families of the Bible, in both the Old and New Testaments, are not much better. In truth, God's ideal for the family is evident in Scripture, but an ideal family to imitate is not.

Enter God's mercy and grace. Without it, the great faithful men of old would have been part of just another dysfunctional family—just like you and me. None of us are deserving of God's grace, not one. And yet he offers it freely.

## God's Redemption

Entering into this fullness is not something you figure out or achieve. It's not a matter of being circumcised or keeping a long list of laws. No, you're already *in*—insiders—not through some secretive initiation rite but rather through what Christ has already gone through for you, destroying the power of sin. If it's an initiation ritual you're after, you've already been through it by submitting to baptism. Going under the water was a burial of your old life; coming up out of it was a resurrection, God raising you from the dead as he did Christ. When you were stuck in your old sin-dead life, you were incapable of responding to God. God brought you alive—right along with Christ! Think of it! All sins forgiven, the slate wiped clean, that old arrest warrant canceled and nailed to Christ's cross.

Colossians 2:11–15 THE MESSAGE paraphrase

Did you hear that? The apostle Paul is shouting the good news—we can't earn our worthiness. Our worth, the possibility of forgiveness, and a right relationship with God have come about because of Christ's saving work on the cross. While we were stuck in our sin, Christ died for us, giving us the hope of redemption. Not all stepfamilies are born out of sinful behavior, but some are. And the good news is that no matter what decisions or sins you may have committed in the past that led to your current stepfamily situation, God wants you back. And he's provided a way through Christ to make it happen.

The portrait of families in the Bible is a series of broken relationships in need of redemption. Not a single family in the entire Old or New Testament was so exemplary that God held it up as a model or pattern for us to follow. Indeed, the great faithful men of the Bible had to rely on God's grace too. And despite their imperfections, God used them for his purposes.

The answer to the question "How does God feel about me and my less-than-perfect family situation?" is this: God loves and forgives the imperfect people in stepfamilies the same way he loves and forgives the imperfect people in biological families. Furthermore, people in stepfamilies are not "second-rate Christians," because there is no such thing as a "first-rate Christian." We're all sinners and all less than perfect. All our families are less than ideal. And we all need a Savior.

You may be plagued by guilt, shame, and remorse over your past and present. You may have had an affair or abandoned your spouse, which resulted in divorce; you may have been neglecting your children since the divorce, and their faith is suffering because of you. You may be harboring anger at your ex-spouse for the hurt he or she caused you and the children. Or perhaps a mean-spirited church leader pushed you away from believing you could be forgiven, and previous friends have isolated themselves from you. You may have lost touch with God and find it hard to pray and spend time with your church family. If so, don't look now, but you're being pursued—pursued by a God who desperately wants you to STEP UP to meet him.

His desire for you is the same as it was for Abraham, Isaac, Jacob, and David—God wants you daily to surrender your will and follow him. His desire for your family is the same as it was for any imperfect biblical family—that you make him the cornerstone upon which the house is built (Psalm 127:1).

If there is distance between you and God, decide today to humbly accept Christ's offer of forgiveness, dedicate your life and marriage to the Lord, and make him the architect of your new home. It's a decision you'll never regret. If you don't, you may be destined to repeat the past. If your walk with the Lord is solid, keep right on stepping.

I hope this chapter has either opened your eyes to God's incredible redemption or encouraged you to continue basking in his grace. Ultimately,

*The Smart Stepfamily* is aimed at helping all members of your family strengthen their relationship with the Creator of life. Truly, what good would it do to develop a healthy stepfamily but have no relationship with God? "What good is it," Jesus wondered, "if someone gains the whole world but loses his soul?" (Matthew 16:26 NIRV).

The stepfamily's journey to the Promised Land begins and ends with stepping up to a redemptive God. No other step is nearly as important. And while no other step costs as much as emptying yourself to carry a cross, no other step is as easy. For our effort to step up is successful only because of our Savior's willingness to step down to the point of our greatest need.

## Questions for Discussion

■ FOR PARENT-CHILD DISCUSSION (Discretion based on the age of the child and the quality of adult-child relationships is advised.)

1. If appropriate for your child(ren), read to them the following opening paragraphs from my booklet for children, *Life in a Blender* (available at FamilyLife.com). Then discuss the questions.

> *So, was Jesus a stepchild? It's an interesting thought and one worth consideration. Think about it: Jesus was raised by a stepdad. Certainly the circumstances surrounding His birth were, well, quite extraordinary. Being conceived by the Holy Spirit and born of a virgin certainly places His "stepfamily" situation in a category of its own. Yet when you stop to reflect on it, the God of the universe allowed His one and only Son to be raised by someone who wasn't His "biological" father.*
>
> *My point: you are not alone.*
>
> *As a matter of fact, most of the major characters of the Old Testament were raised in homes with parent and stepparent combinations. Some of these came about when a parent married following the death of his or her first spouse, but most occurred when their father married more than one woman. While the circumstances of your stepfamily differ, my guess is that you and the biblical characters of old share some of the same confusing emotions and dilemmas.*
>
> *Consider, for example, Ishmael, who was born to Hagar, Abraham's maidservant. I wonder what he was feeling that led him to mock his new younger half-brother, Isaac (Genesis 21:8–11). Why would he do*

*such a thing? I wonder if he was feeling left out, now that Isaac, the "promised child," was getting all the attention. I also wonder how it felt to have his stepmother Sarah try to cut him off from his father when she declared to Abraham, "Get rid of that slave woman and her son [Ishmael], for that woman's son will never share in the inheritance with my son Isaac" (Genesis 21:10).[1]*

- How would you have felt?
- How does it feel knowing that lots of God's people grew up in stepfamilies?
- What are some aspects of our family that are confusing for you? What aspects do you feel both good and bad about?

2. Question for teens and young adults: What messages do you get at church about divorce and living in a stepfamily? If we asked the pastor what he thought of families like ours, what do you think he'd say?

3. Question for teens and young adults: How is our family or are you treated differently from other kids by people at church?

4. Question for teens and young adults: This chapter reminded me that there is grace for our family. How is that helpful to you as well?

### ■ FOR ALL COUPLES

1. How does the survey of Old Testament families make you feel about your stepfamily?

2. On a scale of 1 to 10 (with 10 being the strongest), how strong is your relationship with Christ? How strong is your spouse's relationship with Christ?

3. To what degree have you been alienated from him in the past? What was happening at that time?

4. What messages that you have received from the church have discouraged your walk?

5. In what ways do you feel unworthy of God's grace and forgiveness?

6. What parts of your life (such as self-reliance, pride, or selfish desires) do you hold on to? What is difficult to surrender?

7. What hurts have you had difficulty letting go of? Share about your journey toward forgiveness.

8. Realizing that the ground is level at the foot of the cross—that is, we're all in need of a redeemer—what do you need to do individually and as a couple to begin living in a right relationship with Christ?

9. Whether your relationship to Christ is just beginning or going strong, list three habits that would deepen your knowledge of God's Word and his will for your life.

# Smart Step Two: STEP Down

*Adjust your expectations and learn
how to cook a stepfamily*

Therefore I tell you, do not be anxious about your life, what you
will eat or what you will drink, nor about your body, what you
will put on. Is not life more than food, and the body more than
clothing? Look at the birds of the air: they neither sow nor reap
nor gather into barns, and yet your heavenly Father feeds them.
Are you not of more value than they? . . . Therefore do not be
anxious, saying, "What shall we eat?" or "What shall we drink?"
or "What shall we wear?" . . . But seek first the kingdom of God
and his righteousness, and all these things will be added to you.
Therefore do not be anxious about tomorrow, for tomorrow will
be anxious for itself. Sufficient for the day is its own trouble.

Matthew 6:25–26, 31, 33–34

f the Israelites had known that they would face the Red Sea, be pursued
by Pharaoh and his army, and face great tests of their faith, do you think
they would have ever embarked on the journey to the Promised Land?

More than once they considered going back because the costs of the trip were much more than they had expected. They always are. Perhaps that's why God didn't tell them what was in store. Instead, he simply called upon them to trust him with what stood directly in front of them. All the Israelites had to do was trust God's faithfulness with each step they took. I think we would all find the journeys of life much less worrisome if we could just be faithful to God with what stands in front of us and not fret over what tomorrow may hold.

We cannot help but have expectations of what lies ahead. And because love and romance are natural blinders, expectations are often filled with unrealistic visions for how stepfamily life will proceed. Knowing the stepcouple divorce rate is considerably higher than first marriages, would you form a stepfamily if you believed you would soon join those making up that statistic? Of course not. No one assumes he or she is destined for marital failure or even distress. We assume, whether it is a first marriage or a remarriage, that love will conquer all.

> ### Dating Couples: Knowing Yourself
>
> One dangerous motivation for finding new love is running from the ache of pain. Feelings of guilt, rejection, loss, and sadness can have an intoxicating and blinding effect on your ability to make wise dating choices. For more, read *Dating and the Single Parent*.

During pre-stepfamily counseling, I consider it my job to break through the fog of "being in love" and give couples a realistic picture of the challenges, as well as the rewards, of stepfamily life. But I'm amazed at how easily the challenges are discounted and minimized. "I can see how that might impact someone else," they say, "but we're different. The kids are getting along just fine, and God has obviously brought us together; this must be right." Can you hear the expectation that harmony before the wedding will immediately translate into family harmony after the wedding? *Reader beware:* If you allow unrealistic expectations like this to drive the way you attempt to bring your family together, you are in for a great deal of disappointment.

Whether you are not yet married or are a few years down the road, use this chapter to examine your expectations and listen to what is realistic. Learning to accept "what is" versus "what you think should be" is critical to your emotional well-being and dedication. It also sets you up to relax in the Lord's timing rather than be overtaken by the "blended family" myth.

## Hopes, Expectations, and Realities

In her intriguing memoir describing her journey from single parenthood into a remarriage, Wendy Swallow writes,

> What I thought I was doing by remarrying was going home, back into the warm hearth that is the family . . . but in actuality, though, remarrying isn't about going home. It's about going someplace else entirely new, almost as if you've stepped through a looking glass. Things appear normal, but there are all sorts of strange contortions to life, things that aren't readily apparent on the surface. In the end, remarriage turned out to be quite different than I imagined—indeed, from what most of us would imagine.[1]

Whether a first or fifth marriage, everyone has expectations for how life will turn out. But as the author above discovered, stepfamily life is full of "strange contortions" that don't meet up with our expectations. I suppose you can blame hope. We all hope for the best in life and assume that love will find a way. But hope must be tempered by reality—otherwise, one can be blindsided by stepfamily realities.

Consider Carol, a widow who wondered if she and her boyfriend were ready to get married. Her story was full of hope—and unrealistic expectations. She and Mike had met over the Internet through an online dating service and had not actually met in person yet; she lived on the East Coast and he in the Midwest. Carol and Mike had been cyber-dating for six months. She had five children, ranging in age between fifteen and four, and her husband had been deceased for less than two years. Mike was divorced and had four children (ages eighteen to eleven). His first wife had an affair that ended their marriage, and she was physically abusive toward the children. Ongoing legal battles over his ex-wife's time and impact on the children were far from resolved.

As we talked, Carol said things like, "If you ignore the children, I believe Mike and I have all the ingredients between us to be very happily married." Well, that might be possible, but who can ignore the children? Carol even assumed that moving her children to the Midwest wouldn't be burdensome for them because she homeschools. That's hardly the only consideration for children, especially teenagers. She admitted that her goal was to give her children a father again, and, based on six months of online dating, she believed Mike could be the replacement father her children needed. She also believed that accepting his four children—whom she'd never met—wouldn't be a problem for her.

Carol's hopes were shaping her unrealistic expectations for the new marriage and family. Her attitudes were reflective of common misconceptions about stepfamily life. For example, she assumed that the roles for stepparents are the same as those for biological parents; she expected that the children would adjust to the new family and living arrangements quickly and easily; she assumed that love for her stepchildren, and undoubtedly love between the stepchildren, would develop smoothly; and she believed that a past filled with loss and heartache for all nine children would not be a barrier to their new family's success.[2]

She obviously wanted to be a "blended" family.

### Blending Is Not the Goal

In the U.S. a common term used to refer to the stepfamily is *blended family*. But many stepfamily therapists, educators, and researchers do not use the term *blended family* simply because most stepfamilies don't completely blend—and if they do, someone usually gets *creamed* in the process![3]

Blending is not the goal. When you're in the kitchen, blending is a process by which you combine ingredients into one fluid mixture—think of a fruit smoothie or a cream soup. Rarely can it be said that a stepfamily becomes one in a relational sense. More realistic is a process by which the various parts integrate, or come into contact with one another, much like a casserole of distinct parts. For example, it's to be expected that biological parents and children will always have a stronger bond than stepparents and stepchildren, even if all goes well. And biologically related children will always have a tighter connection than stepsiblings. This is not to say that stepfamilies can't be close, connected, loving homes; many will develop deep emotional bonds. They just don't "blend" in the sense of becoming one fluid family smoothie.

John was a very conscientious stepfather. He impressed me with his commitment to the Lord and desire to be a positive influence on his stepfamily.

Yet he was longing for something deeper. "Why doesn't my stepson show as much desire for a relationship with me as he does with his dad?" John asked. "His dad is a jerk—he breaks promises to spend time with David, he forgets his birthday, and when they are together he drops David off at his grandmother's house. I've been with David since he was four, and even now, ten years later, David prefers spending time with his father. Why does that hurt so much?"

I had spent a fair amount of time with David and knew that he greatly respected and loved his stepfather. Yet the pull to know his dad was tremendous (as is frequently the case with an unavailable noncustodial parent). A blood relationship, for David, was thicker than his mom's marriage. The reason John hurt so much was that he still carried the hope that he and his stepson would be one fluid mixture. They had not and probably would not "blend," but they had already integrated quite well. John was simply placing the bar too high. Stepping down his expectations would have resulted in less hurt and a greater awareness of his current connection with his stepson.

So if blending is not the goal, then how do you cook a stepfamily?

## How to Cook a Stepfamily: What Not to Do

Whether you realize it or not, you likely have an assumed integration style. By that I mean a set of assumptions about how your family ought to come together. Let's use cooking as an analogy to identify some integration styles that generally don't work.

### Blender

We've already noted that this mentality assumes all ingredients can be whipped together into one smooth mixture. This assumes each ingredient will relate to the others in the same uniform fashion. There is no uniqueness granted to the different ingredients and little space for diversity.

"Why can't I build a relationship with my stepdaughter? She was sixteen when I married her mother. The other kids were ten and eight, and I haven't had any trouble building a bond with them." Keeping in mind that time is essential to relationship development, building a bond with teenagers is slow-going because they are gradually moving away from the family. It is quite normal for a stepparent to have close bonds with one stepchild and be working on bonds with another, while experiencing a distant relationship with a third. Relationships will be different within the same stepfamily, not one fluid mixture.

Another blender example is assuming that with the passage of time the losses that children experienced before the new stepfamily will have no lingering effects on their lives.

This blender assumption could be seen as self-serving on the part of adults, but isn't necessarily a selfish assumption; seeing our children's grief is heavy on us. For years after their brother's death, I've watched my two other children struggle to function at school, to sleep, to connect with people who have relatively problem-free lives, to attend churches that are "churchy" and put on airs, to make new friendships with people who never knew Connor—the list goes on and on. I don't like watching them struggle, and I do what I can to help them cope. The truth is, loss has changed us forever, and we can't go back—and I can't expect them to no longer feel the effects. Neither can you.

### Food Processor

These stepfamilies chop up one another's history and attempt to instantly combine all ingredients with rapid speed. When love doesn't occur right away, persons are left feeling torn to pieces; no one remains whole.

A classic example of this mentality is the adult who demands that the stepchildren call their stepparent "Daddy" or "Mommy." It is as if the child is told, "We've chopped up your real dad and thrown him to the side. This is your new dad." Some parents actually think their children will buy that!

Another example is stepfamilies that assume they can't honor traditions that were established in the first family or single-parent family, because it would leave someone out. What they fail to realize is that chopping up the tradition also chops up the people who honored it. It results in another loss and invites resentment toward the new family.

### Microwave

These families refuse to be defined as a stepfamily and seek to heat the ingredients in rapid fashion so as to become a nuke-lear family (pun intended). They avoid labels like *stepfamily* and the implication that they are different than biological families. Some people tell me they resent being called a stepfamily because it makes them feel second rate. There is nothing inherently wrong with being a stepfamily. It is a family formed after loss; someone who is not a biological parent to at least one child has married into the role of being a stepparent. Really, what I think people who resent the stepfamily label are afraid of is not being accepted. They fear that if the children see them as a stepparent, they won't ever be embraced as a full-fledged family member. I understand and sympathize with that fear, but denying the reality of your life only hurts you.

For example, one barrier to healthy stepfamily adjustment is a parenting team that denies in the beginning the limitations of the stepparent's role (see chapter 7). One stepmother demonstrated her microwave mentality in an email, questioning an article I had published: "I was disturbed after reading your article," she began. "I am a stepmother of two wonderful girls. I became their stepmother when they were four and two. Shortly afterward, their biological mother abandoned them, and we have not seen or heard from her in almost four years. Don't get me wrong," she continued, "I consider this a blessing." (For whom, I wondered.) "My point is, I am the girls' mother. No step or halves or any other modifier. . . . Our family can and does function like any other family."

Right now this stepmother obviously feels good about her role and stepfamily. For that I am grateful. But I wonder how she will feel when the school tells her she can't get a copy of the girls' report cards since she isn't their mom, or what if her husband dies and the court gives custody of the children to their maternal grandparents since they are "next of kin"? (See chapter 8 for more on legal matters and stepfamilies.) What if their biological mother reappears after a number of years hoping to resurrect her relationship with her two daughters? Or perhaps the girls are secretly keeping their mother present through fantasies about her. Perhaps they will someday seek her out, trying to discover more about their genetic and cultural heritage (as do many adopted children). Don't get me wrong—I'm pleased that this stepmother feels so close to her stepdaughters. But whether she wants to accept it or not, she lives in a stepfamily, not a biological family.

Coming to accept your unique challenges and opportunities as a stepfamily is a tremendous first step to finding creative solutions to your dilemmas. If you refuse to admit a difference, you inadvertently shut off your ability to learn new, more effective ways of relating.

### Pressure Cooker

This family cooking style results in ingredients and spices (that is, rituals, values, and preferences) being put under pressure to meld together completely. The family is under great duress, and since expectations are so high, the lid often blows off the pot.

I've watched dating parents, for example, plead with their kids to like, accept, and love their dating partner (because it would make the parent happy). The message is "What's good for me should be good for you, now take care of me by liking him." The parent's selfishness is channeled into pressuring the children.

Another example of the pressure cooker mentality is stepfamilies that assume the answer to every conflict in holiday ritual is to combine the traditions. Paul and his children developed a meaningful Christmas tradition in which each person opened one gift on Christmas Eve and the remaining gifts the following morning. However, his new wife, Sharon, and her children held the tradition of opening all the gifts Christmas morning after a special breakfast. In a panic, Paul called a few weeks before their second Christmas together. "I'm dreading Christmas this year. Last year Sharon and I combined our holiday traditions and it was disastrous. To honor my family we had all the children open a gift Christmas Eve, and to honor Sharon's family we had breakfast and opened the remaining gifts. But no one liked the outcome. Everyone acted as if we were at a funeral instead of a celebration, and eventually Sharon and I ended up in a fight that lasted through New Year's Day. What are we supposed to do this year—go to our separate corners and pray no one throws a punch?" I'll discuss surviving holidays in chapter 9, but for now understand that combining rituals works sometimes, but sometimes it doesn't; pressuring or criticizing people who are struggling with the adjustment usually ensures that it doesn't.

### Tossed

Like a salad, this style throws each ingredient into the air with no consideration as to where it might fall. The ingredients keep some of their integrity, yet are expected to fit together with the other pieces. Examples of this style can be subtle or extreme.

When one child is spending time at their other home, the remaining children may believe they can play with the absent child's toys or belongings. Children should be taught that even though someone has been temporarily tossed to the other home, the absentee's stuff is not free game. If Susie wants to wear her stepsister's sweater, she should call her at the other home and ask her permission. If Brooke wants to play with her stepbrother Cole's video game, she needs to call and ask his permission or establish ground rules before he leaves the house. Respecting one another's possessions is important because it teaches people to honor others; it also communicates belonging to the child who is spending time at the other home. "You may be at your dad's house, but you still have a place here."

More extreme examples of the tossed integration style are noncustodial parents who make frequent moves and expect their children to immediately adjust to the disruption in visitation schedules. Parents who expose their children to a revolving door of dating partners or live-in lovers and those who engage in Velcro marriage (a series of stick-and-peel marriages) are also tossing their stepfamily about. This exposes the children to a variety of unstable living environments, changes in school and social arrangements, financial insecurity, and unhealthy relationship models.

## Culinary Insights for Cooking a Stepfamily

### Crockpot Cooking

"So, if all of these integration styles are generally not helpful, what style should we use?" I recommend a Crockpot cooking style. Stepfamilies choosing this style understand that *time* and *low heat* make for an effective combination. Ingredients are thrown together in the same pot, but each is left intact, giving affirmation to its unique origin and characteristics. Slowly and with much intentionality, the low-level heat brings the ingredients into contact with one another. As the juices begin to flow together, imperfections are purified, and the beneficial, desirable qualities of each ingredient are added to the taste. The result is a dish of delectable flavor made up of different ingredients that give of themselves to produce a wondrous creation.

The key to Crockpot stepfamilies is *time* and *low heat*. I've already stressed the importance of being patient with the integration process and not trying to force love, care, or togetherness (the average stepfamily needs 5–7 years to integrate); perhaps you've noticed that the one common element of the food processor, microwave, pressure cooker, and blender integration styles is an attempt to quickly combine the various ingredients (people, rituals, and backgrounds). Such an effort almost always backfires, bringing a backlash of anger and resentment.

Stepfamilies need *time* to adjust to new living conditions, new parenting styles, rules, and responsibilities. They need *time* to experience one another and develop trust, commitment, and a shared history. They need *time* to find a sense of belonging and an identity as a family unit. None of these things can be rushed. People who are trying to prove to their parents, friends, church, minister, or *themselves* that their marriage decision was right for everyone, need their family to "blend" quickly. But they are often greatly disappointed and feel like failures. A slow-cooking mentality, however, brings relief from the pressure to show everyone you can get along because you assume from the beginning that it will likely take years for your stepfamily to integrate. It also invites you to relax in the moment and enjoy the small steps your stepfamily is making toward integration rather than pressuring family members to move ahead.

Cooking with *low heat* refers to your gradual, intentional efforts to bring the parts together. It is working smarter, not harder. To illustrate the Crockpot mentality at work, let me apply some Crockpot approaches to the previous examples of what not to do.

A Crockpot stepfather, as opposed to the blender stepfather, might also be concerned about the slow pace at which he is bonding with his stepdaughter, but he wouldn't allow that worry to drive him to blender behavior. Rather, slow-cooker stepparents understand the cardinal rule of relationship development with stepchildren: Let the stepchild set the pace for the relationship and match their level of openness. If she is affectionate toward the stepfather, let him return her affection. If she remains distant or standoffish, he shouldn't force himself upon her, but search for common interests that naturally bring them together without effort.

The food processor adults had a similar struggle. They hoped the children would want to refer to their new stepparent with a term of endearment.

When this didn't happen naturally, the food processor parents demanded they do so (e.g., "Call me Daddy"). But a Crockpot adult who understands (even while wishing it were otherwise) that the terms children use are indicative of their evolving relationship with the stepparent and their loyalties to the other biological parent, would relax about stepparent titles and negotiate something that works for both stepparent and child. Further, they would be flexible to understand that different children may utilize different terms based on their evolving relationship. A stepparent can be "Daddy" to his youngest stepchild, "James" to his next oldest, and "Mr. James" to the teenager. Crockpot stepfamilies recognize the emotional and psychological attachment children have to biological parents and don't force them to change those attachments.

The microwave-turned-Crockpot mother will accept that her husband will gradually bond with her children. As a Crockpot mom, the formerly frustrated pressure cooker dating mom will not respond with anger to her son for not immediately embracing the man she is dating. She will look past his oppositional behavior to see a boy who is struggling with loss, unable to connect with his biological father, and discouraged with his family circumstances. And Paul, the pressure cooker stepfather who tried to meld two Christmas traditions, would allow his stepfamily to develop an entirely new Christmas tradition. He and his wife, for example, might have a series of family meetings with the children to discuss their preferences. It may be that they decide on an entirely new tradition to honor each family's history by alternating how gifts are opened, or they may decide to let each parent and their children keep their own tradition.

This last idea refers to "mini-family" activities. Early in a stepfamily's integration process it can be helpful to maintain separate family traditions and rituals by giving parents permission to spend time with their children without the steprelations present. Stepparents need to give their new spouse and stepchildren time to be alone without intrusion. The biological parent can play games with her children, while the stepparent enjoys a personal

> **What Kids Need**
>
> The irony of blender and pressure cooker actions is that they sabotage the bonding process. Remember, what "ingredients" in the Crockpot need is time to soften and combine with other ingredients on their own timetable. The more pressure to soften, the less likely they are to do so.

hobby or goes shopping with his children. Such mini-family activity helps children get uninterrupted time with their biological parent and siblings, honoring their need for attention from the ones they love most. It also affirms to children that they have not completely lost access to their parent. As helpful as compartmentalized mini-family activities can be, however, those without a Crockpot mentality often perceive segregated time as an indication of family division.

Troy and Meredith called me with a typical integration struggle—what to do with free time on Saturday afternoons. Prior to the remarriage, Troy and his children—Josh, eleven, and Emily, nine—enjoyed spending their Saturdays doing activities together. Whether miniature golfing, playing softball with friends, or riding bikes in the park, their priority was doing something together. Meredith and her sons—Terry, thirteen, and Joe, eight—had a different preference for free time. They valued independent time away from each other so each could pursue his or her particular interests. Meredith considered it her downtime to relax and read a good book; Terry enjoyed playing with friends, while Joe mastered his latest computer game.

At the time they called, Troy and Meredith had tried everything they knew to create a "blended family." They challenged each other and the kids to take turns spending their Saturdays doing activities together or apart. One week they would all go miniature golfing only to discover that Meredith's kids complained they were missing out on their fun. Joe would then pester Emily when he got bored, quickly turning the outings into arguments. First the kids would whine and complain, and then Troy would suggest to Meredith that she needed to better control her son. She would feel attacked and defensive about her parenting and resent Troy's "controlling" behavior.

The next week they would try to let everyone experience the joys of doing their own thing. But inevitably one of Troy's children would try to join Meredith's children in some activity, resulting in arguments and slamming doors.

"We've tried everything," they insisted.

"No," I responded, "you've just tried the blender cooking style, hoping to create a biological family that does everything together. What you need to do is back off and honor one another's past by spending time with your kids doing what you like most."

"You mean he should go golfing with his kids, while the boys and I do separate things? That wouldn't be a family afternoon at all," Meredith challenged.

My response was sobering. "Yes it would. It would be a stepfamily afternoon." I went on to explain that pressuring the various ingredients to blend was blowing the lid off the pot. Troy and Meredith needed to accept their family as different so they could discover a creative solution. Mini-family activities might not *feel* like a good solution because they were trying to steer their family as they would a biological family. Accepting their stepfamily as one *in the integration process* would help them to see that *for now,* this was the best solution. Plus, the mini-family activity would only last a couple of hours. After cooking a little longer—giving the family time to come together—spending the afternoon together might become more appropriate.

> **Reducing Friction and Tension in the Home**
>
> Learn what you can do in the Smart Questions, Smart Answers bonus material, available at SmartStepfamilies.com/view/learn.

Unrealistic expectations often set couples up to overcook their stepfamily. Trying to force, pressure, or quickly cook the ingredients of your home will likely result in a spoiled dish. But stepping down your expectations and giving your stepfamily time to cook slowly will move you closer to the Promised Land. Relax.

### Cooking Success

One of the advantages that a revised edition of a book gives you is success stories. Through the years this last section on developing a Crockpot mentality has resulted in significant family improvement for my clients, conference attendees, and readers of the first edition of this book. Countless stepmoms, for example, have shared with me how letting go of the high heat expectation that they become an integral member of their family has lowered their anxiety, sense of failure, and blood pressure! And best of all, it helps them to enjoy their family as it is rather than agonize over what it isn't. The paradox, of course, is that when adults who used to be full of pressuring and blender behavior relax, the entire family relaxes a little, too. That in turn creates space for ingredients to soften on their own and the family moves forward. In *The Smart Stepdad,* I shared another Crockpot success story. The example is so clearly articulated and demonstrates such a clear "before and after" change in family expectations that I decided to share it with you here as well.

After reading the first edition of this book, Charles and his wife, Debra, decided to make some changes in their home:

> When my kids came to visit for the weekend, they would hug some and shake hands with others, but after a while, her kids would migrate back to her and mine to me. At first we thought we had to group everyone together all the time so they would like each other. But we learned that it was okay to let them go where it was safe. We let them have their own space, do their own thing, and respected when and how they chose to come together. Things got better when we relaxed and didn't throw on the blender switch. We let them simmer and come together with a long moderate heat.[4]

In the beginning, Charles and Debra thought that in order for the step-siblings to become family their kids' attitudes needed to change. And they did. But *first*, Charles and Debra had to change their mentality from a blender to a Crockpot.

### Questions for Discussion

■ FOR PARENT-CHILD DISCUSSION (Discretion based on the age of the child and the quality of adult-child relationships is advised.)

For this chapter, instead of discussing questions, I suggest your family engage in an activity. Ask all the children to help you in the kitchen with a project. Have a recipe ready for a Crockpot dish of your choice. Let everyone add one ingredient to the pot. As they do, talk about how your family is like this dish. Note to the children that you are not stirring or blending the ingredients by hand but are relying on the Crockpot to bring everything together slowly over time. Also, talk about how long it takes to cook foods in a Crockpot and that for every hour, your stepfamily may need a year. Allow people to ask questions. Reconvene at the end of the cooking time, sit down together as a family, and enjoy the meal. As you eat, wonder with the children what the food would have tasted like at the beginning of its cooking time. Pray together at the end of the meal, asking God to give your family patience as you "cook together."

### ■ For All Couples

1. In what ways has this chapter discouraged you? How has it given you hope?

2. When did you first realize that your expectations were not becoming reality?

3. In what ways have your expectations been met successfully? Celebrate your successes and share what is going well for your home.

4. Which of the following myths have you been guilty of believing? Identify each and express what you hoped would come about as a result.

   • Love will happen instantly between all family members.

   • We'll do it better this time around.

   • Everything will fall quickly into place.

   • Our children will feel as happy about the remarriage as we do.

   • Blending is the goal of this stepfamily.

5. Which of the following integration styles have you been guilty of? What have been the results? Give an example.

   • Blender

   • Food processor

   • Microwave

   • Pressure cooker

   • Tossed

6. How does the Crockpot cooking mentality go against your natural desires and assumptions for how a stepfamily should integrate?

7. In what way is it a relief to know that time is important to the integration process?

8. What "low heat" approaches have you utilized already (even if you didn't realize it was important until now)?

9. What fears do you have that force you into a high-heat mode of response?

10. In what ways do you need to implement a low-heat mentality? What would you have to change about yourself?

11. How appropriate are mini-family activities for your stepfamily at this time? In what way might you implement this idea over the next month? Make a plan and share the outcome with your support group. Evaluate its effectiveness and decide whether to try it again.

■ FOR PRE-STEPFAMILY COUPLES

1. How is this book opening your eyes to the challenges of stepfamily life? List your hopes for how your future stepfamily will be an exception to the rule.

2. Now list reasons why you believe your family will successfully integrate.

3. How might these hopes and reasons create blinders for you?

4. As a couple, discuss the following expectations a stepmother expressed two years into her remarriage. How do you identify with her desires? How realistic do you believe them to be?

   • I thought my husband would appreciate how overwhelming and difficult it would be for me to care for his children.

   • I thought that raising his children would fill my need to be a mother.

   • I thought I would have more say in the children's visitation schedules (e.g., when we watch them for their mother, when they spend the night at a friend's house, etc.).

   • I expected to fit in, to be welcomed by his children, and to be treated well.

   • I expected to immediately take priority over all his other relationships, even his children.

# Smart Step Three: Two-STEP

*Your marriage must be a top priority*

Have you not read that he who created them from the beginning made them male and female, and said, "Therefore a man shall leave his father and his mother and hold fast to his wife, and the two shall become one flesh"? So they are no longer two but one flesh. What therefore God has joined together, let not man separate.

Matthew 19:4–6

Every family, including the stepfamily, is founded on the marital relationship. Yet the complexity of stepfamily life makes nurturing the marital relationship a tremendous challenge. Caution: It is easy for your marriage to get lost in the stepfamily forest, and without a strong marriage your entire family falls apart. As stepfamily educators and friends Gil and Brenda Stuart say, "If you ain't got the marriage, you ain't got nothing."[1]

The divorce rate in America is generally considered to be around 50 percent. However, a recent book by Shaunti Feldhahn calls this assumption into question. In *The Good News About Marriage* she accurately points out that while researchers *predict* that 40–50 percent of all marriages will end in divorce, the actual number of marriages that have divorced (referred to as the "current" divorce rate) is much lower; only 31 percent of all marriages have divorced (25 percent of first marriages and 34 percent of remarriages).[2] That really is good news.

The divorce rate specifically among stepfamily partners, while difficult to calculate exactly because of little research, seems to be considerably higher. Whether preceded by divorce, the death of a spouse, or a non-marital birth, I estimate that at least one-third of all weddings conducted in America today give birth to a stepfamily (it actually might be closer to 40 percent)[3] and that the current divorce rate for stepcouples is around 40–45 percent (most occur within five years).[4] Another way to view the impact of this statistic is through the eyes of children. A significant percentage of all children will watch their parents divorce at some time; half of those children will watch at least one parent divorce a second time.

Without question the stepcouple divorce rate is higher than the divorce rate of first marriages. But why? I believe the intersection of marital dynamics and complex stepfamily relationships, including issues around stepparenting, cause family stress that eventually erodes marital trust and commitment. To protect your marriage from this negative force you must get smart about managing the dynamics between you and surrounding you. That is the focus of this chapter.

## God's Design From the Beginning

The beautiful story of Genesis 2 is of a God who provided a partner for man and for woman. Two people who would complete each other, share intimacy, work side by side in child rearing, and reflect God's love to each other. The mystery of marital oneness (Ephesians 5:31–32) was created by God for humankind. Marriage was created with purpose.

From the beginning God was at the center of the marital relationship. He was the focal point for Adam and Eve's relationship, giving purpose and instruction for life. Marriage, like all of God's activity in this world, is meant to usher people into relationship with him. He loves us with his whole heart and desires to be known by us. Marriage, then, is about knowing God and sharing his love with another, who, in turn, loves us in such a way that we are drawn toward God. In fact, the closer we draw to God as individuals, the closer we come to our mates; the closer we become in marriage, the more intimate we become with God.

This spiritual intimacy is at the heart of Christian marriage and forms the basic divine purpose of marriage for all times, places, and cultures. Healthy, growing marriages seek to build on this foundation. Couples who place God at the center of their relationship, whether a first, second, third, or fourth marriage, put him in charge of their wills, their choices, their money, their vocation, and their parenting. Such couples, while never achieving marital perfection, will undoubtedly experience some of God's richest blessings. This holy love triangle has three parts: each partner's relationship with God and their relationship with each other.

Loving God involves everything we are and have—our heart, soul, mind, and strength. Loving each other involves romantic affections, committed love, and a host of other practical life skills and qualities, including trust, a sense of companionship, a satisfying sexual relationship, and healthy communication and conflict resolution skills. It is beyond the scope of this book to address all the areas of a healthy marriage. For that I would point you to *The Smart Stepfamily Marriage* by David H. Olson and me; it provides a comprehensive look at marriage in a stepfamily based on the largest survey of stepcouples ever conducted (a study guide for groups is also available).

I will focus here on two key barriers to marital oneness in stepfamilies that, I believe, account for the higher divorce rate in stepfamily marriages. Drawing upon the love of God and loving each other through these barriers will greatly strengthen your marriage and help it to grow and mature.

---

### Best Practices for Enriching Your Marriage

To keep the energy in your marriage moving in a positive direction, prioritize two things:

- To strengthen your couple relationship, attend a general marriage enrichment class, workshop, or conference every year.
- In addition, attend a class or conference for stepfamily couples to specifically confront the stressors of stepfamily living.

## Barrier One: Parent-Child Allegiance—*When Children Precede the Marriage*

God's design for the family includes a man and a woman beginning their marriage by separating from their families of origin. As the two "leave father and mother" emotionally, financially, and psychologically and "be joined" to each other, a foundation is laid for their new home (see Genesis 2:18–25). The marriage relationship is established before children are born and continues as the foundation to the home throughout the child-rearing years. Scripture affirms the necessity of what some have called a honeymoon period as the couple solidifies their relationship: "When a man is newly married, he shall not go out with the army or be liable for any other public duty. He shall be free at home one year to be happy with his wife whom he has taken" (Deuteronomy 24:5). But stepfamily couples don't have this bonding time. In fact, because parent-child relationships are bonded by blood and have more history, the marital relationship, instead of being the strongest bond in the home, is often the weakest.

The normal progression in a first marriage is for the couple's relationship to broaden from one characterized by romance before children to one of partnership after children. Without a honeymoon period, stepfamily couples are forced to negotiate their partnership at the same time they are solidifying their romance. Needless to say, the process is complicated, and frequently the couple's personal relationship gets lost in the stepfamily forest.

The challenge for stepfamily couples, then, is to make their relationship a top priority and position it as the foundation of the home. This does *not* mean de-prioritizing children or neglecting them. "Wait a minute," said Carrie. "You mean I have to put my husband before my children? I understand your point, but they are my flesh and blood. He's just someone I picked up alongside the road somewhere." Her tongue-in-cheek meaning was evident, but so was her fear. "I can't do that to my kids. I don't ever want them to think I love him more than I love them."

Her statement calls attention to a number of legitimate fears for biological parents that new spouses/stepparents must understand. First, children suffer significantly when a parent dies or their parents divorce, and biological parents feel guilty because of it. Guilt is a powerful emotion that can easily motivate parents to protect their children from future pain. This effort to protect children can take on many different forms both before and after a stepfamily is formed. Shielding a child from inconvenience, letting them off the hook from consequences, preventing a stepparent from having an equal say in parenting decisions, monitoring the amount of contact between stepsiblings, and controlling money so that children don't go without are just a few examples. Many of these inadvertently align the child with the biological parent to the detriment of the parent-stepparent (and marital) relationship. This is very dangerous to the long-term viability of the family. Gary and Emily know what I mean.

Gary's sixteen-year-old stepdaughter, Amy, walked into the kitchen while he was fixing dinner. He politely asked her to set the table while he finished the meal. She ignored him. A second time he asked, and this time all he got in return was a halfhearted, "I'll do it in a minute." Ten minutes later she showed no indication of helping, so he repeated his request, this time with tension in his voice. Amy's mother, Emily, walked into the room just as he was raising his voice. At first, Emily remembered how important it was to support Gary, so she gave Amy "the look." Amy grudgingly responded. Later, as the family sat down to eat, Gary made a snide comment about how Amy had forgotten the knives. Emily came unglued. "Why do you have to criticize her like that? Can't you just leave well enough alone?" Gary felt that Emily was once again taking Amy's side and became resentful. In an instant Gary's conflict with Amy became Gary's conflict with Emily and ended when he slammed the front door and shouted something about divorce.

Stepfamily couples can learn two things from this story. First, aligning with each other as a couple is delicate sometimes, so hold on to the "little victories." Emily's initial support of Gary's request was a step in the right direction. But Gary, when he pushed for a big victory with a comment about forgetting the knives, turned the situation into a big defeat. Gary should not have criticized Amy's effort at the dinner table. He could have voiced his concern to his wife later (behind closed doors), and together they could have decided on a standard of conduct for the future. Later he confessed that his comment grew out of his frustration that she hadn't accepted him as her stepfather and because she refused to honor his authority. He should have settled for the "little victory." Little victories or big defeats.

Second, Emily's initial effort to support Gary was short-circuited by her need to protect Amy from more harm. Emily's divorce had been difficult, and Amy got caught in the marital conflict often. Emily could have expressed her feelings about Gary's negative comment behind closed doors or done so at the table without attacking, but she lost her ability to respond appropriately when her allegiance to Amy took over.

Let me point out that conflict over loyalty to children is not unique to modern-day stepfamilies. In Genesis 16 and 21, we read how Abraham, on more than one occasion, got caught in the jealousy and competition of Sarah and Hagar. Sarah even approached Abraham and insisted he cut his son Ishmael out of the will because he was born to Hagar. "Cast out this slave woman with her son, for the son of this slave woman shall not be heir with my son Isaac" (21:10). She was protecting Isaac's interests and insisted that Abraham put her first. But the decision wasn't so easy for him. The Scripture goes on to say that "what Sarah said upset Abraham very much. After all, Ishmael was his son" (21:11 NIRV).

Stepfamily couples experience countless instances where the biological parents feel caught between their spouse and their children. Perhaps it is a decision over what treat the family will pick up after Bible class. The kids want ice cream from Baskin Robbins, but your spouse wants pie from Perkins. Any one time this happens may not feel significant, but repeated over time choices like this feel like a statement of loyalty and priority. If you choose to get pie for your spouse, your children may feel slighted and get angry. If you choose ice cream, your spouse may complain. Either way, biological parents feel like they can't win for losing. We'll return to how to handle this situation in a moment.

Eventually biological parents must make choices that elevate the status of the stepparent, and more important, the couple as a unit. Ice cream or pie is not the issue; it is whether the marital team leads the home or not. The real culprit driving the barrier of parent-child allegiance is when biological parents refuse to take whatever risks are necessary in order to move their spouse and marriage into a position of leadership. What risks are involved? Making children angry, upsetting the delicate balance between households, and giving an ex-spouse a foothold to use against you in court. Or it could be feeling guilty about bringing a stepparent and stepsiblings into the child's life, or even emotionally investing in the new marriage.

Notice that it's the biological parent who ultimately has the responsibility to elevate the status of the stepparent and the marriage in the family.

If they don't, it probably won't happen. I'll say more about that later, but first, let's recognize that stepparents with the wrong attitude can make this process even more difficult.

### How Stepparents Contribute to the Problem

The parent-child allegiance coin has another side. Biological parents can feel resentful when stepparents pile on guilt trips or turn every little instance into a major issue.

Jennifer wrote to me, complaining that her husband focused too much on his daughter when she came to visit. At first I thought, *Yes, that's a common problem for fathers who see their children infrequently each month.* She then described how the daughter had the gall to ask her father to take her to an art gallery—*alone.* The stepmother felt that the daughter was intentionally pushing her out; it felt even worse that her husband gave consideration to the request. At that point in reading her email I was feeling a little sympathy for the stepmom, especially if this happened repeatedly over time.

And then I read the next portion of the email. It turns out that the daughter doesn't visit a couple weekends a month as I had assumed, but only a couple times *a year.* She lives in another country. In my mind, that changed everything. Of course, the daughter and the dad want to make the most of their time together; of course, there is need for exclusive time together. And no, the stepmom should not be in competition for that time. After giving his daughter some focused attention, the father can orchestrate

---

### Managing Time

Choices to spend time either with a spouse or children can be stressful. Early in the Crockpot make "both/and" choices to this apparent "either/or" dilemma.

- Share your torn-in-two feelings with your spouse; reassure them that the marriage is your ultimate priority.
- Try to balance time and energy with each; don't keep score, splitting every hair.
- If you have different opinions about how time should be spent, extend grace to each other and try to meet in the middle.

opportunities for his wife to join them, but for the stepmom to turn every minute into a competition for his loyalty is a poor choice. Rather, she should give the gift of time and permission for them to be together.

### Comparing Loves

One of the problematic thoughts in both biological parents and stepparents that pits couples against each other as it relates to parent-child allegiance has to do with comparing and ranking loves. Do you remember Carrie's comment, "I don't ever want them to think I love him more than I love them"? The love a parent feels for a child is qualitatively different than the love a spouse feels for his/her husband or wife. Carrie's fear is misguided because it assumes she has a certain number of love points to give away and once they're gone, everyone else will have to do without. This simply isn't true. God provides us with an endless supply of love.

Children often feel insecure when their parent marries and may even attempt to play the "you love him more" card to manipulate parents into choosing them. But biological parents who know they can love many people at once won't be manipulated. Likewise, stepparents shouldn't force their spouse into an either/or position to determine his or her dedication. They should, instead, acknowledge their personal worth in Jesus Christ, realize that during the Crockpot years children need reassurance of their parent's love, and work with their spouse to find time together. Stepparents cannot afford to be insecure. (Stepfamilies were not made for the emotionally fragile.)

One more thought: On a couple of rare occasions over the past two decades I've seen children who just wouldn't let this issue go. The "I have enough love points for both of you" response from their parent wouldn't cut it for them. If you run into this, give them what I call "the speech" and then move on. It includes a reframing of their concern into something that might make a little more sense to them:

> Because you keep bringing this up, I can tell that you need some reassurance. I do love you. You are my child and I'm committed to you for life. And I'm committed to my husband/wife for life. It's not about who is number one in my life—you both are. Just like all of my children are equally important to me, both you and my husband/wife are equally important. You kids are the most important children in my life and he/she is the most important adult in my life. You're both number one. I hope you can rest in that.

## So What's the Answer?

Even if you give "the speech" and limit comparing the amount of love you have for spouse and child, and if stepparents relax enough not to make every circumstance a life-or-death dilemma, you may still feel caught in the middle and still have to work toward elevating the status of your "us-ness" within the home.

The answer to the parent-child allegiance barrier to marital oneness is unity. Stress in a stepfamily generally divides people along biological lines. When push comes to shove, the allegiance (or loyalty) between parents and children often wins out over the marriage unless the couple can form a unified position of leadership. If they cannot govern the family as a team, the household is headed for anger, jealousy, and rejection. Unity within the couple's relationship bridges the emotional gap between the stepparent and stepchildren and positions both adults to lead the family. If a biological parent is not willing to build such a bridge with the stepparent, the children will receive an unhealthy amount of power in the home. All they have to do is cry "unfair" and their parent protects them from the "mean, nasty" stepparent. This almost always results in marital tension, conflict, resentment, and isolation.

As discussed in chapter 2, stepfamilies are divided into "insiders and outsiders," that is, those who are biologically related and those who aren't.[5] Insiders have a strong bond that pulls them together in the face of stress or conflict. Outsiders often feel that they don't belong and frequently try to force their way in. The biological parent in stepfamilies maintains relationships with both insiders (their children) and outsiders (new spouse and his or her children), and therefore, must position the stepparent as his or her teammate. Including the new spouse in parenting decisions (see chapter 7), setting a date night and keeping it, and taking a few minutes each day to connect as a couple without interruption are a few simple but significant ways to communicate the unity of the couple to the children. If the biological parent doesn't help the outsider stepparent take a leadership position, the stepparent is likely to try to force his or her way in. This almost always results in resentment and resistance from the insiders. Again, jealousy, rejection, and anger are common resulting emotions.

Now let me balance this truth by noting that biological parents must take a "both/and" stance with their children and new spouse. They must invest time and energy in both. Early in the marriage, it is especially important to stay connected with your children, but this doesn't mean the marriage can't be made a priority, even in front of the children.

Returning to the ice cream or pie dilemma, I suggest that stepfamily couples purposefully choose ice cream for the kids' sake early on and privately enjoy pie together. If the stepparent is agreeable to this solution, the couple is still unified in accommodating the children. As the Crockpot works over time, the biological parent can more overtly say no to the children while saying yes to the spouse. For example, "Sorry kids, we're going for pie tonight." Such a transition almost always elicits anger and insecurity from at least one child, if not all. But a stepfamily in which the couple isn't working toward affirming the importance of their relationship before the children is one destined for mediocrity.

Waiting for this to happen is difficult for many stepparents unless you are in agreement about how to handle such matters early on and over time. I'm suggesting that early in the Crockpot you strategically choose your battles. If it's just a decision between ice cream or pie, lean toward what the kids are used to, but if the decision is a parenting authority matter, lean toward making sure your "us-ness" wins. Try to keep in mind that biological parents in two-parent nuclear homes frequently make "ice-cream" sacrifices on behalf of their children. You must do the same. Be unified in your sacrifices for the children *and* make strategic choices to support your marriage.

> **Make Changes With Compassion**
>
> Demonstrating compassion toward a child who is protesting a change in rule or expectation helps to make the changes more palatable. "You are used to getting ice cream, aren't you? And now we're changing that. I get it; that is hard. I feel for you. However, tonight we're considering someone else in the family, so you can either join us for pie or sit quietly while we eat. Your choice."

### Two-Step

As you can tell, the above advice requires a delicate balance of marital teamwork. It is a dance that takes harmony and practice. Now you know why I titled this smart step the "two-step." Couples in Texas are well aware of a dance they call the two-step. Like all dances, it requires that the couple work together to stay in balance. Striving to make your marriage a top priority means balancing commitments to both the children and your spouse. As moving around the dance floor becomes more natural, greater harmony and enjoyment result. But as I've suggested, sometimes learning to dance means fighting some battles.

### Divide and Conquer

Not all stepfamilies struggle with the tug and pull of parent-child allegiance, but for most this developmental task is difficult. It takes a few to the brink of divorce.

I had been working with Jeff and his new wife, Kelly, for a few sessions when they walked in with worried looks on their faces. I had been trying to help them make room for Jeff's fourteen-year-old daughter, Lauren, who had recently come to live with them. The transition had been difficult, to say the least. Prior to Lauren's moving in, the couple had integrated quite well. Kelly brought four-year-old Becky to the marriage, and she had warmly accepted her stepfather. The couple enjoyed three relatively hassle-free years together—until Lauren moved in.

"Lauren wrote me this letter after our last session," Jeff explained. Lauren was very jealous of her stepmother and had been cornering her father about his marriage. At my direction he had already talked with Lauren about how he could love her and Kelly without competition, and he reassured her that she didn't need to be concerned about losing him. "She's really forcing the issue now," he said. He showed me the letter. It started with a classic adolescent manipulative tool—a guilt trip.

*Dear Dad,*

*Listen, I'm sorry I'm such a screw-up! But I really don't think I can do this anymore! I was thinking about what you said: It's (1) God; then (2) your spouse; then (3) your children! I can't live with you [believing] that the second Kelly and I get in a life-or-death situation you would save Kelly over your own flesh and blood. . . . I can't live with you, knowing that would happen. I can't live here knowing that you love Kelly more than me. And Kelly loves Becky more than you. And don't tell me there are different kinds of love, 'cause you put her above me. I can't take this anymore. I knew this girl in school who gave herself up for adoption; I really think I want to do that! I don't want to, but it's the only option.*

*Love,*
*Lauren*

Is it reasonable for a parent in this situation to be afraid? Absolutely. Everyone loses contact with someone when a family ends by death or divorce, and Jeff had lost a lot of time with his daughter. His time with her since the divorce had been very limited. Lauren had also missed her dad. The change of residence represented an opportunity for Lauren to reconnect with her dad, but now his relationship with Kelly appeared to be threatening her chances, so she resorted to guilt and threatening withdrawal to try to orchestrate closeness with her dad. (By the way, before you judge her tactics too quickly, let me note that many adults resort to guilt trips and emotional withdrawal in their marriage, too, with the hopes that they will foster closeness. They don't.)

Before we developed a game plan, I asked the couple to put themselves in Lauren's shoes for a moment. That was a stretch for Kelly, who only saw a manipulative teenager systematically eroding her marriage. Kelly hadn't wanted Lauren to "invade" their home, but didn't have much choice due to difficulties with Lauren's mother. Kelly bristled when I suggested Lauren was frightened and simply trying to find her place in her daddy's heart. She found it even more difficult to hear me say that neither of them should take it personally. "Please understand, Lauren didn't ask for her parents to divorce, and she didn't ask for you to get married. She needs some reassurance." Kelly had to find some compassion for Lauren; the couple couldn't afford to be divided by this maneuver or Lauren would conquer. Not taking this personally and finding compassion was Kelly's task at this point. Jeff had to step up to bat and swing at the pitch Lauren had thrown.

And Jeff did just that. He took a "both/and" approach with Kelly and Lauren, giving personal time to each. He and Lauren spent exclusive time together and renewed their relationship. Jeff also made sure he and Kelly dated on a regular basis no matter how much Lauren complained. In addition, Jeff took a firm role in setting boundaries with Lauren and carried out the consequences even though he feared making her mad and driving her away. At one point he let her know without question that if push came to shove, his loyalties were with Kelly. But since her father had become so involved in her life as well, Lauren didn't fear being forgotten. Eventually, with time and constant effort, Lauren backed away from competing with her stepmom.

Kelly's role as stepparent in this situation was to avoid fighting fire with fire. It is tempting for stepparents who are being pushed out by the stepchildren to fight back by insisting their spouse choose them in all circumstances. Unfortunately, that kind of stepparent easily falls victim to insecurity and resentment if the biological parent doesn't do just that. Kelly needed to stand tall and support Jeff as he dealt with his daughter. She needed to give him space to spend time with Lauren and reassure her of his love. She also needed to express her fears to Jeff privately and appropriately instead of with accusation and contempt. Trusting that he was on her side and giving the Crockpot time to cook were critical. Together they made it through the Sea of Lauren's Oppositions. And so can you.

## Barrier Two: The Ghost of Marriage Past

> The past has very little substance, but it stays close to your heels.
>
> Unknown

> A cat that sits on a hot stove won't ever sit on a hot stove again; neither will it sit on a cold stove.
>
> Mark Twain

It is human nature to view new relationships in light of previous ones. But doing so is like putting on poor quality sunglasses that are tinted yellow or black—everything you see has a yellow or black hue. Viewing a current relationship through a previous marital lens (and family-of-origin lens) sometimes leads to negative assumptions and expectations. Specific behaviors can also be interpreted negatively. If these assumptions are not examined or the lens not taken off, a new marriage can easily be colored by the experiences of the first (or previous). That's why it's critical that people take time to heal and resolve the ending of their marriage, whether by death or divorce, before jumping into another relationship. The circumstances of the loss (death or divorce) make a difference in how long

**Why Wait Two to Three Years to Begin Dating?**

In general, the first year is spent grieving heavily and finding your footing again. The second year one often thinks they're ready to date, but if they wait long enough they discover that it's just loneliness pushing its way out. In the third year people begin to realize that they can be alone and not be lonely or desperate. That's when you're ready to date again. (For more, read *Dating and the Single Parent*.)

someone should wait before dating, but in general I recommend individuals wait at least two to three years before beginning a serious relationship. All too often, however, people rebound from one failed marriage into another and take their tinted glasses with them. When circumstances in the new marriage remind someone of negativity in a previous marriage, the person becomes frightened and reactive. This second barrier to marital oneness in the stepfamily is what we might call being haunted by the ghost of marriage past.

Terri's first husband had an affair. She came home one day to discover he had packed his stuff and moved in with a woman half his age. The fallout from this rejection was almost more than she could handle. But with the help of a supportive church family, she and her eight-year-old son survived.

Bill made her feel good again. They met through a mutual friend and hit it off right from the start. He listened to her anger, supported her through the custody battle, and helped her son with his homework. Terri found herself trusting him with more and more of her life.

After the wedding, though, Terri would ask questions if Bill didn't come home on time. When they talked, she shared her thoughts, but not quite everything. She often felt it wise to watch her step and not become too transparent. After all, look what happened last time. When they made love, Terri offered her body to Bill, but not her passion. In other words, she was willing to meet his basic sexual need, but guarding her heart meant never fully joining her soul to his. A year into the marriage, she deemed it wise to put money in a secret bank account, just in case anything ever went wrong. Finally, Terri invested much of her time in her son, "because his father hurt him so much." Terri was haunted, and her marriage was slowly being sabotaged by her guarded heart and cautious love.

Don's second wife misused money. She continually forgot to record checks in the ledger, maxed out their credit cards, and bounced numerous checks. Even before the divorce, Don's credit was ruined; he had to borrow money from his parents to buy a car for his third wife, Heather. The first time Heather forgot to record an online billpay in the ledger, Don starting sweating bullets. He withdrew emotionally and demanded control over the checkbook. Heather was granted an allowance, but all expenditures beyond that had to be preapproved by him. Taking control seemed to be the only way to prevent another bad situation. But Heather resented Don's controlling behavior.

What's truly ironic about being haunted by the ghost of marriage past and responding out of fear is that it can become a self-fulfilling prophecy. If you treat someone as untrustworthy in spite of their efforts to love and please you, frustration is sure to set in. In his frustration, Bill found himself repeatedly trying to change his wife's mind about his being untrustworthy; she saw this as his being defensive. *I wonder what he's trying to hide?* she thought. Heather's resentment of Don's control became disrespect; she began pulling away emotionally and sexually.

I have a cartoon of a man shouting at his wife as she drives off with her luggage: "Marie, don't leave me. My ex-wife will think she's right when she says no one can live with me." That's a man who is married to one woman but emotionally tied to another. His divided attention has left him unable to meet his current wife's needs and haunted by a ghost. No one can live with him.

### Menacing Ghosts

Do you know what your ghost is? Can you recognize its voice and the fear it imposes? Maybe you have more than one. Whether you have experienced the death of a spouse or a divorce, here are some common ghosts that you might be able to relate to:

- **Protect the Kids.** This ghost seems to have the children's best interests at heart, but in reality, it is protecting you. It says, "What does he/she know? They're just a stepparent to your kids. You better watch out or your kids will experience even more pain. Protect them when you can."

- **Keep Your Eye on the Money.** Especially after experiencing a tremendous loss in income, this ghost urges you to watch every dime.

It says, "You better keep a little money stashed away just in case. You don't want to get stuck holding the bag again. And don't add their name on the house!"

- **Who's in Our Bed?** This ghost is concerned that sex this time around might pale in comparison to previous sexual relationships. It urges couples to "check for compatibility" before marriage and plants seeds of fear within the marriage. It says, "I wonder if he/she is thinking of someone else right now; I wonder how our lovemaking compares. Maybe I need to act sexier to keep their attention. Whatever you do, don't relax while making love, you need to perform well."

Specifically, the divorce ghost also has some predictable whispers:

- **Trust Not, Want Not.** This ghost says "Avoid vulnerability and the dangers of 'wanting.' Being in a position of wanting or pursuing the other person puts you in a vulnerable place—like walking on the edge of a cliff. Better to make sure they want you more than you want them." Careful, calculated guardedness is this ghost's friend.

- **Fear Factor.** This ghost says, "You better watch your back. You never know what's really going on with your spouse or when the other shoe will drop. I advise you to check cell phone bills, read his/her emails, and check to see if their stories are true. Remember, marriage is not forever." A thick emotional shield is this ghost's best protection from further harm.

- **You Know What That Means.** This ghost is quick to interpret the meaning of words and actions in a negative light. It says, "Did you hear that? That sounds just like what old so-and-so used to say, and you know what that means. You better beat them to the punch/watch your back/argue your case before it's too late." Defensiveness and judgment are this ghost's friends.

The widow ghost also has some unique whispers:

- **You'll Never Find Another One Like Him/Her.** Many widowed persons enjoyed their partner and didn't want to live without them. While divorced persons often look for someone different from their previous partner, widows and widowers often find themselves looking for someone much the same. When the partner or marriage takes on a different complexion, the person judges it "less than." This ghost says, "He/she was one of a kind. This person just can't live up to what you had. . . . You see? Did you see that right there? That's just what I was talking about. Good luck trying to make this work. Things just can't be the same."

What this ghost fails to realize, of course, is that this relationship can't be compared to the previous one. Yes, you're the same person, but it's the combination of two people that make up your "us-ness." Yellow and red make orange. But yellow and blue make green. Of course, your marital color is going to be different. Judge this relationship on its own merits.

- **What Would He/She Say About This Person?** Trying to evaluate a new dating partner or spouse through the eyes of your deceased spouse is ultimately an issue of permission. Some widows don't feel they can fully embrace a new relationship without the "permission" of a former spouse. This ghost says, "I know he/she told you before they died that they were okay with you getting remarried, but you don't know if they would approve of this specific person. You just can't be sure." Of course, that is true. You can't be sure. But then, that's not the point. If your former mate approved of you and found you to be competent, trust in any future mate for you would be based on their belief in you, not the person. Assuming they believed in you, then you *have* their approval.[6]

Your ghost, of course, might not sound exactly like these common examples. And that's the point—you have to find your ghost(s). Jennifer's first marriage was physically and verbally abusive. She never knew what to expect. "My ghost says, 'Is he going to snap one day and become the angry man? Keep your guard up and be ready to run.'" She continued, "I still live with fear from the past. It really haunts me even though my current marriage is peaceful. I keep waiting for the other shoe to drop."

After reading the first edition of this book, Veronica, a mid-forties remarried widow, started observing her emotional and behavioral patterns in order to identify her ghosts. She made a list of her fears and shared them with me. In her case, one of her ghosts had roots in the family she grew up in.

"Ghost #1," she wrote in her journal. "See what happens? Husbands get sick and die. You'll be abandoned again, and alone. Better not get too attached. Better keep some financial resources for yourself. Better act tough."

"Ghost #2: It's obvious that your husband doesn't love you as much as he loves his kids. Now, here you are . . . and this after your dad left you when you were eight and wasn't interested in you or your activities. It hurts to see your stepchildren have the love and security you always longed for but never had, doesn't it?"

"Ghost #3: You were hoping your husband would be able to make up for what you didn't have as a child and the horrible pain of losing your first husband. But he won't. He's a person with his own past, needs, and priorities. Who's really going to take care of you?"

### Becoming a Ghost Buster

For many people, having an open, trusting posture toward your new spouse and treating them fairly requires becoming a ghost buster. Jennifer and Veronica can teach us a lot about ghost busting.

First, they were humble enough to look deep in the mirror at themselves, and brave enough to write down what they saw. One reason most people stay haunted is that they focus their attention on the actions of their spouse; that's actually part of the haunting, that is, they are looking for evidence that they can't trust their spouse, so their attention is on the other. Let me skip to the obvious at this point: There's no doubt that you will find qualities or behaviors in your spouse that concern you. They are imperfect. Be less focused on the imperfections of your mate and focus more on becoming the person God has called you to be in the marriage. Love and trust will come much easier to both of you if you do.

A second lesson we learn from Veronica is looking beyond the ghosts of the previous marriage to the ghosts from childhood. All of us have some emotional residue coating us from childhood because our parents and families were imperfect too. Sometimes our family of origin residue is thin, sometimes very thick. But when it gets reinforced with similar experiences in marriage, it hardens into a protective coating that we must crack and shake off if we are ever to become free of it. Veronica was abandoned by her father when she was a child; her husband did the same. Even though the circumstances were very different—her father left her by choice and her husband because of an illness—her experience of abandonment, of being left alone, was the same. This theme in her life story led to the fear that it would happen again. The result? See Ghost #1. Don't get attached (withhold yourself), keep some money (don't invest everything you have or are into this man), and act tough (maintain your protective coating). There may be a number of character defects in Veronica's husband, but even if he were Jesus, she wouldn't trust him or give herself sacrificially to the marriage.

You must examine how you have been influenced by your previous relationships and strive to adjust your responses to similar circumstances. Here are some tips for recognizing your ghosts and then busting them.

- Actively connect the dots between your quick and guarded reactions and your fears. The actions are obvious; the fears that gave birth to the actions often remain hidden and unrecognized.

- Recognize that sometimes you negatively interpret your spouse's motives and behavior. It's not a given, but if a husband or wife says, "Why are you overreacting to this?" or "Wait a minute. I am not your ex!" you may be haunted. When that happens, take some time to reflect. Examine whether your past is still part of your present. Then replace your reactive behavior with more appropriate responses.

Tips for busting ghosts:

- Write down your ghosts and what they whisper in your ear. Become very familiar with this so you can recognize the voice.

- In contrast, strive to recognize the voice of Jesus and what he is telling you to do. Jesus said that he is the Good Shepherd and his sheep follow him because they know his voice (John 10:1–14). Even when there is risk involved in loving your spouse (and there always is), following the voice of Jesus will lead you toward acts of service, a gracious attitude, kindness, patience, gentleness, and self-control. Moving toward his voice and away from the ghost's is how you bust a ghost.

- Ask yourself, "If I had never been hurt before, how would Jesus have me respond in this situation? If I were to treat you as if you are trustworthy, how would I act? If I weren't afraid of being abandoned, hurt, or controlled again, how would I love?" The answers to these questions are a great start toward how you should act and what you are trying to become.

- You may also have to struggle with matters of forgiveness as difficult emotions and memories come to the surface. We'll talk more about forgiveness in the next chapter, but for now, recognize that the work of forgiveness can be an ongoing part of busting ghosts.

- Admit your ghosts to your spouse and enlist their help as you fight to change your behavior. Ask your partner to pray for you and compassionately be patient with you as you strive to change. Admitting to a ghost is an act of vulnerability. While difficult, this in and of itself can be very healing. It not only invites prayer and compassion from your spouse, it overtly tests your belief that the marriage is fragile. If you discover your spouse to be caring and comforting, your ghost has been proven wrong. Confidence in your marriage should go up.

## What If Your Spouse Has a Ghost?

If you are married to someone who is haunted by a ghost, here's how you can help them bust it.

**Spotting a ghost.** I've often said that the answer to the question *How does someone know if they have a ghost?* is that their spouse will tell them! If you are feeling like something unseen is infiltrating your marriage, say so, but do so carefully. If you are feeling unfairly attacked or prejudged by your spouse, softly say something like, "I'm pretty confused about why this subject sets you off the way it does. I'm wondering if it reminds you of anything." Let your spouse process your observation over time; if they haven't spotted the ghost yet themselves, they may need time to make the connection. Again, be soft in your observations. Remember, "A soft answer turns away wrath, but a harsh word stirs up anger" (Proverbs 15:1).

**Once a ghost is identified, be patient.** Naming the ghost is an important first step toward change, but don't expect your spouse to corral that thing immediately. Because change is difficult, you will see it haunting again and again as they strive to move out from under its influence. Offer support, not quick judgment. "But I shouldn't have to suffer for the sins of their ex-spouse," you might object. Unfortunately, marriage means we join ourselves to each other's past—positive and negative—for better or worse; remarriage is a package deal. Stop feeling victimized and start helping.

**Don't take responsibility for their ghost.** Ultimately you cannot do enough to bust their ghost; it's their ghost and they must do the work to manage it. But here's what you can do to be supportive:

- Ask, "How can I mention a 'haunting in progress' when I see it without putting you on the defensive?" This gives both of you a system for acknowledging what's happening without setting you against each other.

- Let the bullet bounce. When your spouse overreacts, remind yourself that it is about the past, not so much about you personally. Like putting on a bullet-proof vest, you can let what was fired at you bounce instead of penetrate. When you de-personalize their comments, you are left with a bruise instead of a piercing hole through your heart.

- Own your part of the exchange. Ghosts are sometimes triggered when you act in a way that mirrors the previous partner. Anything that closely resembles their behavior or attitudes creates a land mine. As your spouse talks about their ghost, learn what you can do to avoid triggering those explosions and monitor yourself closely.

- Love as perfectly as you can. Most ghosts are rooted in fear, but Scripture tells us that perfect love casts out fear (1 John 4:18). Having an unconditional love that reflects the love of Christ will eventually help to root out and destroy your spouse's ghosts.

**Pray with and for your spouse.** Taking ghosts to the Father together as a couple and asking for his wisdom and power to overcome can bring powerful healing. Besides enlisting the power of the Holy Spirit, praying together reminds you that you are a team attempting to chase, face, and displace the ghosts. Prayer strengthens your resolve and unites you.

**Focus on improved behavior before softened emotions.** The process of change for your partner requires them to "act better than they feel." Don't be discouraged when you notice negative emotions set off by the ghost. Instead, focus on their effort to change their responses toward you (behavior). Offer encouragement by saying, "I've noticed you trying to [identify the positive behavior], and I appreciate your commitment to our relationship. Your effort is bringing us closer together. Thank you."

Ghosts are hovering, irritating pests; they are about the past. Love and service are about the present *and* future. That's where you are headed. Follow God and he'll take you there, ghost free.[7]

## Ghost Busting Before the Wedding

I would be doing all of the dating couples a disfavor at this point if I didn't make an important observation (married couples may also find this section insightful as you consider in hindsight the origins of your relationship): Culture has a collective ghost, and it is selling you a lie on how to avoid getting stuck in a bad marriage, while still having a loving, intimate relationship. Ironically, much of it is driven by fear.

Stacy's dating career could be described as casual. She would meet a man and throw herself into getting to know him while, in her heart, simultaneously keeping her options open. The dopamine brain-rush of meeting someone new and connecting through physical touch made her feel wanted and important, but the idea of being tied down to someone made her nervous. She often found herself caught between hope and doubt, between the accelerator and the brake, between sex and the hope that he would want to leave her apartment afterward. After a while, her relationships would fizzle; she would lose interest because the relationship just wasn't going anywhere or the guy would tire of waiting for her to make up her mind about their future.

After being tossed aside by his wife and mother of their two children, Caleb declared to friends in his divorce recovery group, "Never again will I be hurt like that. Never again will I fall in love." Bitterness and fear built twenty-foot walls of self-protection. Fast-forward life a few years and, to his surprise, Caleb found himself attracted to someone. He wondered if he could love and trust again. As quickly as hope would say, "Yes, you can," fear would shift his heart into neutral. Just imagining being vulnerable made his heart tremble. The combination of Caleb's passion for his new girlfriend and simultaneous fear of being hurt again found expression in a "stayover" arrangement. A few nights a week he would stay at her apartment; occasionally she would stay at his, but both kept their separate residences, separate rent responsibilities, and ultimately separate lives.

### Afraid to Be Seen With Our Clothes On

People like Stacy and Caleb are in a dilemma: They want to be in an intimate committed relationship but don't want to take on the risks of marriage. Their solution? Strive for independent togetherness.[8] And they aren't alone.

Commitment is a tough sell these days. Americans prize our national and economic independence, but now that mentality has dramatically invaded our social psyche about marriage, and it's confusing us. We want to be *with* someone, but don't want to be *really with* someone.

Half of U.S. residents are single (whether never married, divorced, or widowed) and nearly one-third of all households have one occupant.[9] And yet, we don't necessarily like being alone. On one hand, we value and cherish marriage—it is still a highly sought-after goal—and yet, we fear the vulnerability it creates. Nearly three generations of people now have suffered under a high divorce rate and many have watched their parents have multiple marital or cohabiting partnerships—and breakups—creating an increasing social fear and distrust of marital relationships. In this collective fear, we've drifted toward dating strategies that supply the benefits of marriage while protecting us from potential pain. Essentially we have normalized a variety of dating arrangements, such as cohabitation and "stayover" relationships that allow us to have sex while at the same time hiding from the risks of permanent commitment. Taking off clothes is how one hides. Carelessly, we are hiding naked.

Relationships that make independent togetherness the primary guiding force behind the level of investment from each person remain surface and, ironically, vulnerable. Noted family psychiatrist Frank Pittman once said, "Marriage, like a submarine, is only safe if you get all the way inside." I say it this way: When I am protecting me from you there can't be an "us."

### The Blindfold of Sex

The dark hole inside independent togetherness is fear. Sex becomes the hiding place, an external behavior that gives the appearance of intimacy, but is really striving for self-protection. Let's consider this observation by comparing it to marital sex. One function of marital sex is renewing the emotional bond of the couple and reminding them of their covenant to each other. From within the safety of permanence, the couple is free to engage in sexual touch that sustains and reinforces the specialness and safety of their relationship.

Outside of marriage, sex has a very different function: It creates a pseudo-bond between the couple that blurs the definition of their developing relationship and confuses physical closeness for emotional safety. Couples with little foundation to their relationship can be fooled into thinking they have more in the bank with each other than they really do. Physiologically we can explain it this way: The hormone oxytocin, sometimes called the cuddle hormone, facilitates bonding in mammals (e.g., between a mother and her newborn child). It is also released when couples are affectionate and escalates dramatically after orgasm, especially in men. In short, it makes you feel connected even when there is no substance to a relationship. Couples having sex outside of marriage are quite possibly writing checks with their lives based on a bankrupt account. In the end, they get hurt and waste a lot of time on a quick but shallow high.

But then, who cares? At least you have a little fun and don't open yourself to soul-level rejection that way, right? Wrong.

In a blind act of self-sabotage, sexuality in dating is not viewed by today's culture as something that contributes to vulnerability; rather, the assumption is that you can enjoy it while maintaining your separateness. You can have your cake and eat it too.

- You don't have to reveal yourself to another.
- You don't have to accommodate your preferences while living in intimate relationship with another.
- You don't risk your accumulated wealth.
- You don't have to lose your independence or identity by getting married.
- You don't have to risk having your child(ren) raised by a stepparent.
- And you don't risk being hurt . . . again.

In short, you can hide naked without consequence.

But this line of thinking is completely faulty. Independent togetherness strategies actually foster pain when what seemed to be real turns out not to be. Sometimes dating couples figure this out and break up (because "he just wasn't the one"), while other couples don't realize what has happened until they have already married and discover they really don't know—or like—each other. Either scenario is completely avoidable.

### Courageous Dating

What is needed is the courage to date well (intelligently and romantically) and make a clear decision for marriage so that each person takes responsibility for leaping into the deep end of the pool. There are, of course, no guarantees of long-term marital success. Intimacy is inherently risky. But without the courage to take risks, love will remain a distant dream.

Here are some quick tips to help you avoid an independent togetherness dating arrangement. For more, read my book *Dating and the Single Parent*.

**Date with an eternal purpose in mind.** Recognize that one ultimate purpose of marriage is to further disciple us into the image of Christ. This reality should change everything. Pursue relationships that keep you connected to God, not withdrawing from him in shame.

**Get healthy.** Does your relationship history testify to the presence of fear in your life? Have you settled for independent togetherness relationships in order to "play it safe"? If this section has you examining yourself, take it before the Lord and ask the Spirit to help you to get healthy. Peel away the layers of your emotions and see what the Lord wants to redeem in you so you aren't paralyzed by it any longer.

**Take off the blindfold.** If you have been hiding naked in sexuality, it's time to move back to sexual purity until marriage. Even if you're in a cohabiting situation and regularly engaging in sex, it's time to stop. The only way to recover an objective perspective about the health of your relationship—and more important, about your true priorities—is to remove the mirage that sex before marriage produces. This level of obedience is very difficult and at times costly (e.g., increasing couple conflict), but I've never known anyone who regretted it (even if the other pulls away in anger because of your obedience—then their true motives have been revealed and you, ironically, are less vulnerable to disappointment).

Maintaining a desire for the best in your dating life—and in your future marriage—starts by trusting that God has your best interests in mind when it comes to his boundaries around sex. God knows what a powerful force our sexuality is. After all, he designed it. By declaring sexual intimacy before marriage a sin, he is not being a simpleton or killjoy; he is trying to protect you from a shallow relationship and personal pain. The only question is, do you trust his motives and his insight? Saving sex till after marriage protects the objectivity of your dating, ripens your commitment to each other, and after marriage becomes a symbol of marital oneness that blossoms into a pleasurable celebration of love. That's worth waiting for.

**Choose to risk, choose to love.** At the end of the day, there are no guarantees in love. We live in a fallen world and you and I are fallen, imperfect people. Because of that, being in a loving relationship sometimes hurts. Marriage, to be successful, needs to be an all-in experience. Dating, on the other hand, is progressively moving toward the all-in experience. Each new depth requires a little more openness, a little more trust, a little more risk. To pull up short of the risk required is to revert back to hiding. If you find the relationship unsafe at the new depth, then by all means, pull back. But then again, maybe a lack of willingness to risk has made it seem unsafe.

Knowing when to risk and when to pull back is never easy. One thing is sure: Love that is motivated by self-preservation never matures into selfless love, and independent togetherness dating relationships never find oneness. If you are dating, this is one ghost you must bust.

## Conclusion

Marriage is tough under any circumstance. Stepfamily marriages can fall prey to the common issues of escalating conflict over money, sex, and in-laws just like all other marriages, yet it's the unique stepfamily challenges that are so insidious for many couples. That's why stepfamily couples must make their relationship a priority and must work harder—and smarter—at their marriage than anyone else.

The above barriers can quickly or subtly destroy a marriage, especially when they work in concert with one another and compound their impact. For example, why would a wife want to make her husband a priority and risk alienating her children when she is haunted by a ghost of mistrust? If she's not sure her husband will be there in two years, why not stick closer to her kids? After all, they're not going anywhere. Truly, the risk of marriage is vast. But so are the rewards for those who keep God at the center of their relationship and love like they have nothing to lose.

## *Questions for Discussion*

▓ FOR PARENT-CHILD DISCUSSION (Discretion based on the age of the child and the quality of adult-child relationships is advised.)

1. If divorced, discussing the topic of marriage with your children could be awkward (e.g., "if God values commitment, why did you guys divorce?") and bring up hard feelings (e.g., over how the divorce occurred or what life has been like since the divorce). Let me encourage you not to hide from the topic of marriage with your kids; it's too important that they have your guidance. Give consideration and prayer to how you will address it with them.

2. In reference to the section on comparing loves, ask your child if they have ever felt loved less than a new stepfamily member. Normalize this feeling while reassuring them of their importance and your love.

3. In reference to the section on ghost busting before the wedding, engage your older children around social messages about sex before marriage and cohabitation. Teach them about the blindfold that sex before marriage creates.

▓ FOR ALL COUPLES

1. Discuss your personal relationship with God and your ideas of what a faithful life would look like. In what ways do you need to grow spiritually?

2. How will your marriage be God-directed? What is your desire for spiritual intimacy?

3. What insights did this chapter give you about your relationship?

4. What fears do you have for your children, and how do you most naturally protect them?

5. What barriers exist because of someone's allegiance to his or her children? Work to establish trust in a unified direction and plan for handling difficult situations. Don't put each other in a corner.

6. Identify and name the ghosts in your marriage. Make a contract to help each other exorcise them from your relationship.

7. How would you act differently if you had never been hurt before, if you could love like you have nothing to lose?

## ■ For Pre-Stepfamily Couples

While conducting pre-stepfamily counseling, I asked a couple what ghosts might be haunting them. They, like most couples before marriage, quickly dismissed the possibility. "I've got a decent relationship with my ex, and he just lets the stuff with his ex roll off his back," she said. He agreed, "Yeah. I just put things behind me and go on. I don't let it affect me much." I doubted that and was soon proven correct.

Within five minutes the couple was arguing about a current issue in which each felt the other was acting like someone from his or her past. The truth is this: We don't want to believe that previous relationships will impact our future ones, but they do—especially if we deny the ghosts that haunt us. Give careful attention to the following questions and honestly identify your ghosts:

1. How many years has it been since the ending of any prior significant relationships (whether to death or divorce/breakup)? Assuming you can keep your sexual passions in check, what are the benefits of slowing down your dating and progression toward marriage?

2. To what degree have you achieved "emotional divorce" with a previous spouse(s) and healing from difficult emotions? (Rate yourself from 1 to 10.)

3. Have you tried to reconnect with former lost relationships (children and/or extended family)? What has been the result?

4. How much did you need to be needed when you first began dating?

5. What scares you about committing again? What ghosts have you identified already?

6. Are you now or have you in the past tried the "independent togetherness" approach to dating? What wisdom did you see in the "Ghost Busting Before the Wedding" section?

# Smart Step Four: STEP in Line (Part 1)

*With the parenting team (co-parenting)*

Parenthood is a partnership with God. You are not molding iron nor chiseling marble; you are working with the creator of the universe in shaping human character and determining destiny.

Ruth Vaughn

The greatest use of life is to spend it for something that will outlast it.

William James

**D**ivorce doesn't end family life; it reorganizes it. This foundational truth first communicated in chapter 2 is nowhere more applicable than regarding the roles adults play in raising children in stepfamilies. You may have been reorganized into different households following divorce, but you still must act as a parental team. This is

> ### When There's Not Another Home
>
> Not all stepfamilies involve multiple-home situations. If your children don't travel between homes, feel free to skip this chapter.

often referred to as co-parenting. To co-parent well you have to get along reasonably well; you may have hated your ex-spouse at the time of the divorce, but now you have to find a way to cooperate with him or her for the sake of your children (it is one of the great ironies of divorce). After all, parenting is about your children's welfare, development, and spiritual nurturance, not your personal needs. I like to say that parenting is all on behalf of the kids. This does *not* give you permission to placate, spoil, or cater to your children; rather it means that your parenting decisions, goals, and attitudes—including finding ways to be cordial and cooperative with people you dislike or distrust—need to be oriented around what will benefit your children and increase their desire for the Lord. Most of that last sentence is not difficult for parents—we want what's best for our kids! It's the part about dealing with people we dislike that is tough.

> **Wise Stepparents**
>
> Stepparents need to understand the principles of this chapter too because you are part of the parental team in your household; you and your spouse need to find unity in how you relate to and cooperate with the other home.

In Genesis 21, Sarah refused to consider Hagar or Ishmael as having a place in Abraham's life. Sarah showed great hostility and selfishness when she insisted that Abraham exclude Ishmael from the inheritance. She was looking out for her son and good old number one. Her actions were driven by fear (of Isaac's not getting the full blessing from Abraham), anger (because Hagar and Ishmael were mocking Isaac), and jealousy (because Hagar had given Abraham the highly prized firstborn son). But why would she act that way? Didn't she know what was coming when she encouraged Abraham to give her a child through a union with Hagar (Genesis 16)? Probably not.

I suspect neither did Abraham see what was coming. He agreed to the union with Hagar and then found himself stuck between two mothers and the children he loved. Modern-day stepfamilies are different in the sense that a remarried man isn't married to two women at the same time, but similar in the sense that men in that situation sometimes find themselves trying to cooperate with two women for very different reasons. His motivation to please his wife and cooperate with her around parenting matters is out of his devotion to her (marital and parental motivation) while his motivation to cooperate with his ex-wife is out of his devotion to his children (parental motivation). The problem in Abraham's situation was that the two mothers had different agendas for their children and their husband. That's the kind of dynamic that divides co-parents and causes conflict or stress.

## Step in Line—With Whom?

I've never done it myself, but I've seen people line dance. I don't try it because I have very little coordination, and I would surely throw off the entire group. After all, if I can't fall in line with others and keep pace with the necessary movements, the effect is lost. The same is true for the adult caregivers in stepfamilies.

There was a time in America when parents had lots of children; today we say children have lots of parents.[1] The parenting team is comprised of everyone who shares responsibility for child-rearing tasks. This primarily includes biological parents and stepparents, but might incorporate grandparents, ex-in-laws, stepgrandparents, and extended family members who aid in the child-care process. The more coordinated or unified they are as "line dancers," the better team they become for the benefit of the children.

Parenting team cooperation is one of the most challenging aspects of stepfamily life. Leftover pain from previous relationships, broken promises, and envy often characterize how ex-spouses and new spouses feel about the adults in the other home. Walls of distrust are built as the bricks of painful emotions and experiences are stacked side by side. Tearing down those walls and setting aside personal agendas for the children's sake is no easy task. Yet adults in separate homes who successfully create a functional parenting team discover their individual homes blessed with increased harmony.

The two key relationships in the parenting team are the co-parenting relationship between the biological parents and the parent-stepparent relationship. The relationships between the biological parent of the other home and the stepparent (e.g., the mother and stepmother), both stepparents (when each ex-spouse is remarried), and grandparents are generally determined by the health of these two key relationships. Let's begin by looking at the ex-spouse co-parenting relationship; we'll examine the parent-stepparent relationship in the next chapter.

## Co-Parenting—What's the Goal?

At a minimum, biological parents should contain their anger and conflict in order to cooperate and compromise on issues of the children's welfare. At a maximum, the co-parents can strive to enforce similar rules and standards of conduct in each of the children's homes. Most co-parents find it difficult to accomplish the former; only a few are able to achieve the latter. Nevertheless, co-parents should do everything they can to build cooperation between the two homes.

I cannot overemphasize the importance of this concept in regard to the well-being of children. Research clearly confirms that children successfully adjust to the ending of their parents' marriage and can fare reasonably well if: (1) parents are able to bring their marital relationship to an end *without excessive conflict;* (2) children are *not put into the middle* of whatever conflicts exist; and (3) there is a *commitment from parents to cooperate* on issues of the children's material, physical, educational, emotional, and spiritual welfare.[2] Bottom line—children need their parents to work together whether married, divorced, or married to other people.

A healthy co-parent relationship does not mean children will not experience emotional or psychological distress. "Numerous studies document that children who experience parental divorce exhibit more conduct problems, more symptoms of psychological maladjustment, lower academic achievement, more social difficulties, and poorer self-concepts compared with children living in intact, two-parent families."[3] Judith Wallerstein's longitudinal research discovered that the effects of divorce are often lifelong and traumatic for children.[4] Even Mavis Hetherington's research, which gives hope to parents by pointing out that 80 percent of children from divorced homes eventually adapt to their new life, acknowledges that 20 percent will continuously display impulsive, irresponsible, antisocial behavior, and depression.[5]

In addition, children face greater levels of family conflict while the stepfamily is integrating (compared to nuclear family children)[6] and are at increased risk for developmental behavioral problems, health problems, and substance abuse.[7] Stepfamily conflict and ex-spouse conflict have a number of negative effects on children and are contributing factors in all of the following statistics. Children in stepfamilies are less likely to complete high school[8] and more likely to have lower educational achievement,[9] leave home earlier,[10] and cohabit before marriage.[11] Finally, it's worth noting that boys are more affected by divorce, but girls seem to be more affected by remarriage.[12]

Parents who want to reduce these negative effects on their children should strive to be effective co-parents because it reduces between-home conflict and increases cooperation. Taming your tongue, for example, is critical to cooperating. Scripture notes that the tongue is a small part of the body but that its impact can be severe. "Think about how a small spark can set a big forest on fire" (James 3:5 NIRV). Conflict containment starts with controlling your speech. You cannot be an effective co-parent without doing so.

### What Does a Healthy Co-Parent Relationship Look Like?

Here's a checklist of Healthy Co-Parenting from friend and co-parenting expert Tammy Daughtry for you to consider. (I highly recommend Tammy's book *Co-Parenting Works! Helping Your Children Thrive After Divorce*.)

The remainder of this chapter will discuss concepts similar to those found in the inventory below.

◼ INDICATORS OF HEALTHY CO-PARENTING[13]

by Tammy Daughtry, MMFT, CoParenting International

Rate your co-parenting relationship on a scale of 1–5 for each of the following. 1 = Not at all, 2 = Rarely, 3 = Occasionally, 4 = Often, 5 = Always.

____ We give our children the freedom to love both parents.

____ I believe my child's well-being is directly affected by the quality of relationship I have with their other parent.

____ The transition between our homes is smooth and positive.

____ We discuss and deal with financial matters in a rational way.

____ We intentionally plan out the details of Christmas and other holidays to minimize the stress.

____ We make it possible for our children to love and maintain ties with both extended families.

____ We enjoy being at our children's functions and are there to enhance our children's happiness.

____ I think the more functional my relationship is with my ex, the less likely it is that our children will engage in high-risk behaviors.

\_\_\_\_ We recognize the developmental stages of our children and let them enjoy their childhood.

\_\_\_\_ We take care of responsibilities as adults and do not put pressure on the children to do our jobs.

\_\_\_\_We allow and encourage our children to take specific clothing, toys, and electronic devices between their homes.

\_\_\_\_ We encourage our children to have photos of their other parent (and family) in their bedroom.

\_\_\_\_ We tell our children it is okay to talk about how much they miss the other parent.

\_\_\_\_ I discuss specific parenting strategies with my ex.

\_\_\_\_ We speak highly of the other parent to our children, with at least three specific compliments.

\_\_\_\_ We prioritize our time with the children and are fully engaged with them and focus on them.

\_\_\_\_ We communicate regularly with our co-parent at predesignated meetings or telephone calls.

\_\_\_\_ I do not get upset when our child seeks out the other parent after a game or event.

\_\_\_\_ We do not allow or utilize the children as messengers or "go-betweens" on anything.

\_\_\_\_ We incorporate other friends and activities into our lives to enhance our self-care and happiness.

\_\_\_\_ When we are both present at the same event we do not use the opportunity to discuss family business.

\_\_\_\_ We are working with our co-parent and stepparents to raise healthy and well-adjusted children.

\_\_\_\_ I can see a positive difference in my children as a result of our co-parenting efforts.

\_\_\_\_ I know why co-parenting is so vitally important to the well-being of my children and stepchildren.

\_\_\_\_ It makes sense to me that the well-being of my children/stepchildren is dependent on the relationship with the other parent(s) involved.

TOTAL POINTS _____

Use the interpretive guide below to gauge your co-parent relationship.

### ■ THRIVING CHILDREN (96–125 Points)

Understanding is maximized, which is leading to intentional application of healthy communication and co-parenting strategies. Parental functioning is high and parental conflict is low. The children are becoming happier and better adjusted every day. Their behavior and challenges are typical of other children of similar age, race, and socioeconomic background. These children are thriving in their developmental stages emotionally and physically, and the parents are doing the hard work of parenting without putting them in the middle.

### ■ STRUGGLING CHILDREN (71–95 points)

Understanding and application are minimal but co-parenting function is being enhanced by regular communication. Increasing the quality of communication will have a significant effect in reducing the children's anxiety. There is still a high level of parentification (children thrust into parental roles) taking place as well as noticeable conflict in the ongoing co-parenting efforts. The children are hurting due to exposure to and involvement in adult matters that they are not developmentally prepared to deal with. Put simply, they need the adults to do the "parent stuff" so they can just be kids.

### ■ DISTRESSED CHILDREN (0–70 points)

Lack of communication, understanding, and application is leading to high levels of stress in both households and high levels of anxiety in the children. Quite often these conditions lead to emotional distress and produce unwanted and unhealthy behaviors in the children. These "acting out" or withdrawal responses are not simple ploys for attention but cries for help from fearful, anxious hearts who don't know how to process or express what they are going through.

Now that you've analyzed your co-parenting from an adult point of view, I'll let the children explain what a functional co-parental relationship means in practical, everyday terms from a child's viewpoint.

Julie, twelve, complained in a therapy session that she couldn't invite both her parents to her music recital. "If they both come they'll just scowl every chance they get. I tried inviting them both last year, and Mom wouldn't speak to me for two days because Dad brought Amy with him. She refuses to be in the same room with them." Julie has had to learn to take turns inviting her mom and dad. Unfortunately, this put her in constant turmoil as she was forced to choose which parent she would invite to certain events. If the other wanted to come but wasn't invited, Julie heard that parent's disappointment and felt guilty. "Why can't they just put aside their differences and tolerate a couple of hours in the same room?" Good question.

Because Terrance's parents always ended up fighting on the phone, he became the middleman to their visitation arrangements. His mother stopped speaking to his father and asked Terrance, at age nine, to communicate her preferences for drop-off and pick-up. Terrance had no choice but to oblige, since he enjoyed spending time with his father on weekends.

In both these examples, children carried undue emotional anxiety and burden because their parents could not set aside their differences and be adults. An effective co-parent arrangement for Julie's parents would mean she could invite both parents to her recitals and not worry that they were fighting or anxious. An effective arrangement for Terrance's parents would include their finding a way to talk rationally about their schedules instead of triangulating Terrance. What you're striving for is a system that allows children to be children and adults to be their parents.

Co-parenting does not mean sharing all decisions about the children or that either home is accountable to the other for their choices, rules, or standards. Each household should be autonomous but share responsibility for the children. It also does not mean that rules or punishment from one home cross over to the other home.

Karen sought therapy in part because her ex-husband, Ted, refused to carry out the consequences she imposed on their children. In one instance, her teenage son lied about his homework, so she grounded him from weekend activities. The scheduled visitation meant her son would be going to his dad's house that weekend, so she called her ex to ask him to honor the punishment and keep their son home on Friday and Saturday nights. Ted refused, saying that was his only time with his son and he wasn't obligated to fulfill her decisions. That angered Karen, and she hoped the therapist could intervene and get Ted to cooperate. Karen was right to ask for Ted's cooperation. But since he refused, she would have to let it go. Karen's therapist explained that if her son was grounded, she should wait until he came back to her home to carry out the punishment. Her home is within her control. Ted's home is not.

You might be thinking, *But at the beginning of the chapter you said that co-parents should strive to enforce similar rules and cooperate regarding the children. Didn't that obligate Ted to honor her request?* Yes, I did say that between-home cooperation, even to the point of carrying out the other home's punishment, is a goal some co-parents obtain. However, that does not obligate either side to do so. If you achieve this level of cooperation, great. If the other home refuses, follow through in your home and move on.

Incidentally, this control issue between Karen and Ted was nothing new. It was as old as their failed marriage. Remember, divorce doesn't end the dynamics of family relationships; it merely reorganizes them into separate households. Well into divorce most ex-spouses are still trying to change, control, or influence their ex in the same manner they did before they divorced. They are still emotionally invested in what their ex does and how they do it. Letting go of control is tough, but it helps co-parents respect each other's boundaries and, ironically, work better as a team.

## Children Living in Two "Countries"

Let's examine stepfamily life from the child's point of view. Children in stepfamilies live in two "countries."[14] They hold citizenship in each country and are, therefore, invested in the quality of life found in both. The parenting team should do everything they can to help children thrive and enjoy each of their two homes. But living in two countries does require some adjustments.

Shortly after my wife and I married, we went with my parents to Kenya for a brief missionary effort. My parents continued to lead an annual trip to Kenya for about seventeen years, coordinating volunteers' mission efforts in East Africa. What I remember most about going to Kenya is the radical change in culture that we experienced. Clothing was different, social customs seemed odd, the economy and systems of government were unknown to us—we even had to learn to drive on the left side of the road. Despite all these shifts in customs, ritual behaviors, and rules of conduct, we learned to adapt quite quickly. Because my parents returned to Kenya year after year, the changes grew more predictable for them and, therefore, were not as awkward as our first trip together. But they always experienced an adjustment period when traveling between countries. One year my father returned to the U.S. and began driving on the left side of the road. The oncoming traffic abruptly reminded him of the change in driving system!

You can see the parallel with children living in two homes. At first, the fact that the two countries have different rules, customs, and expectations may require an extended adjustment. Later, when the territory is familiar, only a brief adjustment time is required, especially when the rules and expectations are predictable.

Can you imagine what travel for my parents would have been like if Kenya and the United States had been at war? Getting on a plane and heading to the "other side," even to do mission work, would have been considered treason. And once they landed, they would have been met with anger and rage as co-workers protested how awful the other country was because of their wartime tactics. How would my parents function under that kind of stress? How would they cope with the external pressures to choose an allegiance to one side or the other? Every comment and criticism would be loaded with a battle for their loyalty, and trust would be defeated at every turn. And what if they decided to be ambassadors between the warring governments—would they have a voice? Depending on how suspicious the governments were and how convinced they were that the other side would never change, their attempts to bring peace would likely fail. What a losing position to be caught in.

> ### Part-Time Stepfamilies
>
> Be careful not to take it personally when part-time children forget your household rules. At times this is intentional, but much of the time it is force of habit; they are used to doing things a different way. Offer a gentle reminder and follow through to reorient them to your way of doing things.

An old African proverb says, "When two elephants fight, it is the grass that suffers." Biological parents who fight and refuse to cooperate are trampling on their most prized possession—their children. Elephants at war are totally unaware of what is happening to the grass, for they are far too consumed with the battle at hand. Little do they know how much damage is being done.

Researcher James Bray has confirmed what many therapists have believed for years. When one parent speaks negatively about a child's other biological parent, the child internalizes the comment. In other words, "a child who hears a parent attacked thinks, in some way, he is also being attacked."[15] A simple comment like, "Your father is late again. He can be so irresponsible," cuts the child as well as the parent. If the child is ever late for anything, she knows (or thinks she knows) how you feel about her. In addition, a negative comment subtly invites children to agree with the comment, which children hate to do. It implies they are choosing one parent over the other, and that brings guilt. Because of the internalized negativity and guilt over having to choose sides, Bray goes on to suggest that the child will eventually act out such hurt and anger in some destructive behavior. I say you can count on it.

> **What Kids Are Thinking**
>
> Said to a stepdad: "I can criticize my dad's poor behavior, but how dare you do that!"

Are you making a POW swap every other weekend? How often do you trample your children's loyalties to the other country in an effort to persuade them to remain faithful to you? How has your new stepfamily affected the amount of time children have in the other home? As citizens of two countries, your children should be privileged to all the rights, relationships, and responsibilities of each of those homes. Your job is to be at peace with the other country so your children can travel back and forth in security.

### Loyalty Conflicts for Children

Understanding loyalty conflicts and striving as a co-parenting team to alleviate excessive loyalty concerns is important to children's emotional well-being after divorce. Even in the best of circumstances, children feel caught between their biological parents and often feel as though they are in an emotional tug-of-war.

Parents implicitly ask their children to "choose" and, therefore, put children in a no-win tug-of-war when they

- badmouth the other parent or household
- comment on or compare living conditions

- invade the other home's time with the kids with constant text messages, phone calls, or showing up at private family activities
- cast blame on the other household for financial pressures or emotional pain
- ask for the child's time when it takes time away from the other parent
- coax the child into not visiting his/her other parent until child support payments are made or custody time is renegotiated
- make children feel guilty for enjoying the people in the other home
- refuse to listen to their happy stories of life in the other home

All of these situations, and many more, teach children to take their emotions underground and train them to play the game of "keep everyone happy by making them think I love them most." Children who internalize this tug-of-war become depressed, discouraged, self-destructive, and unmotivated. Children who externalize their pain become angry and oppositional, have behavior problems, and may turn violent.

Children simply want to be connected to the people they love—no strings attached. The messages adults give children that attempt to gain their loyalty in effect are strings. The goal of the string often is to mend the emotional wounds carried by parents. If your son seems to prefer you to his mother, it somehow affirms your wounded heart (not really, it just *feels* like it). This turns your son into an emotional Band-Aid. If his preference for you satisfies your deep desire for revenge against the woman who ended your marriage and broke your heart, your child has become a toy soldier, fighting your emotional war. Be careful not to let your wounded heart influence you to subtly and nonverbally elicit your son's allegiance. Children lose when they are made the caretakers of wounded parents. Parents should find ways to soothe their pain through their relationship with God and others. You may need help from a therapist, minister, or trusted friend, but never turn your child into your emotional healer.

The binds children feel sometimes create an unhealthy preference for one parent, usually the most distant or under-functioning parent. Boys, for example, often identify with an unavailable father to the dismay of their mother and stepfather. I've often had stable, responsible parents (and stepparents) ask why their child seems to prefer time with the noncustodial parent, who is an irresponsible drunk. Others wonder why their kids desire

140

to be with a parent who shows no real desire to be with them. "We are good to my kids," one mother said. "My husband is good to them; we provide a financially stable home and a healthy environment. Why do they worry about their dad so much?"

Again, the caretaker dynamic applies. Children are often pulled into a helper role with a parent who needs help. Someone, it feels to the children, has to take care of Dad—even if he is a drunk—or he'll have no one. In effect, the irresponsible behavior of the father functions as an invitation to the children to be his emotional Band-Aid. Children are easily drawn into this protective role. Further, they may become harsh toward the high-functioning biological parent and frequently are harsh toward the stepparent. To enjoy time with a stepfather when your dad is alone and sad at home feels to some children to be disloyal. This struggle not to cause the under-functioning parent more pain is accentuated if he tells the children not to "call that man Daddy" or if he criticizes the stepdad in any way. The message is, "I can't stand for you to love him and care for him—take care of me by not honoring him." One five-year-old demonstrated his bind rather well when he asked his stepmother, "Can I love you when I'm here at Daddy's house and hate you when I'm at Mommy's house?"

There is something completely upside-down when parents rely on children to make themselves feel okay. If you find yourself guilty of placing your children in an emotional tug-of-war, please begin to alter your messages to them and take them out of the middle. *You can only trample grass so long before it ceases to grow.* Here are some suggestions:

- Acknowledge to your children your improper reliance on them. Communicate your desire to do better in the future.

- Make a list of ways you have inadvertently burdened your children. Then for each improper tactic, plan a more appropriate response. *For example:* Talking to the kids about your job frustrations and worries is improper. Focus conversations on their activities and interests; assure them of your competency; consult with a career counselor. (A chart in the discussion questions at the end of the chapter helps you develop your new responses.)

- Affirm your children for who they are, not how they care for you.

- Look to God for strength and wisdom as you discover how to heal the wounds of your heart. Remember that he is Jehovah-Rophe, "the LORD who heals you." (See Exodus 15:26.)
- Begin to connect with friends and counselors who can help you heal.
- Shy away from dating relationships that fill your emptiness. Remarriages that develop as two people rescue each other from painful pasts have difficulty long term. Get well before dating someone new.

## Adolescents, Loyalty, and Living With the Other Parent

Stepping in line with the parenting team means understanding the developmental decisions adolescents often face. For many reasons teenagers may not welcome the birth of a stepfamily. One reason is the pressure that is put on them to bond with new family members at a time when they are trying to move away from the family.

Adolescence is a developmental passage in our society when children become young adults striving for increasing levels of autonomy and independence. It is a time of testing values and rules, of building a distinctive identity, and an opportunity to gain decision-making power. All of these developmental forces are moving teenagers away from parental control and away from the family.

Eager stepparents who are bonding quite well with younger children sometimes complain that they don't have sufficient access to the adolescent children. The message teens hear is an expectation that rivals their efforts for independence. Parents and stepparents alike should, again, relax and not force a level of participation or acceptance from adolescent children. Realize they may be stepping back for many reasons. Maintain a Crockpot mentality and enjoy the bonding experience with younger children, while allowing teens to keep their main interests outside the family.

Striving for independence and identity formation is also expressed when teens begin wondering what it would be like to live with the other parent. Some 20 percent of adolescents will move in with their nonresidential parent during the teen years. What to them is further exploration into their history and family background can be easily taken as rejection by parents. "I'm afraid of how Mom will react if I tell her I want to live with Dad," is a statement I've heard from numerous teenagers. "It's not that I don't like being with her, I just want to know my dad a little better."

Understanding this struggle for teens is important for parents because teens have been known to generate family conflict in order to be sent to the other home out of parent frustration. High conflict levels are not fun for anyone, but they seem to be less guilt inducing for teens than facing a parent who feels rejected after a request to live in the other home. Is conflict a good result? No. Is conflict the lesser of two evils for the adolescent? Yes. Show your children that you are emotionally strong enough to listen to their needs, even if it means a loss for you.

Unquestionably, some teens threaten to live in the other home as a way of gaining power. "Fine, I'll just go live with Mom," is a great trump card to a parent who fears losing another battle to an ex-spouse. Parents cannot afford to be manipulated by a teen's threats. If you find yourself in this situation, seek outside help immediately. You will need help deciding how to respond.

In all the above circumstances, consider the individual growth needs of your teenagers. Be considerate of adolescents' strivings for independence and don't force them to give up their social life to bond with new family members. Be discerning about adolescents' desire to live in the other home and let them know that you would entertain a conversation about such a change if ever they desire it. Undoubtedly, watching them go will tear open your heart. But this isn't about you, remember? It's all about the kids.

## Some Important Reminders for Co-Parents

1. Unless systematic parental alienation is taking place, you will never lose your children's affections, so relax about the bonds they are making with stepfamily members in the other home. Blood is very, very thick and nearly impossible to dilute. Your children will not forget about you just because they have a new, rich, and/or entertaining stepparent. You have to *intentionally* be a royal jerk over an extended period of time before your children will consider turning their back on you. Don't worry or compete with the other household for loyalty; you already have it. (If alienation is taking place, see the section at the end of this chapter.)

2. Never make children regret having affections for the other home. Remember that they have citizenship there, and forcing a loyalty

battle only destroys them. Children need your permission to love their other biological parent, and they need to see your psychological stability as they do so. Your permission helps to take them out of the emotional tug-of-war and relieves the pressure to take care of you. They also need your acceptance of the relationship they carve out with their stepparent. A stepparent cannot replace you, so don't force a competition. In fact, the more comfortable you are with the children's relationships in the other home, the more likely it is that they will honor you (and *your* new spouse). Respect given is respect returned. Said another way, permission connects, but possessiveness divides.

3. Relax and let your children open the circle of insiders to include your new spouse at their own pace. Some children will do so more quickly than others (more on this dynamic later), but don't try to push your spouse in or force your children to allow him or her in. You can find ways of getting along long before stepparents become welcomed family members.

4. If you have children who are protecting an under-functioning parent, do not try to force them away from the other parent. While your desire to remove your child's need to rescue is valid, coaching the child away from the other parent feels to the child like a betrayal. Your child may resent you for standing in the way of his relationship. Listen to his worries and affirm his concerns: "I can tell you are worried about your dad. You're afraid he is going to lose another job, huh? Tell me what you are thinking you should do." Express concern and gently *help them to decide* what their boundaries with the other parent should be.

Also, don't feel the need to protect the children from the other parent's actions. Many parents try to preserve the child's opinion of the other parent by covering or explaining negative behavior. This generally puts you in the middle of the child's angry feelings. Help your older children and adolescents to ask the other parent why he or she didn't keep a promise or to explain unhealthy decisions. This empowers children in their relationship. Protecting hides the truth. Children can cope with a parent's actions if they know what to expect, so try not to sugarcoat the truth.[16]

### Guidelines for Co-Parents

The following are guidelines that will help you to help your children move back and forth between their two homes. All co-parents should seek to live according to these guidelines.[17] Consider how you might make each a reality in your situation. Remember that you are responsible for your contribution to how you and your ex interact. Change your part of the interaction even if you believe your ex-spouse is to blame for the negative exchanges that have occurred in the past.

1. Work hard to respect the other parent and his or her household. Agree that each parent has a right to privacy, and do not intrude in his or her life. Make space for different parenting styles and rules, as there are many healthy ways to raise children. Do not demean the other's living circumstances, activities, dates, or decisions, and give up the need to control your ex's parenting style. If you have concerns, speak directly to the other parent (see Borrow a Script and Stick to It, later in this chapter).

2. Schedule a regular (weekly to monthly) "business" meeting to discuss co-parenting matters. You can address schedules, academic reports, behavioral training, and spiritual development. Do not discuss your personal life (or your ex's); that part of your relationship is no longer appropriate. If the conversation turns away from the children, simply redirect the topic or politely end the meeting. If you cannot talk with your ex face-to-face due to conflict, use email, text, or speak to their voice mail. Do what you can to make your meetings productive for the children. Learn more about the structure of T.E.A.M.M. meetings in the Smart Questions, Smart Answers bonus material available at SmartStepfamilies.com/view/learn.

3. Never ask your children to be spies or tattletales on the other home. This places them in a loyalty bind that brings great emotional distress. In fact, be happy when they enjoy the people in their new home. ("I'm glad you enjoy fishing with your stepdad.") If children offer information about life in the other home, listen and stay neutral in your judgment.

4. When children have confusing or angry feelings toward your ex, don't capitalize on their hurt and berate the other parent. Listen and help them to explore their feelings without trying to sway their opinions

with your own. If you can't make positive statements about the other parent, strive for neutral ones.

5. Children should have everything they need in each home. Don't make them bring basic necessities back and forth. Special items, like clothes or a comforting teddy bear, can move back and forth as needed.

6. Try to release your hostility toward the other parent so that the children can't take advantage of your hard feelings. Manipulation is much easier when ex-spouses don't cooperate.

7. Do not disappoint your children with broken promises or by being unreliable. Do what you say you will do, keep your visitation schedule as agreed, and stay active in their lives.

8. Make your custody structure work for your children even if you don't like the details of the arrangement. Update the other party when changes need to be made to the visitation schedule. Also, inform the other parent of any change in job, living arrangements, or other situation that may require an adjustment by the children.

9. If you plan to hire a baby-sitter for more than four hours while the children are in your home, give the other parent first right to that time.

10. Suggest that younger children take a favorite toy or game as a transitional object. This can help them make the transition and to feel more comfortable in the other home.

11. Regarding children who visit for short periods of time or spend time in another home:

- Sometimes it is tempting to only do "special activities" when all of the children are with you for fear that some children may feel that they aren't as special as others. Do special things with differing combinations of children (it's all right if someone occasionally feels disappointed he or she wasn't able to go).

- When other children come for visitation, let the lives of those living with you remain unaltered as much as possible.

- Keep toys and possessions in a private spot, where they are not to be touched or borrowed unless the owner gives permission (even while they are in the other home).

## Top 10 Things Kids Wish They Could Say to Their Divorced Parents

**Tammy Daughtry, MMFT**
**CoParenting International**

1. Don't say mean things about my other parent—I want and need to love you both!
2. When you criticize my other parent it makes me angry at YOU!
3. Don't make me pick who I want to spend time with—it's not fair and I will get hurt if you do that. And don't "keep track" of my time like I'm "on the clock." It can't always be 100 percent fair. Please just love me when we are together and don't make me feel bad about not spending the same amount of time with each of you.
4. Handle your financial conversations in private—I don't want to hear about it and I don't want to be your messenger.
5. Don't use money to win my love—be a stable and loving parent and I will love you no matter who has the "most" money.
6. Don't keep me from seeing the other parent—if you do, I'll grow up and resent you.
7. Get a counselor to help you with your problems—I need you to be strong and stable for my well-being. I don't want to hear about your dating and your disappointments. I don't want to hear about your problems at work or how much we are struggling financially. Talk to someone else. I need you to be my parent and mentor and lead me in the way you want me to grow up. Don't make me be YOUR parent.
8. The harder you make it on my other parent, the harder you are making it on me.
9. Laugh and smile—I want to enjoy my life, and your mood impacts my mood. Find a way to be happy and enjoy your life—I need to have fun and enjoyable memories with you.
10. Don't forget that I have a divided heart now and I live between two completely different houses, rules, traditions and attitudes. Be patient with me when I forget things or need some time to adjust from house to house. Please buy me enough stuff that I don't have to live out of a suitcase my whole life. If you want me to feel "at home" in both places, please set up a full home for me, even if I am only there a few days a month. Things like toothbrushes, shoes, clothes, my favorite cereal, and having cool décor in my room—these all help me feel welcomed and "at home" in both homes. Don't compete or argue about these things, just help me not to feel like a visitor when I am with either parent. Make it as easy on ME as possible![19]

12. Help children adjust when going to the other home:

    • If the children will go on vacation while in the other home, find out what's on the agenda. You can help your kids pack special items and needed clothing.
    • Provide the other home with information regarding your child's changes. A switch in preferences (regarding music, clothes, hairstyles, foods, etc.) or physical/cognitive/emotional developments can be significant. Let the other home know what is different before the child arrives.
    • When receiving children, give them time to unpack, relax, and settle in. Try not to overwhelm them at first with plans, rules, or even special treatment. Let them work their way in at their own pace.[18]

13. If you and your ex cannot resolve a problem or change in custody or visitation, agree to problem solving through mediation rather than litigation.

## Building the Co-Parental Relationship

"Now we know what we're trying to accomplish as co-parents, but how do we get there?" is one question I'm often asked. Another is "Sounds great to me—I'd love to have that kind of relationship with my children's parent. But he won't try. Everything I do always backfires or gets sabotaged. What can I do about that?" Believe me, I understand, it takes two to make any cooperative relationship work. Nevertheless, do what you can. (*Notice:* Rarely does someone admit that he or she contributes to a difficult co-parent relationship. Pointing the finger of blame is always easier; we are usually blind to how we contribute to the difficulties.) This section will help you understand the emotional issues at play and provide practical ideas for building a better co-parental relationship. Please know that some situations require a different set of rules. If the other home has systematically alienated you from the child's life, the rules of engagement change. More will be said about the extreme circumstances of parent alienation at the end of this chapter.

### Dissolving the Marital Bond/Retaining the Parental One

As you attempt to build or strengthen your co-parent relationship, it may be helpful to understand the emotional tasks of ending your previous marital relationship while still maintaining your parental one. When a man and woman marry, they form a husband-wife relationship. Later, when children are brought into the marriage, the same two people form yet another relationship. This father-mother relationship is focused on the partnership of raising a child, while the husband-wife relationship is based on romantic love, companionship, and sexuality. The boundary between these two types of relationship is blurred and weak. For example, most couples are well aware of how disagreements over discipline or which values to teach children can easily turn into marital rifts that pit husband against wife. What starts out as a parental issue quickly becomes a marital issue.

> **"My husband's ex-wife relies on him too much. What do I do?"**
>
> Find the answer in the Smart Questions, Smart Answers bonus material, available at SmartStep families.com/view/learn.

The challenge for couples after divorce is to dissolve their marital relationship while retaining their parental one. This is a terribly difficult task to accomplish for most people. In effect, the couple redefines their relationship to one of parents only (partners trying to raise a child), not lovers. This is especially difficult when old buttons get pushed and past marital pain is resurrected through parental disagreement. Unless ex-spouses actively set aside their previous marital agendas, they will easily fall back into personal attacks and manipulative ploys. Again the elephants start fighting, and the grass gets trampled.

How many times have you heard of someone withholding visitation to a former spouse because the ex is a little behind with child-support payments? In effect, one parent holds a child hostage until the child-support ransom is paid. "But you don't understand. My ex was always irresponsible with money and is selfish even today. The only reason he doesn't pay is because he can't stand to part with material things." So you're going to change him by withholding his children? Does that sound like an old marital issue that's supposed to be buried in a grave somewhere, or a parental one?

Putting to death the old marital bond with all its pain, power, and privilege is difficult. Yet it is just what the doctor ordered for effective co-parenting to begin. Separate your marital past from your parental present and there will be less conflict between you. (For a specific example of this in action, see "Letting the Bullet Bounce" later in this chapter.)

## Ex-Spouses: What's Your Type?

Family researcher Constance Ahrons has identified five types of ex-spouse relationships. Consider her descriptions and see where you and your ex fit.

*Perfect Pals:* These couples are high interactors/high communicators, and comprised just 12 percent of the research sample. Even though these couples were divorced, their friendship behaviors continued. They still considered themselves good friends, spoke once or twice a week, and were interested in each other's lives. They remained connected with family and old friends. Not many of these couples remained in this category, but moved on to less cooperative relationships. Also, five years after their divorce they had not recoupled with new partners. (Indeed, it's difficult to establish a new relationship while holding on to a former spouse.)

### What Kids of Perfect Pals Are Thinking

It's weird. My parents get along better now that they're divorced. I'm not sure why they divorced.

---

*Cooperative Colleagues:* These moderate interactors/high communicators represented 38 percent of the research sample. While not considering each other best friends, these couples did cooperate quite well around issues that concerned the children. Some talked frequently, others minimally. For the most part, they were able to compromise when it came to dividing up time with the children. In handling conflict, they usually didn't end up in vicious battles, but resolved issues or avoided them. A common denominator for these couples was the ability to compartmentalize their relationship; that is, they separated out issues related to their marital relationship from those related to their parenting relationship. Their desire to provide the best situation for their children took precedence over their personal issues.

### What Kids of Cooperative Colleagues Are Thinking

These kids think nothing of being connected to family members in both homes or engaging with one home while with the other. They are blessed with permission from each parent to enjoy the other: "Mom, I'll miss you this weekend, but I'm really looking forward to the camping trip with Dad and Sharon."

---

*Angry Associates:* These moderate interactors/low communicators (25 percent of the sample) communicated only to make plans for their children and usually got angry doing so. Conflict was the major issue for these couples. Unlike cooperative colleagues, they were not able to compartmentalize their anger, but found it spreading to most aspects of their interaction.

### What Kids of Angry Associates Are Thinking

Careful not to give either parent cause for eruption, these kids are calculating and anxious about what might upset their parents: "Dad, I'm sure Mom didn't mean anything by it . . ."

*Fiery Foes:* These low interactors/low communicators made up about 25 percent of the sample. Fiery describes these ex-spouses well. They communicate very little and when they do, it usually ends up in a fight. Legal battles over the kids and highly litigious divorce proceedings are common, with each deepening their anger toward each other.

### What Kids of Fiery Foes Are Thinking

These kids display a wartime vigilance as they monitor their parents' hostilities and try to prevent combat. Never at rest, they're usually depressed, withdrawn, or highly anxious. They think, *I'll just skip my birthday this year. That will cause fewer problems.*

*Dissolved Duos:* These ex-spouse pairs stop contact entirely. It is common for one ex-spouse to move away and maintain little or no contact. There is no two-household arrangement here; it is truly a single-parent family.[20]

### What Kids of Dissolved Duos Are Thinking

"Why did my dad leave? What is it about me that he doesn't like?"

Did you find your type or the one that most aptly describes your current ex-spouse relationship? What type are your new spouse and his or her ex? Which of these types should co-parents strive for? Cooperative Colleagues works best. If you look closely at the description, you can see why: They have the ability to compartmentalize personal issues relating to their marriage and parenting issues relating to their children. They are able to dissolve their marital issues while continuing to work together as parents. They simply don't allow old marital junk to spoil their ability to cooperate.

What if you find yourself an Angry Associate or a Fiery Foe? Take control of yourself and make changes to your part of the relationship. Improving your ex-spouse relationship, even if you have an "impossible" ex, is not completely out of your control. You can always—and God expects you to—control yourself and not give in to anger or pain. Yet the obstacles for some are many. Let me offer some tools to help you to be a Cooperative Colleague.

### Spoiled Leftovers From the Past: Coping With Anger, Hurt, and Guilt

Relational attachments come in many shapes and sizes. The highest attachment is, of course, selfless covenant love. What surprises most people is the realization that hurt, anger, and guilt can tie two people together as tightly as love.[21] The root of such attachments is pain; it binds people together in disharmony. Even more surprising is the realization that conflict, bitterness, and control are the umbilical cords through which anger and guilt stay alive. As criticism and defensiveness pass back and forth between ex-spouses, hurt and the bond of disharmony are kept alive. One of the greatest ironies of bitterness is that it imprisons you with the person who hurt you. Over time you actually contribute to your own pain and misery.

If you are the leavee (your ex left you), you probably feel more anger, rejection, and hurt. If you cannot set this aside and compartmentalize your feelings, you can easily spoil the co-parental relationship. If you were the leaver (you initiated the divorce), you may feel guilt over your actions, especially when you see your children's pain. You may find it difficult to separate from your decision and fully invest in your present stepfamily situation, in which case your new spouse may feel insecure with your commitment, and your stepchildren may feel rejected by you. Your guilt may even lead you to keep your ex-spouse from being angry with you. For example, some feel obligated to their ex and go out of their way to accommodate him/her regarding money, time schedules, or taking care of maintenance tasks for their ex-spouse's home. For both the leavee and the leaver, whether you feel rejection or guilt, your pain is dictating your responses. You are locked in a prison cell of pain, and your continued negative interaction is keeping the key beyond your reach.

### Learning to Forgive

So what do you do? How do you let go of the old marital hurt so you can cooperate as co-parents? Let it go with forgiveness. I know this is where I'll lose some of you. Your back is already bowed, your blood pressure is going up, and you want to close

**Leavee or Leaver?**

Rarely do our actions or experiences fit nicely into categories like these. In truth, you are probably some of both—a part of you was left and a part of you participated in the leaving. Recognize each aspect and take responsibility for it.

the book. "After what he did to me, how dare you suggest I forgive?" One woman heard me discussing the necessity of forgiveness as a tool to improve co-parent relationships, and she was offended. She called to say, "My ex left me for another woman and now she is my kids' stepmother. There's no way I can forgive him for that and I won't accept her place with *my* children." As she talked further I could tell that she was intentionally trying to badmouth the stepmother to her children, since she broke up their family.

Please understand, I don't make the suggestion to forgive lightly, nor do I believe it an easy task. I was a crisis counselor after the Westside School shooting in Jonesboro, Arkansas, and for years after worked with a number of the families who were so painfully impacted by that event. Never have I seen such pain or crying out to God. Never have I felt so inadequate as a therapist. My passion for those who lost so much on March 24, 1998, would not allow me to flippantly urge them to "forgive and move on." To discount the value of lives lost in such a way would be reprehensible. Yet acknowledgment of a loving God who cares deeply about our losses and the ability to offer forgiveness to the two young boys who perpetrated the tragedy eventually became the backbone of healing for those whom I counseled.

Your pain is real too, and your anger may be completely justified. Yet you can't be for your stepfamily everything God calls you to be if you're carrying around a burden of anger, hurt, and guilt.

Forgiveness is an unnatural act of a will that has been shaped and molded by a forgiving God. There is nothing human about it. Forgiveness doesn't restore the broken relationship or repair the emotional damage done. It simply writes it off. And it only becomes practically possible to us when we realize what God has forgiven us. Even after having his debt canceled by his master, the unmerciful servant of Matthew 18:21–35 was not able to cancel the debt owed him by a fellow servant because he didn't fully appreciate his gift of forgiveness. Paul reminds us in Colossians 2:13–14 that while we were dead in our sins, God made us alive with Christ. "God made [you] alive together with him, having forgiven us all our trespasses, by canceling the record of debt that stood against us with its legal demands. This he set aside, nailing it to the cross." Only when we realize what stood between us and God (our sinfulness) and how God removed that through the cross, can we ever realistically apply forgiveness to that which stands between us and another person. Be humbled by the magnitude of your forgiven debt and you'll discover that the unnatural act of forgiving is possible.

> **New Spouses and Secondary Pain**
>
> After hearing stories and seeing the negative consequences of a former spouse's behavior, new spouses (stepparents) who were not direct recipients of hurtful actions can still find themselves angry at their spouse's former spouse. This "secondary pain" deserves to be acknowledged and forgiven.

### Some Practical Observations About Forgiveness[22]

*Forgiveness begins with a decision.* Saying the words "I forgive Lisa for abandoning me and our family" starts a process of forgiveness. The challenge, then, becomes living that choice. Please know that emotional release—a letting go of pain and hurt—follows the intellectual decision to forgive, not the other way around.

*Choose to forgive one offense at a time.* All too often we face a mountain of hurt that cannot be overcome. Make a list of the boulders that comprise that mountain and strive to forgive them individually. Take it in manageable pieces.

*Communicating your forgiveness is optional.* For some, relief comes just by having made a personal decision to forgive. Others need to communicate their decision to bring closure to the process. Do what is best in your situation.

*Forgiveness and accountability are not mutually exclusive.* We can forgive someone and still hold him or her accountable for his or her actions (not for revenge or personal gain). For example, you can forgive an ex-spouse for driving drunk with your children in the car, but you don't have to then subject your children to future possible harm. Work with your ex and/or the court system to ensure safety (e.g., another person must be present when driving) until your ex demonstrates more responsible behavior.

*Forgiveness takes one; trust and reconciliation takes two.* Mercy can be extended to someone without reestablishing trust. Many resist forgiveness because they believe they will be forced into making themselves vulnerable to the other person again. If a bank employee steals from a bank, he can be forgiven and still not be given his job back. There is nothing wrong with learning from your past experience with someone and protecting yourself or others from hurt. Just check your motives.

*Forgiveness is empowering.* Holding on to hurt and pain enslaves us to the person who hurt us. Conflict and bitterness keep our hurt alive. The result is a helpless victim. Have you ever been guilty of constantly blaming your poor life circumstances on someone else? That's what victims do—constantly complain about how others have ruined their life. In doing so, victims alleviate themselves from personal responsibility for the condition of their life.

Forgiveness moves us from victim to empowered victor. It breaks the chains of imprisonment and severs the umbilical cord that gave life to the pain. When you forgive, you no longer have to react to the other out of pain, but have free choice to decide the best course of action. For example, an ex-spouse might continue to act as a Fiery Foe, but you do not have to return fire (as in the past). Forgiveness is the key that opens your prison cell door. Ex-concentration camp victim Corrie ten Boom said, "To forgive is to set a prisoner free and discover the prisoner was you."

While forgiveness is fresh on your mind, take a moment and complete this action point: Write brief answers to the following questions.

1. What offenses or leftovers from the past are you carrying with you? (Make a list.)
2. Which of these can you decide to forgive today?

3. Decide how you will continue to struggle with forgiving the remaining items.

4. What personal acts do you need to repent of, release to God, or seek forgiveness for?

### Learn How to Invite Cooperation

Some parents, after reading this material, can simply call their ex-spouse, share this book, and have a rational meeting to discuss how they might better implement the Guidelines for Co-Parents (earlier in this chapter). If that is within your power, by all means set up the meeting soon. Angry Associates and Fiery Foes, however, will understandably fear a face-to-face meeting, believing it will erupt into World War III.

"You just don't understand. My ex is a jerk and won't listen to anything I say. If I mail her a copy of your book she'll throw it away. I have no control over her attitude." True, you have no control over your ex's attitude, but you may have some influence. Years ago I wrote "An Open Letter to Parents Who Are Divorced." It was designed to remind parents of their vital role and invite ex-spouses to consider how they might better cooperate. I had no idea how useful and productive the letter would be to angry, fiery co-parents.

**Here's the plan.** The letter is now available online (find it at SmartStep families.com/view/open-letter). Send the link to your ex-spouse with this written or verbal message: "I have been reading a book on stepfamily life and co-parenting. The author of the book recommended that I share this with you; otherwise, I wouldn't impose. I also want you to know that I've realized I have been violating a few of these principles and am committing myself to do better. Specifically, I've noticed that I am guilty of [provide two examples of mistakes you have made and what you intend to do next time. For instance, you could say, "I shouldn't cut into your visitation time by bringing the kids over past five p.m. I'm sorry. My new goal is to be on time, every time. Also, I'm going to stop saying negative things about your new husband. I now see that that puts the kids in a tight spot."] I appreciate your time. [sign your name]"

There are, of course, no guarantees that sending the letter will create immediate change; you are simply trying to open the door to change. To that end, be sure not to send the link with a message like "Boy, do you need to read this. You're a terrible co-parent and it's tearing up our kids." Obviously, this will re-ignite your battles and close the door to change. Admit your mistakes without asking your ex to evaluate his or her parenting. Admit your failings with no strings attached. This quietly invites the other parent to consider his or her own behavior without pressure from you. Above all, keep the goal in mind, do your part, and pray that the Lord will soften your ex-spouse's heart.

### Be Businesslike If Necessary

Many co-parents have learned how to handle difficult ex-spouse relationships. Some use note cards while speaking on the phone to help keep them on task. Others avoid personal contact altogether, relying on text messages, voice mail, letters, or email. No matter what your avenue of communication, treat the contact as you would a business deal: Don't get personal, seek the win/win solution, and stick to discussing the kids. Having a business mentality may help you to avoid being sidetracked when your buttons get pushed.

> **Should You Admit Mistakes in Writing?**
>
> Those of you in Fiery Foe, highly litigious circumstances may not want to admit mistakes in writing because it may be twisted and used against you in court. Just leave that part of the cover letter/email out.

One good business principle that applies in many circumstances is to try to find the common ground. Whenever possible, agree with some aspect of what your ex is saying, even if you disagree with the main point. "You're right, every teenager wants the independence a car provides; I'm just wondering if he should be rewarded with one right now given his poor grades." If you can't "close the deal" because of personal pain or attacks, politely take a time-out from negotiations (e.g, "I'm afraid I'm not thinking straight at the moment and need to take a break. I'll call you back later/tomorrow to discuss this further."). Return to the table later when you have gathered yourself.

### Borrow a Script and Stick to It

Stepfamily expert Patricia Papernow has designed some scripts to help co-parents deal with each other and the differences between their homes in a constructive manner.[23] Before calling your ex, for example, have a written script in your hands to guide your responses. This will help you manage yourself during the conversation.

Here are some of Dr. Papernow's scripts to help you communicate.

### ■ 1. LETTING THE BULLET BOUNCE

After answering the phone, you hear your ex say, "I can't believe you forgot to send Jennifer's Halloween costume. We're going to be late, she's crying, and once again you are irresponsible! When are you going to grow up?"

Your response: [Take a deep breath and gather yourself] "I know it's a pain. I'm sorry. Do you want me to bring it over, or do you want to pick it up?"

*Note:* I call this letting the bullet bounce, because your ex is attacking you, and if you let the bullet penetrate, you will react defensively. Putting on thick skin is a premium in stepfamilies. Don't respond to the accusation; get to a behavioral solution. And next time remember to send the Halloween costume.

### ■ 2. MOM'S HOUSE RULES/DAD'S HOUSE RULES

You say to your son: "Homework *before* watching TV."

He says, "Dad lets me watch TV before doing my homework."

Take a deep breath and say, "That may be true in your dad's house. And in this house, the rule is homework *before* TV."

*Note:* It's okay to have differing rules and expectations. The temptation is to argue with Dad's rule or judge his motives by saying, "That's because your dad likes to watch TV all the time himself." Don't worry about Dad's rule. Stick to yours. Also, notice the use of the word *and* instead of *but* preceding "in this house . . ." The latter creates defensiveness; *and* is much more conciliatory.

### ■ 3. THE "LOOKING FOR INFORMATION" PHONE CALL

Sometimes situations like the one above require further information from the other parent. The biological parent should make the call; how you make that call is important to maintaining a cooperative relationship.

If you call and say the following, you are igniting a battle: "I can't believe you let Johnny watch TV before doing his homework."

Rather, call and say, "Hi. I'm calling for some information. Johnny and I had a little run-in, and he says that in your house it's okay to watch TV before getting his homework done. I'm wondering if that's true, or if he's trying to get away with something."

If you are Cooperative Colleagues, the response may sound like this: "Yeah. I figure he needs to unwind a little bit after basketball practice."

You say, "Okay. I can understand that. That's what I needed to know. Thank you."

If you are Angry Associates, the response may sound more like "He comes home tired from basketball practice, and he's just a kid. Why should he have to do it anyway—homework isn't that important right now."

You say [after taking a deep breath], "Okay. Thank you."

*Note:* This second response is by far the most difficult. However, it is likely that arguing is not going to convince the other parent to change (has it ever worked before?), and you don't need to try to control them anyway. You got the information you were seeking, and it wasn't pretty. Hang up and work with your son within your home.

Say to your son: "Moms and dads are different. I have lots of rules about chores in the house; your father has more rules about manners at the table. I'm concerned about your grades and wonder what you can do here to improve them. [Discuss the possibilities.] What might you do while in your dad's house to get your homework done?"

### ■ 4. Off the Hook and Out of the Middle

Parents can sometimes tell when kids are getting caught in negative battles between adults. However, many times children themselves are not aware of a loyalty bind nor can they articulate it, so parents may not know their child is caught. Here are some possible ways to respond when you notice your child is in the tug-of-war.

*To your children:* "It seems to me that you are kind of caught in the middle between your mother and me. I know that is a tough place to be. I'm wondering how you feel about it. [Listen and affirm.] When

**What do you do when kids lie to those in the other home?**

Find the answer in the Smart Questions, Smart Answers bonus material, available at SmartStepfamilies.com/view/learn.

do you feel stuck the most? I'm sorry you have to hear negative things. I want you to know if you hear me say something about the other home that makes you feel bad, you can ask me to stop. And you can ask your mom to stop too. If not, you'll be in a bad spot between us. Do you want to talk about it? [Listen and validate feelings.] By the way, you have my permission to love your mom and respect or love your stepdad. That's important for you, and I'm okay with it."

If your child responds, "Come on, Dad. You know Mom won't stop even if I ask her to. Once she gets started, she can't stop," reply by saying, "You may be right. But I think it's worth saying out loud to her that it makes you feel bad."

*To your ex-spouse:* "I know you would never mean to hurt the kids. But your comments like [give specific examples] are putting them between us. Please stop. I'm learning not to say negative things in front of the kids, and I hope you will do the same. Thank you for your time."

If your ex isn't convinced that negative comments hurt the children, don't try to defend yourself to the children. That only forces them into the middle again. The children will form their own opinions as they grow, and they tend to finally respect the parent who manages their tongue.

### ▪ 5. RECONNECTING

When noncustodial parents have been disconnected from their children for an extended period of time, many wounds are created. If you have been absent from your child's life and now want to reconnect, understand that it won't be easy. As children grow into adolescence and adulthood, they can develop emotional walls that have protected them from feeling your rejection. Your ex-spouse may have great anger toward you for disappointing the children and being unavailable to help raise them. Consider the following script as you hope to reconnect.

*Communicate to your ex-spouse:* "I apologize for not being involved like I should have been. I know I have cheated you and our children out of a lot. And I'm sorry. I am hoping to reconnect with the kids but will not force myself on them. I will just let them know I'm changing, and they can contact me when they are ready."

*Write a letter to your child:* "I know this is tough to hear from me after I've been away for so long. I can see you are holding close to your mother right now. That is as it should be. Sometime I hope things will change enough that you feel you can reconnect with me. I love you. When you're ready to call, I'll be happy to talk to you."

*Note:* Once you have stated your desire to reconnect, don't make it tough for kids to reach back and find you. Send birthday and holiday gifts with short, friendly messages. Don't induce guilt by saying, "Happy birthday. Why haven't you called?" Short emails can also help you stay at a safe distance until your children decide to step closer.

There are times, however, when you cannot reconnect and it's not your fault. There are extreme situations when one parent systematically pushes the other out; in those situations of alienation, most of the well-natured reasonable strategies presented so far in this chapter need to be recalibrated.

## Alienated Parenting

In memory of our son, Connor, who died at the age of twelve, Nan and I have invested in an incredible ministry that rescues trafficked children—slaves, to be more blunt—in Ghana, West Africa. Sold into slavery, many times by their parents, these children as young as four years old work in the fishing industry twelve to fourteen hours a day, eat one meal a day, receive no education, are stripped of their personhood, and never see their parents again. They are *taken.* When most people first hear us talk about the plight of these children, they are dumbfounded and outraged. How insidious to hold a child hostage. Indeed.

> Learn more about this effort at *ConnorsSong.com*.

Sometimes it is divorced parents who hold their own kids hostage from the other parent. They systematically and intentionally alienate the other parent, home, even extended family from the child—and just like the slave masters of Ghana, justify their actions as prudent and necessary. I have written elsewhere about when parents are "occasionally blocked" from spending time with a child or receiving their entire visitation time (see *The Smart Stepdad*), but I am not referring to that now. Nor am I talking here about when a child becomes a prodigal and on their own volition stops returning a parent's phone calls or responding to attempts to connect.

Parental alienation is far more insidious and destructive because it involves the intentional brainwashing of a child by one parent against the other.

A mother approached me at a conference. "What do I do," she begged. "My four-year-old son came home from his dad's house the other day and started saying, 'Mommy, you have a hard heart. You are a bad mommy. You have a hard heart.' We have a great relationship, but ever since his father remarried, his stepmom has started putting these thoughts in his head about me. I am so scared that he is turning away from me."

A valued friend of mine, Richard, has a PhD in marriage and family and is an expert trainer in marital relationships, but his degrees and training came after he and his mother became victims of alienation. When he was just five years old his parents divorced. His father, from a wealthy and highly influential family in Miami, systematically set about to poison him and his siblings against their mother. They were discouraged from visiting their mother and were repeatedly told how their mother had mental problems and that he loved them, not she. Richard vividly remembers his father offering trips for deep sea fishing and the like to dissuade him from visiting his mother. His father intercepted her letters, gifts, and attempts to spend time with them and then accused her of not loving them enough to bother to see them. He even insisted that the kids stop calling her Mom (and punished them with raging guilt if they did) and instead refer to her as "Mrs. Smith."

This depersonalization and marginalization of their mother removed her from their life and caused my friend to despise her. My friend grew up resentful to God that he didn't have a mother like other children. The other great sadness in this story was that Richard's stepmother, who herself was a divorcée, did not desire to be a mother figure and fulfill the emotional needs of Richard and his siblings. He was left to grow up void both of a mother and a caring stepmother.

### Parent Alienation Syndrome

Each year tens of thousands of new court cases are ignited as a result of one biological parent alienating their children from the other. The distorted and self-justifying reasons parents do this varies, but the results are similar. Alienated children rapidly downgrade a once close relationship with a parent (for example, before the divorce) to nothing; they have an absurd devotion to negative attitudes and beliefs about the parent even in the face of evidence to the contrary (e.g., they accuse a parent who pursues them of not caring); they offer trivial explanations for why they reject a relationship with the parent; and/or they extend hatred of the parent to that parent's extended family (grandparents, cousins, etc.) without justification.[24] We all understand how parents who consistently break promises and disappear from a child's life deserve a child's anger and hurt, but truly alienated parents usually haven't earned this response.

If you are living this nightmare, you already know it, but you are desperately searching for answers. While a complete discussion of how to manage parent alienation syndrome is beyond the scope of this book, I do want to offer an important perspective to help you get started in finding help. Earlier in this chapter I addressed healthy co-parenting. In that section I stressed the importance of not bad-mouthing your ex-spouse, especially in front of the children, as it naturally puts them in the middle and adds to their distress. If you are an alienated parent, please hear this: That general principle no longer applies to you. The extreme nature of alienation necessitates that you take a stronger, more assertive posture with your children in order to break the spell they are under. In his seminal and highly recommended book on this subject, *Divorce Poison*, Dr. Richard Warshak tells parents that in the face of alienation, avoiding speaking against the other parent is the wrong approach. "It does not work," he says. "Often, it makes things worse."[25] Being reasonable in the face of an unreasonable opponent only adds to your vulnerability. Parents, he suggests, should maintain a commitment to shielding their children from unnecessary and destructive communication, but notes that the only way to break through the trance of systematic alienation is to assertively confront the reality of the situation.[26]

I once coached a dad to stop passively allowing his ex-wife to control the children's thoughts about him by directly saying to them, "I'm sorry, your mother is wrong about me. I do not hate you. I love you very much. I have sent you many letters only to discover that your mother has hidden them from you. I tried to go to your basketball game last week, but she told me the wrong school—I showed up but the game wasn't there, and by the time I got to the right place the game was over. I'm not sure why your mother says this to you, but please know that what she is saying is not true." Without question, this puts the child in a tight spot, but without direct confrontation, his children would be unlikely to snap out of the trance their mother had put them under.

If you are an alienated parent, I strongly recommend that you pick up a copy of *Divorce Poison* by Dr. Warshak so you can apply the multitude of prescriptions he offers to alienated parents.

Let me return to the story of my friend, Richard. Alienated from his mother by his manipulative father, Richard found himself at the age of thirty crying out to God for a mother in his life. Despite a PhD in marriage and family, Richard never realized what his father had done until the moment he was questioning God as to why he never had a mother in his life. In the midst of his prayer, Richard believes the Holy Spirit opened his eyes and broke through the trance he had been under. Richard remembers the Holy Spirit telling him, "What you always wanted in a mother you always had. You just rejected her." Richard was so disconnected he asked of the Holy Spirit, "Well, who is it?" The Spirit simply said back to his heart, "She gave birth to you."

> ### What Kids Are Thinking
>
> All kids get caught in the middle between their parents to some degree. But alienated kids have stopped trying to walk the fence; instead, because they are manipulated, they jump on one side. Don't give up reaching over the fence to break the spell they are under.

At midnight, Richard called his mother. She answered the phone and was surprised to hear from him. He said to her, "Mom, I realized something tonight." With tears in his eyes and heart he said, "You are my mother." Now, with tears in her eyes and joy in her heart, she lovingly told him, "Welcome home." What he uncovered was a mother's never-ending love, the truth of her persistent attempts through the years to be reunited with her children, and the depth of his father's manipulation. The lost years grieved his heart, but he found his mom.

If you are an alienated parent, I am grieved on your behalf for all that has been lost. You may be tempted at times to give up hope, to withdraw your affections in order not to go crazy in agony over the one you have lost. As a parent who has lost a child to death, I can most certainly sympathize with your despair. But do not give up trying. There is no telling what God may do—or when—in order to reunite you and your child. Keep praying and searching.

### Stepping in Line

This chapter and the next suggest that a key step in stepfamily success is taken when all the adults on the parenting team put their needs aside and consider the children. Remembering that it is all about the children keeps the focus of adult interaction where it should be. The first key relationship in the parenting team is the co-parent relationship. The next chapter will discuss the second key aspect: the parent-stepparent relationship and their roles as caregivers.

### Questions for Discussion

■ FOR PARENT-CHILD DISCUSSION (Discretion based on the age of the child and the quality of adult-child relationships is advised.)

*Note:* Asking kids of any age about between-home and co-parenting matters is delicate; when the subject is brought up, kids naturally feel caught in the middle. To help lower their fears, set up the conversation by telling them (1) they don't have to answer any question that makes them uncomfortable; and (2) start by owning your mistakes as a co-parent and make the conversation about their feelings concerning you, not the other parent.

1. I know from time to time you feel caught in the middle between your mom/dad and me. What is going on when you feel that way?
2. We all feel our anxiety somewhere in our bodies. For example, when I am anxious about something I feel it in my stomach/headache/lower back/bowels. Where do you feel yours?
3. Before we talked today, I completed this exercise. I'd like you to check me on my answers. Help me understand you better. [Review your responses to the "Burdens My Children Face" exercise below.]

### Burdens My Children Face

Make a list on the left side of co-parent stressors for your children. On the right, list what you might do to improve the situation. Consider, for example:

- Ways I put them in an emotional tug-of-war
- Expectations put on them to take care of others or me

165

| ■ Unhealthy Burden | ■ My New Plan |
| --- | --- |
| 1. | 1. |
| 2. | 2. |
| 3. | 3. |
| 4. | 4. |
| 5. | 5. |

## ■ For All Couples

1. On a scale of 1 to 10, rate your co-parental relationship on your ability to contain anger and conflict in order to cooperate and compromise on issues regarding the children's welfare.

2. List two or three things you might do to improve this rating.

3. When a remarriage takes place, the visitation routine is often disturbed. Indeed, fathers, on average, drop their visits to noncustodial children by half within the first year of their ex-wife's remarriage. Regularity of contact is critical to children's self-esteem and reduces feelings of loss. What disruptions in access to both parents have your children experienced? What can you do to improve the access and regularity (predictability) of this contact?

4. Consider whether your children have your permission to care about others in their two homes. If not, what needs to change within you in order to grant that permission?

5. What fears do you have about losing touch with your teenagers? If they wanted to live in the other home, how would you react?

6. Review the Healthy Co-Parenting checklist and rate your co-parenting relationship on each. Overall, how would you rate your situation? What needs to improve most?

7. Review the Guidelines for Co-Parents and create a checklist of items you need to develop or work toward. Affirm yourself and your ex for the things you are currently doing well.

8. Review the list of Things Kids Wish They Could Say to Their Divorced Parents. Which would your children say to you?

9. On a scale of 1 to 10, how well are you able to compartmentalize old marital issues and current co-parental ones? What triggers are you most susceptible to?

10. Share some of the forgiveness issues you have had to face or are currently struggling to release.

11. Which scripts might be helpful to you in the future? Why?

12. Alienated Parenting: If you are experiencing alienation, you already know it. Your heart is burdened. You need a clear plan of action. Discuss who you need to consult or what books you need to read in order to develop this plan.

### ■ FOR PRE-STEPFAMILY COUPLES

1. Openly discuss your present co-parent relationships. How cooperative have you been in the past with your ex? What issues are problematic? How well are you able to contain your anger and responses with your children's other parent?

2. With whom do you need to step in line prior to your remarriage?

3. What are your hopes regarding how quickly your children will accept their new stepparent? Do you think this is realistic?

4. How did you contribute to the breakup or divorce of your last relationship?

5. To what degree have you emotionally resolved the ending of your first marriage?

6. To what degree have you resolved what happened to your future spouse in his or her previous relationship?

7. The presence of moderate to severe anger and/or guilt is a good indication that you have not emotionally de-coupled from your former love relationship. How de-coupled are you and your ex-spouse?

8. Alienated and stressful co-parenting: If you are the potential stepparent and the person you are dating is already facing a situation of alienated parenting or a Fiery Foe ex-spouse situation, you must weigh the burden it will bring to your life and to your children should you marry. Do not minimize this situation as you consider a future together.

# Smart Step Four: STEP in Line (Part 2)

*Parent and stepparent roles*

> But Sarah saw Ishmael making fun of Isaac. Ishmael was the
> son Hagar had by Abraham. Hagar was Sarah's servant from
> Egypt. Sarah said to Abraham, "Get rid of that slave woman.
> Get rid of her son. The slave woman's son will never have a
> share of the family's property with my son Isaac." What Sarah
> said upset Abraham very much. After all, Ishmael was his son.
>
> Genesis 21:9–11 NIRV

Parenting in stepfamilies is a two-, three-, or four-person (sometimes more!) dance. Parent-stepparent harmony is the crux of successful parenting within your home—whatever the condition of your co-parental relationship(s). The two most critical relationships in any stepfamily home are the marriage and the stepparent-stepchildren relationships. The marriage must be strong to endure the many pressures stepfamily couples face and provide a backbone of family stability. Marriage, we might say, is the Crockpot itself; without the pot, nothing gets cooked. Almost as important is the stepparent-stepchildren relationship. The stepparent's presence and the role they play in the family is critical because it dramatically affects the level of stress in the primary triangle of relationships between parent, stepparent, and stepchild(ren). Less stress equals more harmony in parenting; more parental harmony in turn leads to more harmony in the marriage.

Many people assume incorrectly that stepparenting is the sole responsibility of the stepparent. This assumption inadvertently pits husband and wife against each other when the stepparent flounders or upsets the children. Lest there be any confusion, let me say very clearly that stepparenting is a two-person task. Biological parents and stepparents must work out roles that complement each other and play to each other's strengths. Just as in two-biological-parents homes, parents and stepparents must be unified in their goals and work together as a team. Stepparents who are struggling need biological parents who will step up to the plate; biological parents need stepparents who will partner with them in the task of raising responsible, God-following children. Stepping in line in your home means planning and parenting together. This principle was again validated when a study of more than a thousand children in stepfather households found that children are better able to adapt to changes brought on by the introduction of a stepfather, and are more open to connecting with him emotionally, if they see a strong, united, and cooperative alliance between their mother and stepfather.[1] In other words, parental unity is an important aspect of the "low-level heat" that facilitates the Crockpot cooking process.

## Just in Case You Think You've Got It All Together . . .

I'm convinced that children are God's tool for humbling adults. We could pretty well sail through life feeling in control of almost everything if we didn't have children. But competent, self-assured, capable people can be reduced to Jell-O when face-to-face with a typical two-year-old. Throughout the child-rearing years, humility comes to parents in many forms: the helplessness of trying to get a six-month-old infant to stop crying at three in the morning; the powerlessness of struggling with a sixteen-year-old daughter who keeps breaking the rules; the inadequacy you feel when your nine-year-old son says, "So, do you and Mom have sex?" And nothing can embarrass us more than the surprises kids throw at us at the most inconvenient times. I'll never forget carrying a constipated three-year-old out of worship (during the quiet, reflective time of Communion, no less), only to have him announce at the top of his lungs why we were leaving: "Poo-poo!" Once you have kids, your life will never be the same.

One challenge more humbling and frustrating than raising children is raising stepchildren! Throughout the family's integration years, stepparents are often the most rejected, least affirmed, and most taken for granted adults in stepfamilies. At any given moment, stepparents may have all the responsibility for daily child care that biological parents have, but very little authority to manage the child's behavior. They are expected to make the same sacrifices as biological parents but reap very few rewards. "Thanks for washing my clothes for school today" doesn't come often enough.

Stepmothers are at an even greater disadvantage than stepfathers for a number of reasons. First, children tend to maintain more frequent contact with their noncustodial mothers. Second, children's attachment to their biological mother is believed to be stronger than their attachment to their father, making the acceptance and bonding with a stepmother even more difficult. Third, because society expects women to achieve a higher relational standard than men, stepmothers feel greater pressure to build a strong attachment with stepchildren. Despite societal changes in women's roles throughout the world, women still bear the primary responsibility for child care, maintenance, and nurturance of children. Stepmothers are not excused from these responsibilities, and they try to fulfill society's expectations by working hard at building a relationship—only to discover a strong loyalty to the biological mom standing in the way. No wonder stepmothers report greater dissatisfaction with their role and exhibit higher levels of stress.

> **Knowing Yourself**
>
> "I thought I was going to be the best stepmom God ever put together, but I have had such a hard time loving his kids—and I feel just horrible about it."

Unguided by norms, role clarity, or realistic expectations, the stepmother works to "make up for the past" experiences of the stepchildren, only to come to the awareness that she is overwhelmed, frustrated, and less committed to them than she believes she should be. . . . The lack of role models for women who become stepmothers means that women have nowhere to turn for meaningful advice.[2]

Truly the job of a stepmother is a challenging one. Family therapist and stepfamily educator Jean McBride says one woman described it well: "Being a stepmother is like setting your hair on fire and then trying to put it out with a hammer!"[3]

*"I feel more like a maid than a mother."*

*"I feel that every time I try to set some rules, it's like a declaration of war with my stepchildren."*[4]

But remember, the journey for stepmoms and stepdads alike also offers rewards; not all children feel negatively toward stepparents.

*"When I was four years old my father died, and two years later my mother met my stepdad. There were six of us kids to raise, plus he had three from his previous marriage. When they got married, he helped her raise us and treated us like his very own kids. I never knew my father; Ted is the only real father I ever knew. Though we have had our ups and downs, I would never trade him for any other father in the world."*

*Stepdaughter*

*"He's only been my father for about six years. He seems like my real father. He takes me fishing, hunting, and four-wheeler riding. I think the only things we haven't done are skate and golf. If I want something and he can afford it, he gets it for me. He shows me love and discipline. Even when he disciplines me, I can tell he still loves me."*

*Stepson, age nine*

Children nominating their fathers for their church's "Father of the Year" award wrote these last two quotes. The respect and appreciation of these stepchildren is evident. I share it with you as a reminder that there is a Promised Land. All the hard work and discomfort of stepparenting can pay off. It may not happen as quickly as you'd like, but you can get there.

172

So how do stepparents and parents work together to generate this type of recognition? What are some common pitfalls, and how can stepparents avoid them? Let's begin by establishing some rules to keep you on the same side. Then I'll examine the role biological parents have in empowering the stepparent, the evolving role of stepparents, and conclude with an overview of the overall parenting process. The next chapter will discuss some common challenges stepparents face.

## The Parental Unity Rules

These rules will help you work together and keep you on the same side as a parental team. Remember, united you stand, divided you fall.[5]

### Rule 1: Be Proactive

Don't wait until problems occur to discuss behavioral expectations, preferred methods of punishment and consequences to be enforced, and the values you wish to instill in the children.

### Rule 2: When in Doubt, Call a Parental Powwow

Tell the children, "I don't know. I'll get back to you on that" so you can have a parental meeting to discuss the situation. This response communicates to the kids that you seek, respect, and honor each other's input in parenting decisions, and it will speak volumes about your unity as a couple. This will help to dissolve their efforts to "divide and conquer" the marriage. Even if it's inconvenient or uncomfortable, go the extra mile to ensure parental agreement. You won't regret it.

### Rule 3: If the Biological Parent Doesn't Appreciate How the Stepparent Handled a Given Situation, Have a Private Discussion

The biggest mistake a biological parent can make is to make negative, critical comments about the stepparent in front of the kids. The second mistake is to reverse the decision. Either of those responses robs their authority, which is already under scrutiny by the kids. Listen openly to the stepparent's explanation of what happened (kids often leave out significant details). If you don't agree with how something happened or a decision made, acknowledge the stepparent's good intentions and then discuss an alternative plan for the next time: "I appreciate that you were trying to teach Rebecca a lesson. I understand what you were attempting to accomplish, but given Rebecca's personality, I'm wondering if you could handle it a little differently next time." Refrain from turning this into a competition. The goal should be to find a solution that you can both support.

### Rule 4: Making Changes

From the time they are born, children are learning the expectations and behavioral management style of their parents. They become accustomed to rules and expectations over time and settle into them. When rules change, children adapt (after a bit of grumbling) because they give their parent the right to make the changes. When stepparents enter the picture and influence changes, children often struggle with the stepparent's authority to make those changes. That's when they complain or protest to their biological parent. Biological parents must take seriously how they support the status of the stepparent to their children. Here are some guidelines to help couples communicate the changes, especially when the stepparent's opinion has obviously contributed to the change.

**Dating Couples**

Once you're serious about marriage, begin bringing your parenting systems in line. Doing so before the wedding communicates that you, the biological parent, are clearly behind the changes. Communicate rule changes separately from the future stepparent and give your kids many months to adapt to the new expectations.

**Remember to powwow in order to find unity in the new expectation.** Then decide how to communicate the changes.

**In general, communicate changes in rules or expectations to the children together.** It's best if the biological parent takes the lead in sharing the change with the stepparent standing beside them. This is particularly important in the early years of your marriage. The stepparent can certainly add to the conversation, but the biological parent's voice should be clearly heard.

If a child disrespects the stepparent, correct them in front of the stepparent. This clearly communicates to both the stepparent (who will appreciate being backed) and the child the expectation that children respect their stepparent.

**A biological parent may need to communicate the change privately, without the stepparent present.** This should happen if:

- A child continually challenges the new rule (e.g., "you're just doing this because he/she wants you to"). The biological parent should be empathetic, but gently follow through. "You are right. You now have to wash your own laundry because he/she brought it to my attention. But we have discussed it thoroughly and I am in agreement. I'm sure you are bummed about this—I can't blame you. But this is how it's going to be from now on."

- A child is highly sensitive to the issue at hand or feels on display or embarrassed about the circumstances. For example, restricting computer use because the child visited inappropriate websites or working through boyfriend/girlfriend matters may be best handled by the biological parent alone. Again, powwow together as a couple to determine the best way to handle these situations.

These general guidelines will help to keep you on the same side as you parent the children. Even still, each of you must understand your role as it relates to the other.

## Biological Parents: Champion the Stepparent's Role

In each of the books *The Smart Stepmom* (with Laura Petherbridge) and *The Smart Stepdad*, I included two chapters for the biological parent. People often asked me, "Why does a book for stepparents include chapters for the biological parent?" "Because," I replied, "stepparents cannot be successful unless the biological parent sets them up for success; much of stepparenting depends on the biological parent doing their job."

Biological parents hold four keys that aid stepparents in their role. Essentially you must champion their place in the family. If you don't, they may experience defeat, frustration, and resentment toward you.

### Key 1: Be the Parent

Before championing the stepparent's role you first have to function consistently in the role of primary parent. You did this during the single parent years and before the wedding, and you have to continue doing so after the wedding, especially around matters of nurturance, affection, and punishment. Until the stepparent has had time (more on this later) to develop a bond with the kids and earn respect as an "authority," you need to clearly be the authority. Look at it from your kids' perspective: you are the safest, most well-defined parent figure in their life. Be that parent.

Here's the problem that presents for those of you who haven't been *that parent*. Making the change to become *that parent* may be met with resentment from your kids and a blaming of the stepparent even though it isn't their doing. Let's say, for example, that during the single parent years you lowered your expectations and your children got used to not obeying. Trying to reinstate your expectations comes along at the same time a lot of other changes in the family occur. This makes it difficult for kids to adapt to the change and easy for them to blame the stepparent. Nevertheless, you need to do what you must to become *that parent* because the parental standards of the home will follow your lead. Find the courage to be strong for the sake of your kids.

> **Part-Time Biological Parents**
>
> If you are a nonresidential, part-time parent, making changes and raising the standards with your children is difficult, because the temptation to remain a Disneyland Daddy or Magic Mountain Mommy is high, and you have limited opportunities to follow through. Be proactive and plan to spend a number of months shifting expectations. If you have a respectable relationship with the other home, let them know what you are trying to do and ask them to be patient with the process.

### Key 2: Declare Your Spouse (the Stepparent) Your Lifelong Partner

As discussed in chapter 5, a healthy marriage paves the way for healthy parenting. But since your relationship with your children preceded the wedding, your marriage is the least bonded and most vulnerable relationship in your home. You must protect it, honor it with time and energy, and declare it a top priority. If you don't, your children might assume they can pull on your loyalties any time it suits their selfish desires. For example, if a child learns that acting sad over the losses they've experienced draws your sympathy, makes you soft on punishment, and likely to defend

> **Parenting and Birth Order**
>
> Learn more about parenting and birth order changes when a step-family forms in chapter 8.

them to the stepparent, they will use it to their advantage. Children need to know you sympathize with their grief, but they also need to know their place in the family.

### Key 3: Pass Power to the Stepparent

The main challenge to stepparenting is earning or building a relationship with a stepchild that affords the stepparent needed authority to make rules (and impose consequences for disobedience). Until such a relationship is built, the stepparent must live on borrowed power from you. If you haven't yet done so, begin communicating to your children the expectation that they respect their stepparent. Say something like, "I know Bob is not your dad. However, when I am not here, he will be enforcing the household rules we have agreed upon. I expect you to be courteous and respect him as you would any authority figure." Then back up your expectation with action. I'll say more about this "baby-sitter" role later in this chapter.

### Key 4: Build Trust in the Stepparent

Roger loved Cheryle very much, but he wasn't sure why she was critical of his two daughters. Cheryle complained that Roger was too easy on them and she feared they would grow up to be "spoiled, boy-chasing girls." Roger believed that Cheryle's real problem was jealousy; he interpreted her criticism of the girls as her attempt to step between Roger and his daughters. Therefore, he ignored her input and discounted her efforts at discipline.

For some biological parents, the greatest barrier to entrusting their children to their spouse is a fundamental lack of trust in the stepparent. In first-marriage, two-biological-parent homes, couples don't seem to question the motives of their spouse. They may not agree with each decision or response, but they don't question their spouse's love for the children or parenting motives. Stepparents are not always granted that same benefit of the doubt. Open yourself to the stepparents' input. Listen to their "outsider" perspective and strive to see the love behind their actions.

## The Wise and Prudent Stepparent

> It takes five years to learn how to parent a five-year-old. I just got one yesterday, and no matter what I do, I am five years behind.
>
> David Mills, therapist

Proverbs 1:1–4 makes an interesting comparison between the wise or prudent person and someone who is simple-minded. The wise person has good sense and is skilled in living. The simple-minded person on the other hand lacks judgment due to inexperience or naïveté. The following section describes the qualities of unwise, naïve stepparents and contrasts them with wise stepparents, skilled in their role. Take them to heart so that inexperience need not result in heartache.

### Unwise Stepparents Make Becoming an Insider Their Goal

It's perfectly understandable to want to be considered a part of the family, but stepparents who make it their goal to quickly become insiders often end up terribly disappointed. It is one thing to find ways of getting along or to be respected by stepchildren with moderate authority; it is another to want stepchildren to want you in their innermost family circle. This desire leads stepparents to force their way in and put pressure on the biological parent to help bring them in. Simply put, these stepparents try too hard, rather than accept the relationship that develops.

**Wise stepparents enjoy the relationship they have now.** The cardinal rule for stepparent bonding is to let the children set the pace for their relationship with you.[6]

> **"My stepson doesn't follow rules or treat me with respect. What do I do?"**
>
> Find the answer in the Smart Questions, Smart Answers bonus material, available at SmartStep families.com/view/learn.

178

If they welcome or seek affection, then give it in a way that matches their comfort. If they remain distant and cordial, honor that as well. If they follow your rules and respect your decisions, continue to assert your given authority. If they challenge your authority, find ways to live on borrowed power from the biological parent while slowly growing your attachment over time (see key 3 above). Effective stepparents know that building a connection with stepchildren takes time, and they aren't focused on "deepening the bond" to the point that they miss the relationship they currently have. Learn to find the nuggets of good in the relationship you have now. Be patient and keep seeking to grow with your stepchildren, but don't add too much pressure.

### Unwise Stepparents (and Their Spouses) Expect Too Much of Themselves

Parents and stepparents tend to assume that children want a close, warm relationship with the stepparent. Biological parents want their children to be happy with their stepparent, and stepparents assume they need to be someone special to the children. Kids say otherwise.

When asked how the stepparent role *should be performed*, parents and stepparents generally envision the role in similar ways. In one study, close to half of them said the ideal stepparent role should be one of "parent" as opposed to "stepparent" or "friend." In contrast, 40 percent of stepchildren identified "friend" as the ideal role. Far fewer children thought a "parent" role was ideal.[7] "Parents" give hugs and expect obedience to their rules; "friends" offer support and encourage positive values in a child's life.

**Wise stepparents have realistic expectations for their role.** Stepparents need to learn to relax into their role and not expect too much of themselves. To expect too much is to set themselves up for disappointment and frustration. Parents also need to relax and let stepparents and stepchildren carve out their relationship.

James Bray discovered that most stepchildren in the early years of stepfamily life view the stepparent like a coach or camp counselor.[8] Such people have limited authority with children and provide instruction, but they are not "parents." However, just because your stepchildren don't give you unsolicited hugs does not mean you don't have a decent relationship. Having stepchildren who only talk to you when they want something is not necessarily an indication that you are a poor stepparent. It represents where you are today. Relax and trust the Crockpot.

### Unwise Stepparents Rush Into Authoritative Parenting

You may be familiar with what parent educators call *authoritative* parenting, identified as the most effective parenting style. The authoritative parent seeks to maintain firmness with respect for the child; boundaries, while providing limited choices; and rules with stated, consistent consequences that are balanced by nurture and love. Authoritative parenting at its best is a mirror of the parenting God gives us. Love and grace stand side by side with law and discipline.

*Authoritarian* parenting, by contrast, is characterized by high rules, harsh discipline, and excessive control. This strict parent essentially says, "You do it because I said so."

*Permissive* parents represent the other end of the parenting continuum. They provide very few limits or rules and give children unlimited choices. These parents make excuses for their child's behavior and assume the child will find his or her own way in life.

The authoritarian and permissive parenting styles have consistently been shown to produce children who lack self-control, have poor decision-making abilities, and who struggle with value-centered living. Stepparents don't want to adopt either of these styles. So, one would naturally assume that since authoritative parenting is best for children, stepparents would need to begin there. Surprisingly, research suggests this is not so, at least not at first. It is a matter of timing.

**Wise stepparents grow into their role.** Stepparenting changes as relationships grow. Authoritative stepparenting, especially within the first six months after remarriage, does not have the same positive outcome that authoritative parenting does in biological families (at least with most children).[9] Authoritative parenting requires stepparents to set rules and determine structure for children's lives, as well as display high levels of affection. This kind of parenting is based on a bonded relationship, which does not exist for stepparents until the Crockpot has had time to help the stepfamily integrate.

Early in remarriage, the most successful stepparent-stepchild relationships are those where the stepparent focuses first on the development of a warm, friendly interaction style with the stepchild. Once a foundation of mutual respect and affection is established, stepparents who then attempt to assume a disciplinarian role are less likely to meet with resentment from the stepchild.[10]

Closeness and the authority to discipline develop over time, and neither should be rushed. For example, stepparents are often eager to build a relationship and commonly seek one-on-one activities with stepchildren. Bray discovered that stepchildren were usually uncomfortable being alone with a stepparent.[11] They preferred family group activities to intense one-on-one experiences. After a period of time, one-on-one opportunities are received more openly. The length of time required for stepchildren to build a relationship with their stepparent depends on a number of factors that will be discussed later in this chapter.

The research evidence suggests that the best stepparent initially works through and with the children's parent. Initially, maintaining an emotionally non-threatening, distant relationship is best. After a couple of years, stepparents can begin to spend more time in direct child care and rule setting. Agreement between the spouses as to the timing of this role shift is important. Marital consensus and mutual support always provide the strength a stepparent needs to become more authoritative. (A more complete discussion of wise stepparenting can be found in "A Prescription for Evolving Parent and Stepparent Roles" later in this chapter.)

I should note here that there are exceptions to this guideline based on age and gender of the stepchild. Stepfathers of young stepsons who move into authoritative parenting fairly quickly tend to have positive outcomes. Instead of being disengaged, stepfathers can move more rapidly into leadership with young stepsons. This is generally not, however, the case with stepdaughters. Relationships between stepfathers and stepdaughters became more conflicted over time, regardless of the parenting styles used by the stepfather. And even if early stepfather-stepdaughter conflict is minimal when the girl is young, it seems to erupt around adolescence.[12] In addition, it seems that stepmothers and stepdaughters have the most difficult time bonding their relationship, in part due to strong mother-daughter bonds and competing female gender roles in the home.[13]

The point is this: Stepparent-stepchild relationships vary widely given a number of factors. You won't be able to discern every factor, so remember to listen to each child's cues and read his or her openness to you. If you let the child set the pace—and you honor the limits of your role—the Crockpot may eventually bring you closer together and increase your authority. But keep in mind—it also may not (which is why the biological parent's role as primary authority is so important). Accept what you have, make the most of it, and pray for a deepening relationship over time.

### Unwise Stepparents Punish Before Building a Relationship

By my estimation, this is the most common and one of the most destructive mistakes stepparents make. I've established that parental authority develops gradually over time and increases through bonding and the development of a trusting relationship. (If you want to test my assertion, just go to a neighbor's house and try to punish his children. Just because you live next door doesn't mean you have any say over those children. You can claim authority, but the level of authority the neighbor or his kids grant to you will be much less than what you claim.) Susan Gamache calls this *parental status,* that is, the degree that stepfamily members consider the stepparent a parent to stepchildren.[14] Parents might expect stepchildren to readily accept discipline from their stepparent, and stepparents might *claim* to have as much authority as the biological parent, but what really counts is how much authority children will accept from the stepparent.

I've heard stepdads fall back on Scripture and claim that "since I am the man of the house I should have the power of a father." Please remember, the children have a father (even if he's deceased); you're an added parent authority in their life. If you want to exasperate your stepchildren quickly (see Ephesians 6:4), push yourself on your stepchildren, claiming authority you don't yet have. Rather, the ability to lead and influence children comes the old-fashioned way—you earn it. Trust, respect, and honor grow out of a relational history, and there is no quick way to establish that. Stepparents must be dedicated to building a relationship over time.

**Wise stepparents gradually move into disciplinary roles.**[15] Influence comes with relationship and grows over time. Let's look at three positive relationship phases of parental authority.

**1. The baby-sitter role:** Baby-sitters have power to manage children only if parents give them power. When our favorite baby-sitter, Amy, used to watch our three boys, I reminded them in front of her that she was in charge while we were away. "She knows the rules, and if you disobey her, you are disobeying me. She has my permission to enforce the consequences. Plus, she'll tell me about it later, and you'll have to deal with me, too." After saying this before a number of date nights, my kids would finish the sentence before me. "We know, we know. Amy's in charge." Biological parents who have passed power to the stepparent and back it up with action will generally find their children to be cooperative with the stepparent (even though they may not value the stepparent yet).

There is, however, something very different about a stepparent and a baby-sitter. The latter is not part of the rule negotiation process; baby-sitters don't get a say in what rules should be or what discipline strategies the parenting team will utilize. Stepparents do. They have full membership in the parenting team and, therefore, are part of the decision-making process.

> ### Smart Stepparent Best Practices
>
> For more on how stepdads can be a spiritual leaders, see the bonus material "How Does Scripture Apply to Stepfamilies?" at SmartStepfamilies .com/view/learn.

Parents and stepparents, therefore, negotiate rules *together* behind closed doors and should pursue general agreement in their decisions. Early in the Crockpot, the biological parent then communicates the rules to the children with the stepparent standing in support. That way if a rule is broken, as far as the children are concerned, it is the parent's rule not the stepparent's. If a consequence is to be enforced by the stepparent, to the children it is the parent's consequence. Baby-sitting stepparents, then, are extensions of biological parents.

In a classic example, a ten-year-old girl scowls at her stepfather when he asks her to begin her Saturday chore of cleaning the garage. She barks, "I don't have to do what you say. You're not my dad," and then walks toward a friend's house. His response: "You're right, I'm not your dad. But I am the adult here right now, and this is the rule your mother communicated to you at our family meeting last month, remember? It's your choice. You can clean the garage by three o'clock or pay your brother to do it from your allowance." The stepdaughter clearly has a choice to make. She may choose obedience (and probably grunt and groan the whole way to the garage) or if she keeps walking to her friend's house, the stepfather arranges to have her little brother clean the garage for extra pay. When Mom returns home later that afternoon, she should support the action taken. "I expect you to obey the rules even when I am not here. Your decision to leave cost you ten bucks. Tell me what you plan to do next time."

When both adults bring a child(ren) to the stepfamily, they still negotiate rules together, but each takes the lead role with their own children. Simultaneously they are the primary parent to their children and the "baby-sitter" to the other's children. It is important to note that this arrangement will not work if the couple does not adopt consistent rules. You cannot afford to have one set of rules for his kids and another standard for hers. Consistency without favoritism is key.

> ### Parenting the "Mutual Child"
>
> When couples have a child together (the "mutual child") they will each parent that child from a position of strong attachment and authority. How adults respond to stepchildren versus the common biological child may vary, but strive to be equitable. See the section on parenting the mutual child in the next chapter.

The stepparent/"baby-sitter" system maintains the pre-stepfamily parenting arrangement with the biological parent acting as the primary nurturer and disciplinarian. Most critically, it allows the stepparent time and emotional space to focus on relationship development with the stepchildren. The stepparent can learn about the child's interests, share talents and skills, and engage in family group activities without having to worry about negative confrontations with the children.[16] Researcher James Bray says one of the most important stepparenting skills is *monitoring the children's activities*.[17] This involves knowing their daily routine, where the children are, who they are with, and what extracurricular activities they are involved in, but does not necessarily include being involved in the child's emotional life. Monitoring stepparents check homework and daily chores and befriend stepchildren, yet refrain from emotional closeness that is unwelcomed by the child. The posture of monitoring engages the child in a non-threatening way (which is vital early on) and slowly connects hearts.

2. The **"uncle/aunt" role:** After a moderate relationship has developed, stepparents can find themselves in the "uncle or aunt" stepparenting role. If my sister comes to my house, and Nan and I are away for a few hours,

she carries some authority with my children simply because she's their aunt. She is not a full-fledged parent, but carries power through her extended family kinship. Stepparents can gradually gain a basic level of respect that allows children to accept them as extended family members by marriage. Stepparents can become more authoritative, clearly communicating limits and encouraging family discussion of rules. Furthermore, as personal bonds deepen, shows of affection and appreciation can become more common. One-on-one activities can become more frequent and personal connections increase.

### Transitioning Roles

"How does a stepparent move from the baby-sitter to the uncle/aunt role?" The transition from one role to another is not formal; no one makes an announcement that stepdad is now "uncle-dad." More likely, you wake up one day and feel that something has changed. One stepmom said to her husband, "I don't know exactly what is different, but I think this is getting easier." Celebrate the growth and keep cooking!

3. **The "parent" or stepparent role:** Eventually, *some* stepparents will gain "parental" status with *some* stepchildren. Achieving this status is usually a combination of stepparent qualities that foster trust and respect over time and dynamics of family structure, that is, things no one controls. For example, younger children who have many years with a stepparent tend to grant stepparents a higher parental status than adolescents or part-time children who only have a few years in the stepfamily Crockpot. In addition, it is my experience that stepchildren who have a deceased parent or children with one biological parent who has dropped out completely from their life are more apt through the years to grant this level of status to their stepparent. Just as these dynamics work to the benefit of some stepparents, they work against others. Don't concern yourself with structural matters of your home that you can't control. Rather, focus on being the person God has called you to be and be content with that.

It is important that stepparents not consider themselves failures if they do not achieve parental status with every child. It is quite common to be considered a baby-sitter by an older child, an aunt by a middle child, and a parent by the youngest child. This experience can be confusing to say the least, so be sure you and your spouse are a solid parenting team. Discuss circumstances often and work together to make adjustments over time.

## A Prescription for Parent and Stepparent Roles

A few years ago, I developed a chart to visually demonstrate the changing roles of parents and stepparents over time (see next page).[18] This chart summarizes many of the principles I have laid out in this chapter. Research supports this general model, but acknowledges that there is no one universal best way to stepparent. Some of you may discover as you read this chapter that your family has broken all the rules yet still managed to experience low levels of family conflict. Others may realize that mistakes were indeed made and they need to retreat from their current approach, regroup, and begin implementing this model immediately. Everyone should continually ask God's guidance as you strive to lead your home.

### Parental Status

The vertical axis on the left of the chart is labeled Degree of Authority to Discipline and represents a person's parental status.[19] The higher you go, the more authority you have. (This status is the intersection between the authority a stepparent would like to assert ["asserted authority"] and how much authority a child will grant them at the moment ["accepted authority"]). Notice that biological parents have parental authority from the beginning of stepfamily life. After all, they're Dad/Mom and always will be. Stepparents, however, in most cases begin only with as much authority as a coach, teacher, or camp counselor. Even after marriage biological parents, labeled "Single Parent With Help," continue their role of single parent, only now they have a live-in baby-sitter to help. Biological parents remain the primary nurturer and disciplinarian and should spend special time with each child. Stepparents ("Baby-Sitter Role") initially focus on building relationships with their stepchildren and monitoring their activities and interests. Over time some stepparents move to higher levels of authority. Note the jagged line representing a multitude of up-and-down experiences with stepchildren. The variables impacting increasing authority vary widely, and many are beyond your control. Ride the waves with faith and hope.

As stepparents develop a greater bond with stepchildren and move up the vertical axis, biological parents will need to release more control to stepparents. This is difficult for many parents who have been their children's primary—or only—provider for a long time; they may not know how to

# A Prescription for Evolving Parent and Stepparent Roles

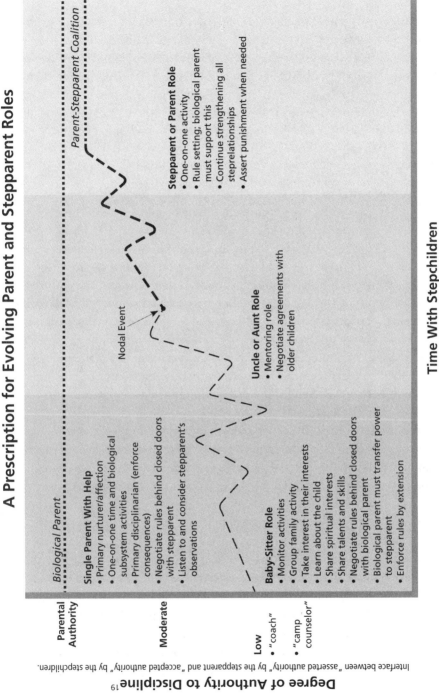

*Biological Parent*

**Single Parent With Help**
- Primary nurturer/affection
- One-on-one time and biological subsystem activities
- Primary disciplinarian (enforce consequences)
- Negotiate rules behind closed doors with stepparent
- Listen to and consider stepparent's observations

**Baby-Sitter Role**
- Monitor activities
- Group family activity
- Take interest in their interests
- Learn about the child
- Share spiritual interests
- Share talents and skills
- Negotiate rules behind closed doors with biological parent
- Biological parent must transfer power to stepparent
- Enforce rules by extension

Nodal Event

**Uncle or Aunt Role**
- Mentoring role
- Negotiate agreements with older children

*Parent-Stepparent Coalition*

**Stepparent or Parent Role**
- One-on-one activity
- Rule setting; biological parent must support this
- Continue strengthening all steprelationships
- Assert punishment when needed

**Parental Authority**

**Moderate**

**Low**
- "coach"
- "camp counselor"

## Degree of Authority to Discipline[19]

Interface between "asserted authority" by the stepparent and "accepted authority" by the stepchildren.

## Time With Stepchildren

Length of time required to increase parental authority will vary according to age of child, previous family experiences, relationship with noncustodial parents, child's temperament/personality, parenting style variations, and child's overall stepfamily satisfaction level.

let go. Indeed, some parents block the stepparents' increasing authority, even after they've pushed for it. Giving up control is difficult.

Some parents decide not to make room for the stepparent, while some stepparents, frankly, don't desire to have a close relationship with their stepchildren. Don't assume you as a couple have the same expectation for the stepparent's level of closeness with the children. Talk about your relational preferences and periodically evaluate your changing goals.

### Time With Stepchildren

The horizontal axis of the chart focuses on the amount of time step-parents have had with their stepchildren. Many people wonder if this begins with dating or the actual remarriage. Dating is important, but true step-family relationships start with the wedding. During courtship children can be tolerant, even encouraging, of their parent's new romance because "she's happier while with him." While the couple dates, however, the children are usually out of the picture, spending time at Dad's house. The dating partner stays friendly with the children, and everything seems to go along fine. But after the marriage, when everyone is thrown into the same pot, roles change. The intensity of relationships increases dramatically, and nearly everyone experiences unexpected anxious emotions.

A number of variables influence how long it takes for stepparents to move from one role to another.[20]

**Age of Child.** As previously stated, younger children accept stepparents more quickly than older children. Children five and under may need just a year or two before viewing stepparents as "parents." It's not uncommon to find children who call their noncustodial parent "Dad" and their step-parent "Daddy." Adolescent children, on the other hand, may require a number of years before ascribing full parental status to their stepparent. Others never get that far.

A child's openness to a stepparent, of course, has a major influence on the success of the marriage. In fact, it seems that "the best time to remarry is before a child's tenth birthday and after his or her sixteenth; couples who marry in between often find themselves on a collision course with the teen's developmental agenda."[21] A small window of attachment and feeling their close parent-child bond threatened (especially preadolescent girls and their mothers) just doesn't make for quick acceptance of the stepparent.

In the end, remember that no one can predict how long it will take to build a working relationship with your stepchildren. Accept what you have and make the best of it.

**Previous Family Experiences.** The family you grew up in (called "family of origin") has had dramatic effects on you, your choice of mate, and your marital behaviors—whether you know it or not. Similarly, previous family experiences impact children and their willingness to trust, honor, or open themselves to new relationships. Spend some time reflecting on what your children and stepchildren have experienced, and talk with your spouse about how it has impacted the children. Learn to be sensitive to their wounds and needs.

**Relationship With Noncustodial Parents.** Loyalty issues come into play here. If stepchildren have a poor relationship with a noncustodial biological parent, they may find it awkward and guilt-producing to enjoy a stepparent. If stepchildren have a positive relationship with the other parent, that too can generate resistance to the stepparent. Ultimately, it is ideal for the other parent to give the child permission to bond with the stepparent. This helps children make space in their hearts for stepparents. But for many noncustodial parents, giving permission is difficult.

One of the most common reasons noncustodial parents criticize and coach their children away from a relationship with a stepparent is fear. Noncustodial parents have lost contact with their kids and may resent a stepparent for having more time with the children than they have. Loss creates the fear of more loss. If stepparents will articulate a supportive message to noncustodial parents and then live up to it, fears can be diminished and criticism may decline as well.

For example, call or email the noncustodial parent and communicate the No-Threat message: "Bob, I want you to know that you don't have to worry about my getting between you and your kids. I respect you as their father, and I will never intentionally do anything to keep you from them. I will expect them to speak respectfully about you when in our home and will do my part to make sure the visitation schedule stays on track. If I inadvertently cause a problem, please let me know, and I'll rectify the situation. You are important to your kids." This informal non-aggression pact helps the noncustodial parent know what to expect from you. If negative comments about you continue from the noncustodial parent, stay in control of yourself and take the high road of righteousness. "Pile up burning coals" of kindness on their heads, even in the face of their critical words, until your good cannot be ignored (see Romans 12:20).

**Child's Temperament and Personality.** Some children are outgoing, some more reserved. Variations in personality between siblings can play a significant role in their willingness to open themselves to new relationships with a stepparent and/or stepsiblings. In addition, a child's interests in sports, music, art, computers, etc., may create an immediate connection with a stepparent that can help bring them together in a non-threatening way.

**Parenting Style Variations.** Stepparents who have more structured rules and are more demanding than either of a child's parents make bonding difficult. Julie's stepchildren complained that since moving into "her house," she always made them take off their shoes. They never had to do that before their father married Julie. "Yeah," said the youngest, "and she won't let me drink my milk in the living room."

This is not to say that stepparents cannot assert their preferences for household rules. Not drinking milk in the living room is a reasonable rule, and children can adjust to the change. Stepparents should simply understand that pulling the rein a little tighter slows the bonding process; choose your battles carefully and make sure your spouse, the biological parent, is also on board for the change in rules.

**Child's Overall Stepfamily Satisfaction Level.** How much transition and loss has the new stepfamily brought to children? What is the level of conflict within the home and between homes? How well are stepsiblings getting along? How well are personalities within the stepfamily mixing—do people have a lot in common or are they strangers under one roof? Are noncustodial parents involved and secure with the amount of contact with their children? If most of stepfamily life is positive for stepchildren, the likelihood of accepting a stepparent increases. If most of stepfamily life is tense and stress-producing, stepparent acceptance decreases.

### Orchestrating Nodal Events

The evolving roles chart indicates that there can be nodal events that catapult the stepparent-stepchild relationship to new levels.[22] Nodal events are extraordinary occasions or circumstances that, for whatever reason, transform bonding or trust. A death or tragic situation in a family, for example, can force family members toward one another in a way never before achieved. Likewise, a positive experience, for example the birth of a mutual child, can do the same. The question is, can parents and step-parents orchestrate nodal events that potentially accelerate the stepparent-stepchild bond?

To answer that question, let me tell you a story. After losing our son, Connor, Nan and I found ourselves, by God's grace I believe, working with rescued slave children in Ghana, Africa. The work is very rewarding; it also brings some semblance of beauty from our ashes.

Some time ago, I returned from a two-week trip to Ghana, where my wife and I, in conjunction with other nonprofits, including Touch A Life Foundation, Go Team Ghana, and Art Feeds, built an art center for rescued trafficked children. The Connor Creative Art Center is a place of healing, restoration, and creative learning for children living in the care facility. (By the way, the art center is shaped like giant Lego-like building blocks; it's so cool!) The designers for this project included five former designers from ABC's *Extreme Makeover Home Edition* TV program and two professional carpenters. Before the trip I had never met any of them face-to-face. For two weeks we worked side by side completing the interior of the art center. We worked fifteen hours a day, slept little, drank water out of bags, and lost weight in the hot African sun. And we forged relationships that bonded us for life. I barely knew those people, but today I would do anything I could for them. We entered the trenches of hard, eternally focused work as strangers, but we came out family.

**Radical Road Trip.** Sometimes stepfamily relationships need a kick in the pants to move them beyond the status quo. But in order for the experience to be powerful enough, it must be out of the ordinary. It must be what I like to call a radical road trip. A day trip to feed the ducks or a day spent water-skiing on the lake probably won't cut it. An extreme experience is needed, something radical to break through the barriers.

A mission trip that takes you to a remote part of the world or a work-camp experience in an unsafe part of an unfamiliar city just might be what is needed. The benefits, of course, are many. First, an extreme mission trip teaches a multitude of spiritual lessons that cannot be learned in church. Serving those less fortunate and seeing how another part of the world

**Dating/Engaged Couples**

Can you plan a radical road trip before marriage? Absolutely. Doing so can propel relationships forward, but then again, it may not. Don't feel defeated if it doesn't; for some children, it just isn't real enough until after your wedding.

lives has its own wisdom, brings us closer to the heart of God, and teaches gratitude, thoughtfulness, and respect for others. Second, the intensity of the journey—we hope—will push through any prickly barriers that exist between stepfamily members and move them to a place of trust, cooperation, and mutual respect. Nothing pushes people together like facing an extraordinary challenge together. Go create your own self-serving "crisis" and serve the Lord at the same time.[23]

## Summary of Points to Remember

- This model of parent-stepparent roles seems to work for most stepfamilies. There is no universal way to work out your parent-stepparent roles. Be sure you are unified in evaluating your approach and step carefully together.

- Early on, biological parents need to remain primary caregivers and disciplinarians. Handing off the children to the new stepparent often sabotages his or her ability to build a relationship.

- Early on, parents should empower stepparents by communicating to the children their expectation of obedience. Later, even if you disagree with what the stepparent has done in your absence, support their position with the children. Then take your disagreement behind closed doors and work out a unified plan and consequences for the next offense.

- Stepparents need to grow into their relationship with stepchildren. Be friendly and support the house rules. Seek to be adaptable to your stepchildren and enjoy the relationship you have.

- Encourage and insist that children maintain regular, consistent contact with the parent living in the other home. Do your best to have a functional co-parent relationship.

- Let children set the pace for their relationship with the stepparent. Consider each child individually. Give and expect affection, nurturance, and emotional sharing only to the degree children appear open to it.

192

- Parents should consider stepparents' input into child rearing. It is easy for parents who are used to having complete control over their children to discount the stepparents' perspective. Keep in mind that, as outsiders, stepparents can see things your blind spots prevent you from seeing. Listen and consider their input.

- Stepparents need to learn to be a nonjudgmental sounding board for parents. When parents get frustrated with their own children, they may confide in the stepparent. However, stepparents who begin to agree and add their own frustration may find their spouse reversing position to defend the child. The parent-child bond is indeed a protective one. Stepparents would do well to listen and affirm without criticizing the child. "I can see you are angry at Jane for lying to us. What do you suggest we do?"

- Finally, but most important, effective parent-stepparent teams begin with healthy marriages. Take time to nurture your relationship, date on a regular basis, learn to communicate and resolve conflict, and enjoy a healthy sexual relationship. Make your marriage a priority!

## "But We're Already Stuck. What Do We Do Now?"

You've done all you could, proceeded with what you thought best, but have now discovered you've made a number of mistakes. Perhaps you are facing some resistance or open defiance from an angry child. So what do you do now?

### First Step: Evaluate Yourselves As a Parenting Team

Together with your spouse, examine the interaction between you as a parenting team.

- Are you cooperating poorly?
- Do you frequently disagree about rules and consequences?
- Does one of you feel sabotaged by the other?
- Does the biological parent frequently feel caught between his or her children and the stepparent?
- Do the same conflicts repeat because they aren't getting resolved?

If you answered *yes* to two or more of the above, the root of the problem likely is not the children (but certainly may be complicated by the emotional condition and behavior of the children). You have a weak parental alliance, and you must work out a mutual plan to act as a team.

Failure to function as a team is the key cause of child behavioral problems in nuclear families and in stepfamilies. Plan a time together or with your support group and decide what aspects of your parenting need to change. You may also decide to seek outside help as you work through some difficult circumstances. Remember that there are lots of ways to parent kids well. The critical element is your ability to do it together.

### Second Step: What If the Stepparent Has Overstepped His or Her Bounds?

If this chapter has helped you to see that you as a stepparent moved into punishment too quickly, and it has hampered your relationship with your stepchildren, consider these points of action:

- Pull back from punishment and your high expectations. Let the biological parent take over being the heavy while you refocus on relationship healing and development.

- Ask your stepchildren for forgiveness and admit your misguided attempt to join the family. Seeking forgiveness displays character and models commitment to your family. A stepdad may say something like, "Hey kids. I want you to know I'm learning how to be a better stepparent. In fact, I've learned that I've been making some mistakes, like not letting you talk to your dad each night before bedtime and being a little too bossy. Can you forgive me? I really want to do better. Here's what you can expect at this point. . . ."

- Biological parents may also need to seek forgiveness for being underinvolved and abdicating their primary role to the stepparent. Together you can tell the kids how each of your roles is going to change and what they can expect.

- Implement the changes slowly. Stepparents must realize that forgiveness may be slow in coming, and even then, children may have hard feelings from the past. Don't drop your boundaries to win them back. Continue to seek relationship and model respect. Remain flexible with your new plan, as you may need to make adjustments along the way.

- If necessary, consult a Christian family therapist who is knowledgeable in stepfamily therapy. (It is important to ask any therapist what specific training they have had regarding stepfamilies. Many therapists have no specialized training and utilize a first-family model of treatment. That will only make matters worse. An article that addresses this matter is available at my website: www.SmartStepfamilies.com/view/findtherapist.)

I often tell parents that raising children is a work in progress. No one ever has all the right answers, and all parents and stepparents yell, scream, plead, and lose their cool at some point. None of us is perfect. That's why we must rely on a perfect God for wisdom and guidance. I cannot emphasize enough the necessity for parents to study the Scriptures on a daily basis. The more we are transformed into the likeness of Christ, the greater chance we will become who our children and stepchildren need us to be. We must be filled with the Holy Spirit and guided by God's nature. Only then will we be able to set an example for our children that leads them to the Father. Press on with your work in progress.

### Questions for Discussion

■ FOR PARENT-CHILD DISCUSSION (Discretion based on the age of the child and the quality of adult-child relationships is advised.)

1. For older children: On a scale of 1–10, how much do you think I trust your stepparent? Give me an example of what makes you think that.

2. Knowing I'll be okay with any answer you provide, how much do you trust your stepparent on a scale of 1–10?

3. What rules have changed for you since becoming a stepfamily? Which ones have been the most difficult to adjust to? What is still confusing for you?

4. What aspects of your stepparent's role have been the most difficult for you to accept?

5. If you were to pick, which of the following terms best describes the role you think your stepparent *should* have? (1) Baby-sitter (2) Uncle/Aunt (3) Parent.

6. Currently, what role are they trying to play? What role do you think I want them to play?

7. How are different children (e.g., "mine," "theirs," or a mutual child) parented differently in our home?

### ■ For All Couples

1. Stepparents, what are your most common frustrations? Now share the rewards you've experienced so far.

2. Review the Parental Unity Rules. Which ones are you managing well right now and which could use improvement? Brainstorm ways you can improve.

3. Biological parents: In what circumstances have you become paralyzed as a parent in the past?

4. Review the four keys to Champion the Stepparent's Role. Which are you managing well?

5. Review the descriptions of unwise vs. wise stepparents. Rate yourself using the following scales and discuss what you'll be doing differently when you improve in each area.

| | | |
|---|---|---|
| *Becoming an insider is my goal.* | 1———7 | *I enjoy the relationship I have now.* |
| *Expect too much of myself.* | 1———7 | *Have realistic expectations for myself.* |
| *Rush into parenting.* | 1———7 | *Growing into my role.* |
| *Attempt to punish before I have relationship.* | 1———7 | *Moving gradually into discipline.* |
| *Trying to replace the non-custodial parent.* | 1———7 | *Encouraging noncustodial parental contact.* |
| *Taking on the peacemaker role.* | 1———7 | *Accepting difficulties and facing them.* |

6. Look again at the chart A Prescription for Evolving Parent and Stepparent Roles. How well are you working together as a couple? What role is most suitable for the stepparent at this point in your integration?

7. What is the stepparent currently doing to build a relationship with each child?

8. In what way does the biological parent need to be more supportive of the stepparent or more involved with the children?

9. Review the Summary of Points to Remember toward the end of the chapter. Commend yourself for what you are currently doing well and challenge yourself with areas that need improvement.

### ■ FOR PRE-STEPFAMILY COUPLES

1. In what way have you been assuming the children will be the same (or better) with the stepparent after the wedding?

2. How does it frighten you to read that emotional shifts after the wedding can complicate the stepparent-stepchildren relationship?

3. How can you protect yourself from getting drawn into the unwise stepparent's ineffective behaviors?

4. Look again at the chart A Prescription for Evolving Parent and Stepparent Roles. What principles do you agree or disagree with? Discuss how you might implement the baby-sitter role even now.

5. Share your expectations for your role as parent/stepparent and the other's role. Begin developing a plan for what role each of you will play with each child. Be aware that you will likely need to adjust your plan after marriage.

6. Discuss what a radical road trip would look like before you marry. Is that possible?

7. What should you do if you are off track already with the dating partner/future stepparent's role? See the section "But We're Already Stuck" and discuss how it pertains to you.

# Smart Step Four: STEP in Line (Part 3)

*Unique Parenting Roles and Issues*

My son, hold on to good sense and the understanding of what is right. Don't let them out of your sight. They will be life for you. They will be like a gracious necklace around your neck. Then you will go on your way in safety. You will not trip and fall.

Proverbs 3:21–23 NIRV

According to Wikipedia, Heinz 57 is a shortened form of a historical advertising slogan "57 Varieties" by the H. J. Heinz Company. It was developed from a marketing campaign that told consumers about the numerous products available from the Heinz company.[1]

Stepfamilies have a lot of varieties as well. When the various parts or origins of adults and children, including previous marriage or singleness, divorce or death, children, no children, and/or "ours" children are thrown into the same Crockpot and mixed together, we discover not 57, but 67 possible stepfamily configurations. (This helps to explain why not everything in this book pertains to you and your family.)

These "67 Varieties" obviously result in many unique parenting dynamics, issues, and roles that don't fit into the more general parenting and stepparenting dynamics I have discussed so far. Much wisdom is needed to know how to maneuver through and around them. This chapter will address some of the key unique parenting matters not discussed in previous chapters, including:

- Adult stepchildren
- Part-time parenting and stepparenting
- Birth order changes and children
- Stepparenting adolescents
- Parenting the mutual child
- Sibling relationships
- Adopting stepchildren
- Legal matters in stepparenting

> **Military Stepfamilies**
>
> For more on this family situation see the Smart Questions, Smart Answers bonus material available at SmartStepfamilies.com /view/learn.

## Adult Stepchildren

Through the years I have posted articles on SmartStepfamilies.com that address what is commonly referred to as later-life or adult stepfamilies (stepfamilies where the children were already adults when their parent married). Some of the most passionate comments we receive about any topic are made in response to these articles. Adult children who feel they are being slighted and forgotten, and stepparents who can't understand why their adult stepchildren are acting like immature children, pour out their frustrations. If you have adult children, you may be disappointed that they're not as enthusiastic about your new love as you are. But you also need to hear from the other side—the adult child—if nothing else, to understand their perspective. Most of what you've read so far in this book about the emotional reactions of children applies on some level to adult stepchildren as well. But let's dive a little deeper into what adult children are experiencing. I'll let them speak for themselves.

One woman who anonymously called herself "step-daughter-in-law" posted:

My father-in-law began dating a few months after his wife died and didn't tell my husband; he then forced an introduction to a woman he would later marry. This woman and my husband got off to a bad start. She then expected "insta-family" and demanded respect and the title of grandparent, all the while slamming the door in my husband's face (literally), informing us (through my father-in-law) that we are not welcome to go to their house, and refusing any invitation to our house. She also didn't allow my father-in-law to come to our home or to activities involving our children.

If a foreign country kidnapped a family member and controlled every interaction while holding them hostage, we'd call them a terrorist. That's what the new spouse was doing—but what's worse, the passivity of her husband gave her permission to do so. No wonder this adult daughter-in-law, and no doubt her husband, was hurt and threatened by the marriage.

And then there was this post from Amanda, who was wrestling with her feelings. On the one hand she wants good things for her mom, but it is coming at such great cost to her, her brothers, and the grandchildren.

Hello Ron, I have always enjoyed reading your articles and now I am entering into a stepfamily situation! My dad passed away in April 2003. Diagnosed with stage-four terminal cancer in January, he died just eight weeks later. I was pregnant with our second child, and Dad passed away only thirteen days before she was born. Mom has been my rock. We have always had a close bond, and that bond became even closer after the loss of Daddy. She has not dated or seemed interested in dating in eight years. But last December she introduced her "friend" to me, and it was very noticeable to all that he was more than a friend. It was extremely hard seeing her with someone. He is a great man and seems to care a lot about her. He lost his wife suddenly in July of 2010. Mom met him through her sister who lives in West Virginia.

They dated throughout this past year and a ring was given in June. Mom has decided to move back to West Virginia and marry him. My two brothers currently live within fifteen miles of Mom and we live just a couple hours away. My older brother has four children who adore Mom and we have two girls who are extremely close to her; they are having a difficult time with her moving fourteen hours away. I need advice. I hate to see Mom move so far away from her three children and six grandkids. She seems so "in love" that I'm not sure she has thought this out. He has two adult children with grandkids and we have yet to meet them. How awkward will that be? Meeting them for the first time at our parents' wedding! I need advice on this!

Are my feelings selfish or are they legit? Never in a million years did I think I would have a stepfamily. Thanks in advance, Amanda.

Amanda's feelings *are* legitimate—and what is she feeling? Loss, loss, loss.

- Her mother, who has been her "rock," is rapidly disappearing.
- Her extended family (brothers, nieces, and children) is upset, anxious, and shaken by all that is changing—and likely by what it means that their mother can just walk away like this.
- She is concerned for her mother, unsure if this marriage is a wise decision.
- She is anticipating new family members whom she has never met and may not like, and wondering how this stepfamily situation will impact her family.
- Her mom's decisions undoubtedly resurrect pain over losing her father—and now she fears that she is losing her mom to another man, another state, another family.

What results from these feelings is an emotional gap between the parent and children; the parent is excited about the new marriage while the adult children are not. Never mind that they are adults, this is a hard transition for them because it comes at a great cost.

- The family identity is being shaken . . . again.
- Every change means more loss.
- Your shift in priority leaves them and grandchildren feeling neglected, perhaps abandoned, and pushed out of the center of your life. New emotional attachments compete with old ones.
- Sometimes this gap is transferred to siblings who disagree about a parent's marriage. One welcomes the marriage and one rejects it. This happened to a friend of mine who at the age of forty-eight became a stepson. He was glad his mom remarried a few years after his father died. "I like the guy," he said. "He takes care of my mom. We play golf together." His sister, however, was upset and jealous from day one about the relationship. She had a close relationship with her

mother and felt tremendous loss when she threw herself at Harry. This difference in perspective made holidays and special family days very tense for my friend, his sister, and the extended family.

And then there are all the idiosyncratic feelings associated with the death or divorce that preceded this union. If the marriage followed the death of a parent, like Amanda they may feel a resurgence of loss for the parent who has died. In addition, after the death they may have taken emotional or financial responsibility for the widowed parent only to be losing that role now that a stepparent has entered the picture.

If divorce paved the way for this marriage, their parent's choice to love another may awaken old wounds and wishes. "You left Mom, and now you want me to be happy with your loving another woman." If the parent who is remarrying abandoned the marriage, this new marriage may feel like another abandonment. This anger can be especially intense if the other parent has been debilitated by the divorce. Being happy for one parent is a loyalty conflict that feels like throwing bitter salt in the debilitated parent's wounds. All of this means the child becomes more opposed to the marriage.

> **About Finances**
>
> Both parents and adult children should be concerned about estate planning and inheritance matters when a parent marries again, but talking about money matters can be awkward. Don't avoid the subject. Engage the conversation sooner rather than later. See chapter 10 for guidance.

I can hear the protests from later-life couples now: *But why can't my kids, who are grown adults, be more mature than this?* I'm not excusing immature behavior, but adjusting to a parent's later-life marriage is not as easy as it sounds. When there is a heavy burden from the past on a child's heart or loyalty issues at play, they tend to revert to more of a childlike posture when dealing with their parent anyway. And in the best of circumstances, when like Amanda they have had a good relationship with their parent, when trying to find their fit in a parent's new marriage, the adult child thinks of themselves more as a child.

What then is the implication of all this? First, don't be surprised by strong reactions by adult children. You may feel that they are raining on your parade, but many of their feelings are legitimate and need to be ac- knowledged. Second, you should see this as an opportunity for healing. A strong reaction is telling you something. Resurrected pain from the past needs to be dealt with; healing needs to occur between the biological parent and child; forgiveness needs to be granted or sought. In all things be filled with compassion and understanding. Express your awareness to the child for how hard this must be and listen to them. Then, apply Crockpot patience and strategies as you slowly begin working toward a developing family identity. Third, make decisions that lower the price tag of acceptance for the kids. For example, a quick dating experience and a fast engagement raise the price. As I've said throughout this book, many parents with younger children do this, but I find that later-life couples with adult children feel greater permission to do this because they assume their children will not be significantly disrupted by the union. Rather, slow down and respect them with the pace of your dating and the timing of major decisions.

## Bonding With Adult Stepchildren

For more on developing a relationship with adult stepchildren, see Susan Gamache's Smart Question, Smart Answer in the bonus material, available at SmartStep families.com/view/learn.

Fourth, the new stepparent should extend the hand of friendship to them. Not forcing themselves on the adult children, but pursuing connection. Assuming they are open to it, the stepparent can take them to lunch, share in their interests, share photos, videos, and family stories with them. Get to know their kids and take an interest in their activities. And, as I've said in previous chapters, it's best to let the adult child set the pace for how much time the stepparent spends with them or their children and how much affection is shown. Stepparents should meet them where they are.[2]

In addition, before and after the wedding, stepparents should give the biological parent time with their children—alone. This compartmentalization of relationships helps adult children (and grandchildren) to maintain their bonds without the constant sacrifice of having to share them with the stepparent. More often than not a stepparent will join in family gatherings. But an occasional break is helpful, especially in the early years of the marriage.

Finally, be proactive to discuss the terms or names you will use to refer to one another. Adult children need to feel their territory respected in this just as younger children do. Find something mutually agreeable and comfortable. Share how you would like the other to introduce you to others.

Also, decide what names you will encourage the grandchildren to use or follow their lead. Young grandchildren may use uncomplicated terms of endearment (e.g., "Grandpa"), or you may find a variation on a family term that suits everyone (e.g., "Papa Joe"). Once you have agreed to a term, recognize that it represents their current level of openness to you and the marriage. Respect those limits and trust the Crockpot to open their hearts further as time passes. Find more on appropriate terms for stepparents in the Smart Questions, Smart Answers bonus material available at Smart Stepfamilies.com/view/learn.

## Part-Time Parenting and Stepparenting

Part-time parenting and stepparenting is difficult, sometimes extremely difficult. Nonresidential parents and stepparents alike find remaining connected to kids and keeping influence with children a challenge. For example, when a stepchild's visitation schedule brings them into the stepparent's home only a few nights each month, the stepparent can continuously feel like an outsider. "I feel whatever relational gains I make during the weekend are easily lost when she goes back to her mother's house," said one stepmom. "It's two steps forward and one step back all the time." That feeling is quite understandable given the tentative nature of the stepparent-stepchild relationship. But sometimes the circumstances surrounding visitation make biological parents anxious too.

Jackson, a father of two adolescent sons, found himself paralyzed by his part-time schedule. After Jackson and his first wife divorced, she and their boys moved over 1,200 miles away. Through the years, Jackson felt his relationship with his sons slipping; they weren't able to talk much on the phone and when they did talk, their mother made her physical presence—and the expectation that they not talk very long—very evident. Plus, the visitation schedule only allowed Jackson six weeks in the summer with his kids, one week during Christmas break, and one week during spring break. The lack of time made Jackson discouraged; parenting them with confidence when

> **Nonresidential Stepchildren**
>
> Learn more about parenting nonresidential children in the Smart Questions, Smart Answers bonus material available at SmartStep families.com/view/learn.

they came to his house was very difficult. Jackson's wife, Cathy, was the first to notice . . . and complain.

"Why don't you discipline your children the way you discipline mine?" she demanded of him. "It's not fair that you let them get away with things you won't let my daughter do. And she's noticing it—and asking why. What do I tell her?"

Jackson tried to explain his position. "You don't understand. It's not fair to expect me to parent my kids the way I parent yours. Your daughter is with us all the time and I can follow through with her. My kids are here for one week; that's all I get with them, and I don't want it to be filled with conflict or expectations. My kids don't call me much as it is; I can't afford to lose the time I have."

Upon further reflection, Jackson realized that he had a great many fears about losing contact with his sons. He viewed their relationship as fragile and not able to bear much distress. He knew his ex-wife tried to hoard the children as much as she could and that she told them untrue things about his life, trying to alienate them further. Plus, he wanted them to leave his home with positive feelings toward him and his wife, not negative ones. While all of these feelings were understandable, unfortunately they resulted in boundary-less parenting on his part, a sense of unfairness in the home, resentment from his wife, and feelings of dread within everyone before each visit.

Whether you are a part-time stepparent or biological parent, here are a few suggestions to help you navigate part-time parenting.

### It Is Critical That You Hear Each Other

Parents and stepparents alike need to listen to and be heard by their partner. It is common for partners to have very different perspectives and feelings about the part-time schedule. A biological parent may look forward to the weekend or six-week summer schedule, while the stepparent lives in fear of the tension it brings to the home. Both perspectives are legitimate and understandable and need to be heard, but fear sometimes prevents couples from sharing. A biological parent might, for example, misjudge their spouse who is sharing their anxiety over the next visit as saying they don't like being with the kids. Fearing that the children will then feel rejection, the biological parent might become critical of the stepparent. This only adds to the anxiety in the home and pushes the couple apart.

Instead, both parent and stepparent should strive for objectivity and empathy toward their spouse, remembering that different perspectives about the situation are common. "I can hear how anxious you are about my kids coming this weekend; what can we do to make things go a little more smoothly for you?"

### Paralyzed Part-Time Parents Should Strive for Balance

If you, like Jackson, find yourself afraid to discipline your children due to the fear

> **Knowing Yourself**
>
> Be aware of your fears as they relate to children and your marriage. Are you concerned that the kids will feel unwanted? Do you fear being left behind when the children come for the weekend? These emotions can block your compassion and optimism; be aware of them and ask the Lord to give you strength to overcome them.

that doing so will alienate them further, explore with your spouse what a balanced response might look like. Find a balance between following through on important values and expectations and letting go of more peripheral ones. Finding this balance can only be achieved through careful and intentional conversation with the stepparent. Follow-through is vital if you are going to maintain your influence as a parent. Take the risk of acting like a parent so your children will respect you as one.[3]

## Birth Order Changes

From a developmental standpoint, shifts in birth order can be problematic for children.[4] This common shift in role and position for children is often unrecognized by adults, but it has a potent impact on children. Nine-year-old Tara was the oldest in her family until her mom remarried a man with a thirteen-year-old son, Josh. During the single-parent years, Tara gained special status with her mother by learning to set the dinner table and changing her younger brother's diaper. She became Mom's helper in many ways, and her efforts were rewarded with a special mother-daughter bond. Once Josh entered the family, Tara's mom thought having him help her in the kitchen would give them a chance to bond. Without realizing it, Tara soon became overlooked and lost a significant role in the family.

Have you ever been displaced at work? Perhaps a new employee has stepped in and captured the boss's attention. Or a competing salesperson has subtly pushed you out and taken your place. How would you feel if your boss decided to move someone alongside him who, despite your laying the groundwork for a project, got to reap the rewards? Or perhaps you've been in a work situation where the new employee didn't pull her weight and the burden of training her or cleaning up after her mistakes fell on you. Can you feel your stomach tightening?

Not all shifts in birth order are this extreme, but they all represent change. Let me remind you that change brings more loss, and loss added to substantial previous losses generates weariness and insecurity. It is the continual process of change that disheartens children, and that is what parents need to be sensitive to.

In order to consider how shifts in birth order have impacted your children, try one of the following ideas:

- If your children are old enough to articulate their feelings (and you are courageous enough), sit down with them and ask how their role in the family has changed since adding stepsiblings. Discuss with them how you treat them differently now and what responsibilities they have lost or gained in the new family. Give them permission to be sad or angry over what has changed, but don't promise to restore the past (having a new family requires change from everyone). Empathize and feel sorry for their losses, but support them with a vote of confidence that they can manage the change in role or position.

- Whether you can speak with your children or not, make a list of each child's roles before and after the changes occurred. Strive to be sensitive to old roles and restore jobs or tasks when possible or replace them with new jobs. This builds a sense of importance as the child contributes to the home and receives your approval for doing so.

- During the early years, spend time every week with each child away from stepsiblings so as to affirm their uniqueness.

## Stepparenting Adolescents

Parenting teenagers is always a challenge, even in biological families. Stepparenting adolescents is even more fun (um, maybe that's not the best word for it). But it might not be as bad as it seems. I'll explain what I mean by that, but first let me remind you of a few things I've already discussed throughout the book that very much apply to stepparenting teens.

In chapter 6 I mentioned that the normal developmental function of adolescence is to prepare kids for leaving home. Developing autonomous thinking, an independent identity from their parent, and the ability to make decisions on their own are important processes to prepare them for life away from their parents. This natural movement away from the family can make bonding difficult; forming a stepfamily identity necessitates moving closer together, while adolescence is pushing people apart. The implications for stepparents are many. Let me briefly remind you of a few of the principles discussed in chapter 7 that are relevant here.

- Early on, even before marriage, be intentional about befriending teens and young adults. Fostering shared interests and topics you can discuss together is critical to finding acceptance and openness from the adolescent. Engage them in activities they enjoy, and spend one-on-one time with them just as soon as they are open to it.

- Regarding areas of their life in which they are inclined not to let you in, stand "just outside the circle." Don't try to push your way in or they will lock you out. Instead, be around the activity or area so you are aware of what's going on.

- Regarding discipline, it is critical early on that you respect the limits of your role and practice "baby-sitting" when it comes to punishment (see chapter 7). Let the biological parent be the heavy and live on borrowed power until you have your own. While smiling say, "Your dad wants your chores done before he gets home, and I'm here to make sure that happens."[5]

- You must work on strengthening your marriage (see chapter 5). If your relationship is not prepared to handle the stress of parenting, ultimately your marriage will fracture and your ability to parent with it.

### Tastes Like Butter, But It's Not

In the mid-1970s Chiffon margarine had an advertising slogan that claimed their product "tastes like butter, but it's not." The message: Based on taste alone it's hard to tell Chiffon margarine and butter apart. The difficulty in stepparenting adolescents is that some of what you experience, like stepparent rejection or defiance, tastes bitter, but it's not. Let me explain.

"What happened to my baby?" Susan asked me. "Josh used to worship the ground I walked on, and then one day he changed into this sarcastic, prickly kid I didn't like." That's when her husband, Josh's stepfather, chimed in. "Josh and I used to get along pretty well, but now all I get is attitude." So, what do you think? Is it margarine or butter?

Given the ambiguous nature of the stepparent role, normal thorny adolescent behavior can immediately be diagnosed by adults as stepparent rejection. It could be, but sometimes it's just the tumultuous nature of adolescence shining through (oh joy). I love the title of a book my friends David and Claudia Arp have written for parents about the challenges of parenting teens: *Suddenly They're 13: Or the Art of Hugging a Cactus.* That title says it all. Prickly attitudes and behavior from adolescents are normal; don't be too quick to judge it as being a stepfamily issue. So, how do you know the difference? One way is to notice how pervasive the attitude is.

"I wish my husband wouldn't take Josh's petulance so personally," Susan continued. "Josh is just as much a pain to me as he is to Jeff." While it's true that some teens can target negativity toward the stepparent with more intensity, Susan's perspective is right on. If the teen is treating their parent and stepparent equally bad (again, oh joy) it's probably not stepfamily related. Jeff would do well not to take things personally so he doesn't overreact and inadvertently make things worse.

As a matter of fact, I think that's a powerful posture even if the surge in attitude is stepfamily related. Assume the best and respond to the child as if this is just normal prickly teenage behavior. Don't get me wrong, it's still a pain! But this posture of confidence empowers you as a parenting team to respond objectively and decisively instead of being pushed back on your heels. "You may not talk to us that way. Hand me your iPod." "You can argue with me all you want, but you're still not going. Keep arguing and you'll also not attend (fill in the blank). It's your call." (Then turn and walk away.) These are the wonderful words all of us parents of adolescents must use and stand behind.

There are other complications of parenting adolescents, as well.

### Teen Depression, Sadness, and/or Anger

The multiple losses children in stepfamilies have experienced can take on a dark side when coupled with hormonal changes and the social insecurities of adolescence. Ryan talked about feeling depressed: "I have no friends. My mom and dad still fight all the time, and my stepmom treats me like I'm second class compared to her kids. Life sucks." The ongoing parental and family conflicts surrounding Ryan brought about a depression that sometimes expressed itself in withdrawn behavior and sometimes irritability and anger. All very understandable, I would say. Obviously, there need to be some changes in the family dynamic, and Ryan needs some direct attention regarding his concerns—someone to help him cope with what can't be changed. (A youth pastor or family therapist may be able to help.)

### The Struggle to Let Go

I often remind parents that we are working ourselves out of a job, that is, if we do our parenting job well, our children will launch out of our home into independence. The irony of this for stepparents is that when it comes time to push the bird out of the nest, it can feel like defeat. "I've worked so hard to bond with this kid," a stepmom shared, "it feels weird to let her go." Yes, it can. But let her go, you must.

### Striving for "Mom/Dad" Status

If you have been involved in a stepchild's life for many years, you may inwardly long for the day when they begin to refer to you as Mom or Dad. If that doesn't happen after a number of years, some stepparents are tempted to emotionally withdraw with hurt feelings. If this coincides with adolescence, the child can experience this as rejection by the stepparent. Stepparents need to understand that only a third of stepchildren ever grow into using the Mom or Dad label for their stepparent and that many years together doesn't increase the percentage.[6] The Mom/Dad label is generally reserved by children for their biological parents. Stepparents need to do themselves and teens a favor and let go of this expectation so it doesn't lead to unnecessary hurt feelings.

Finally, in thinking about parenting adolescents, I'm reminded of the words of one of my favorite parent educators, Roger Allen, who once said,

---

### Additional Tips for Surviving the Adolescent Years

1. Biological parents and stepparents should talk frequently during their child's adolescence. Bounce your perspective about the child's behavior off the other to see if there might be another side to consider.
2. Teens need a safe place to process their emotional sadness. Bringing up losses or extended family struggles that have resulted from the death or divorce gives permission for grieving together. This provides a child perspective and support.
3. Stepparents may need to grieve what will never be. A child moving out of the home before you've had sufficient time to bond or not ever hearing "Mom/Dad" are just two examples. Biological parents should not be defensive about their child; rather, listen and grieve with your spouse.
4. Have a family meeting to discuss the changes taking place with your adolescent. Be flexible with boundaries when appropriate to show respect for their increasing independence while also maintaining the expectation that the child show respect to both parent and stepparent. (Learn about family meetings in the bonus material at SmartStepfamilies.com/view/learn.)

---

"I have good news and bad news about the terrible two's. The good news is that it only lasts around 18 months—usually between ages 18 months and 3 years old. The bad news: kids are subject to relapse at any given point in time—usually around age 15."[7] All I can say is, "Amen."

## Parenting the Mutual Child

Have you ever had a couple walk up to you and ask, "Should we have a baby together?" I have. It was odd at first, but then I realized what they were really asking. Couples asking this question are acknowledging the complexity of their family and showing awareness that their home is still in the process of becoming a family, and they want to know if it's wise to have a mutual child (what is sometimes called an "ours" baby). So, is there any validity to that concern?

The results to date of social research on this subject are mixed; there is no clear direction offered from stepfamily studies. But we do have some limited impressions. For example, stepfamilies experience a wide variety of emotional and relational changes after a mutual child is born. When relationships within the home are generally stable and positive before the pregnancy, the mutual child has a greater chance of bringing a positive impact to the home. In fact, half-siblings may consider the mutual child a full sibling, which can bring a great sense of joy to everyone. By contrast, adult or older half-siblings have widely varying relationships with a mutual baby. Some are close and have frequent contact, while others are distant and neutral about the new child. Infrequent contact with the stepfamily, a lack of involvement, and the differences in age-related interests are common reasons for the emotional disconnection between a stepchild and a mutual child.[8]

If the relationships within the stepfamily home are generally divided, a mutual child can bring further division. Children who already feel slighted may feel jealous of the time and attention a new child receives, thereby causing resentment toward a half-sibling. The biblical story of Joseph and his half-brothers illustrates this dynamic. They all shared the same father, Jacob, but ten of Joseph's eleven brothers were born to women Jacob didn't cherish, and they resented the special treatment Joseph received. Division in the family can also increase unexpectedly if a stepparent, who now has their own biological child, finds themselves pulling away from the awkward relationships with their stepchildren and focusing on their biological child. The natural bonding that occurs between parent and child brings to light the tentative and frustrating process of stepparenting. Stepparents would do well to avoid pulling away and continue to invest in stepchildren and their biological child alike.[9]

And what of the mutual child—what unique pressures does he or she experience? Being related to everyone puts the mutual child in the center of the family's experience. This *hub* position cuts both ways. On the one hand, it is a privileged position, and the child gains more attention than the other children (especially part-time children). This affords the child more influence and control in the home. On the other hand, this child may feel a constant pressure to create bonds between family members and ensure that everyone gets along.[10]

Finally, we know that having a baby in a stepfamily—as in all families—provides both a protective function for the marriage while at the same time contributing to lower satisfaction levels. When couples have a child together, it tends to decrease the chance of divorce as couples now share an added reason to remain together. On the other hand, marital satisfaction diminishes somewhat given the increased responsibilities of parenting. (For more on having a mutual child, see *The Smart Stepmom* and *The Smart Stepdad*.)

## Adopting a Mutual Child

While stepfamily dynamics are similar when a couple adopts or births a mutual child, there's always something unique when a child is adopted. Work with your adoption agency to anticipate how adopting might impact both the child and your stepfamily.

As you can see, the addition of a child impacts the family in many ways. At the end of the day, no one can tell you whether you should or should not have a child together. It is a matter of faith. Couples show wisdom when they continue learning about stepfamily life and honestly assess the climate of their home, but the final decision should be one of mutual prayer. Both the decision to have a child and the process of raising it is, in the end, part of our walk with the Lord. Seek his guidance and follow.

### Harmony and Hazards in Parenting the Mutual Child

The birth of a mutual child sometimes sheds light on how hard people have been working as parents. As was mentioned earlier, a stepparent who didn't have children of their own before the marriage often discovers how much easier it is to bond with, feel affection for, and parent a mutual child once one is born into the family. They didn't realize how fragile and self-conscious they were in parenting stepchildren until they have their own.

In a similar way, partners who each brought a child to the marriage and have found it difficult to negotiate their parenting rules and standards around each other's children sometimes discover a harmony in parenting the mutual child. Again, the change in parenting dynamics—mutual attachment to the child, mutual trust of the other's good will toward the child, the lack of loyalty conflicts with biological parents in another home—can make a huge difference.

As you can imagine, these differences facilitate some positive dynamics around parenting, but they do create some hazards as well. Part-time stepchildren may become bitter as they watch their father spend much more

214

time with half-siblings. Of course, limited visitation is to blame for this, but in their minds, they are being slighted or don't matter as much to their father. In response, some children become critical of their dad or their half-sibling, while others withdraw to their mom's house, where they don't have to face the situation. Here's one more example of a parenting hazard: A stepparent who for whatever reason has forgone their parenting preferences (e.g., bedtime, foods served to children, etc.) in the parenting of their stepchildren may feel entitled and empowered to assert those preferences in the parenting of the mutual child. One stepdad (now father) told me, "I couldn't keep my wife's ex from buying his kids an iPhone when they turned thirteen, but I'm sure not going to allow that when my son gets to be that age."

> **How to Deal With a Bully in Your Home**
>
> Find the answer in the Smart Questions, Smart Answers bonus material, available at SmartStepfamilies.com/view/learn.

Having a mutual child creates new parenting challenges. But the prescription for managing these challenges is essentially the same as presented earlier: Parental unity is a must. Negotiate the rules and standards of the home and treat all children equitably to the best of your ability.

## Sibling Relationships and Parenting

In general, think of the sibling relationships in your home as a microcosm of the larger stepfamily. Much of what we know about stepsibling relationships (and it isn't much) parallels the larger dynamics of the developing stepfamily. Let's consider a few examples. First, as we might expect, biological ties between half and full siblings create a stronger bond and loyalty than between stepsiblings. Just as in the larger stepfamily, there is a natural insider/outsider dynamic between those who have some biological connection to each other (half and full siblings) and those who don't (stepsiblings). When taken to the extreme, this can create coalitions of insiders who shun the outsiders, fostering jealousy and hostility. In addition, biological siblings naturally have more frequent interaction within the stepfamily—and even into adulthood—than do half or stepsiblings. Something about sharing a parent (and a mutual residence) cements family members together. Perhaps that's why, should the stepcouple divorce, step-siblings tend to grow distant.[11]

Second, there is a Crockpot at work in the sibling relationships. Young children (under the age of six), who naturally have more time in the Crock-pot with siblings and who enter it at a developmental age in which they are open to new people in their lives, are more likely to develop and maintain closer relationships with stepsiblings over time than children who enter a stepfamily in the elementary or teenage years. In fact, the connection is so strong, it more closely resembles full-sibling relationships.

Third, as I've mentioned numerous times throughout the book, becoming part of a stepfamily represents loss to children; gaining a stepsibling can add to that. Having a stepsibling reduces, for example, an adolescent's sense of belonging in the family. Getting less time with their parent and moving between homes (as opposed to a half or stepsibling that might not move between homes at all) might be contributing factors to this sense of distance to the family. One observable outcome of this lost sense of belonging is the trend for stepfamily adolescents to leave home at a younger age than children from biological families. Now that I've said that, let me balance the discussion. For some children, gaining a stepsibling is cause for celebration. "At last, a little brother!" "Now I have someone to play with." "Finally, the girls outnumber the boys around here." All of these are viewpoints that children may adopt as a result of becoming part of a stepfamily.

### Parenting Stepsiblings

Just as stepsibling relationships parallel the larger stepfamily dynamics, parenting should reflect the larger "low-heat" cooking strategies outlined throughout this book. Essentially, encourage relationship between step-siblings in order to bridge the natural gaps that separate them; this will deepen bonding (make it feel more "real"), encourage loyalty, break up coalitions, and make their ongoing involvement with the family more likely.

Early on foster opportunities for kids to develop common interests (e.g., play dates), take them to one another's sport or musical performances so they can encourage one another, and orchestrate outings for teens, for example, to encourage relationship building. If they take to one another immediately, great. If not, keep bringing them together around activities they enjoy, but just as with stepparenting, don't demand connection or affection for one another; let them figure it out.

Over time your family needs to create new rituals and traditions. Likewise, be intentional to create rituals and traditions between siblings. For example, one stepmom whose stepkids were fragmented by visitation and school schedules during the week took them for ice cream every Friday after school. It gave her some special "let's celebrate making it through the week" time with the kids, but also developed in them an expectation of fun together. This simple ritual became part of the growing sibling identity.

> **How do I parent kids with different personalities?**
>
> Find the answer in the Smart Questions, Smart Answers bonus material, available at SmartStep families.com/view/learn.

Another example is the couple who built up birthdays as a special time to celebrate the person. They engaged the stepsiblings the preceding month around how they could make the child with the birthday feel cherished and appreciated. Everyone participated in planning surprises and buying gifts. Of course, the birthday was special for the child, but more than that, the planning ritual around the birthday fostered warmth in the siblings toward one another.

What about rituals that encourage physical touch or hugs? A number of dynamics intersect when giving or receiving physical touch with stepfamilies, so the overarching principle here is "try it and see." Young children have the least concern over this type of behavior and are the most coachable: "Hug Joey and tell him 'Good night,'" is not difficult to do. Teenagers, however, have an entirely different level of awkwardness about this and need space to figure it out on their own. (The dynamic of stepsibling attraction is also something to be mindful of; I have an entire section on this topic in chapter 11.) So what should you do? Try a number of things and see what sticks. *Try* having siblings hold hands during a prayer, *try* giving good-night hugs, *try* group family hugs, and *try* wrestling on the living room floor. Then let kids figure the rest out on their own.

If you notice a sibling coalition excluding or mistreating another child, actively pursue breaking it apart. Martin had two daughters, ages eight and six, who were the twin queens of the household. The girls didn't much

## Adult Stepsiblings

Adult stepchildren should be allowed to negotiate their own relationship with stepsiblings. It's not uncommon for them to be cordial, but not close, given busy lives, raising their own families, and living in different areas. Family holidays and special occasions may help, but respect their time and interest limitations.

like it when Sonja, their stepsister, was introduced as another queen in the family. The sisters deliberately mistreated Sonja, left her out of play time, and said hurtful things to her. Appropriately, Martin took charge of the situation and made it very clear to his daughters that they were not to treat her this way. He and his wife put consequences into place and followed through to stop the negative behavior, but that didn't do anything to bridge the relationship gap. They couldn't push the girls into liking each other, so they started going on family outings in order to gently engage the girls around fun activities. Having the parents there helped to buffer the awkward stepsister dynamic. After a few months, the girls began to find their own connections.

Finally, be intentional to coach children through their inevitable sibling conflicts. Helping them to manage the conflict teaches problem-solving skills (which they will use the rest of their life), but also helps to bridge the insider/outsider gaps between stepsiblings. There's more about reducing friction in your home in the Smart Questions, Smart Answers bonus material at SmartStepfamilies.com/view/learn.

## Adopting Stepchildren

"Should I adopt my stepdaughter?" Paul asked. "I love this little girl and I want her to know how precious she is to me. I don't ever want her to feel like she doesn't have a father." I really appreciate guys like Paul; he's got a heart as big as Texas and the maturity to go with it. He wants to do the right thing.

In circumstances like this, I wish I had a definitive answer to what Paul should or should not do, but I don't. This is in part because variations between stepfamilies (e.g., their loss journey, composition, age of children, etc.) make a big difference in whether the family is suited for adoption, and partly because there is little research about stepfamily adoption (it's another area of stepfamily life that hasn't been studied very much). We don't even know how common it is for stepparents in the U.S. to adopt stepchildren because the government does not distinguish stepparent adoptions from other "kinship adoptions," for example, when an aunt adopts her nephew.[12] We do know what is generally required for a stepparent adoption to take place. In general, adopting a stepchild requires the consent of both biological parents, unless one parent has not fulfilled their parental responsibilities or is otherwise incapable of consenting to the adoption (e.g., is deceased or mentally incapacitated).

In practical terms, this means that the nonresident biological parent holds the power to stepparent adoption. But that's okay, in a way, because stepparent adoption should never overpower the will of either the nonresident biological parent or the child. Neither do you want grandparents or extended family resenting a change in last name for the child. You never want an ambiguous entrance into adopting a stepchild. What I mean is, if the path is not exceedingly clear, you probably shouldn't walk down the road. In Paul's case, for example, he had a strong desire to bond with his stepdaughter, but the path to adoption wasn't entirely clear.

> **Legal Considerations**
>
> Adoption creates a clear legal relationship between stepparent and stepchild and the power to make parental decisions for the child. Otherwise, stepparents should pursue permission to act in parental ways. See the next section on legal matters.

Her biological father was inconsistent in his involvement (what I referred to in *The Smart Stepdad* as a disengaged or deactivated dad), but periodically showed up. On some level, he still wanted to be involved in her life. This makes adoption by her stepfather legally impossible and relationally unlikely. On the other hand, a clear path would include:

- A biological father who has for years proven an unwillingness to parent.

- A clear decision by the biological father to relinquish his parental rights.

- A clear reason for stepparent adoption (there are many good reasons—for example, establishing legal rights to the child, medical or financial benefits, preventing stigmatization, and acknowledging family unity).

- A clear, established bond between stepparent and his stepchild.

That last point is extremely important. Both parent and stepparent should think of adoption of a stepchild as the capstone to the stepparent-stepchild relationship, not the path to one. Unfortunately, some stepparents use adoption as another blender strategy: They think that adopting the child will foster bonding, connection, and a sense of family among everyone. It doesn't. All of that should occur before you adopt. When love and trust are established over time and a biological parent has relinquished their rights, a clear path to adoption is evident.

Another well-intentioned but nearsighted agenda for some parents and stepparents is adopting with a health agenda: they think adopting will improve the child's self-esteem. Preliminary evidence suggests this is not really true. A national study comparing nonadopted stepchildren, adopted stepchildren, and children adopted by first marriage couples (not in stepfamilies) found no difference between children on any measure of well-being, at any age.[13] Therefore, do not feel pressure to adopt. Rather, focus on being a healthy stepfamily. If after years of family bonding and strength, a natural path to adoption appears in front of you—and both adults and child are in favor of it—then give prayerful consideration to it. If the decision to adopt is easy, then it's probably the right one.

## Legal Matters in Stepparenting

Family law and policy around marriage and original families is clear in Western cultures. However, family law regarding stepfamilies is ambiguous and diverse from state to state.[14] Laws pertaining to stepfamilies are created through the filter of the biological unions that preexisted the stepfamily. In particular, understanding parental rights in the U.S. is paramount to understanding U.S. law regarding stepfamilies. "Family law resists formal recognition of nontraditional caregivers such as stepparents, regardless of their psychological or functional roles in a child's life, largely because of robust legal precedent that protects and seeks to maintain legal parents and responsible parenting on the part of biological or adoptive nuclear parents."[15]

To determine parental rights, two basic tenets are used. The *parental rights doctrine* gives biological parents fundamental rights to procreate and make parental decisions for their children and the *parenthood as an exclusive status* tenet sets the maximum number of parents that a child can have at two and can only be changed by terminating the rights of one parent (as in the case of stepparent adoption). These tenets result in legal ambiguity for stepparents. For example, you may have developed a deep emotional and psychological attachment with a stepchild, but you can't grant them permission for a dental checkup. (But in all fairness, legal precedent in support of biological parents is not easily altered. How could the law grant stepparent practical authority without undermining the authority of the nonresidential biological parent?) In addition, if you die without a will, your stepchildren will likely not be able to inherit from you because intestacy (without a will) and probate laws do not recognize stepchildren as qualifying for inheritance. Instead, state laws will divide assets between a spouse and any biological children or family members.[16] Again, this leaves stepparents with a legally ambiguous relationship with stepchildren.

To make matters more confusing, federal and state policy send mixed messages to stepfamilies. Federal policy recognizes stepchildren as dependent children, which has implications for receiving federal aid, employee benefits, income taxes, and federal money programs. However, states treat stepparents and stepchildren as having no legal relationship. As one precedent-setting case put it, stepparents and stepchildren are "legal strangers."[17] Stepparents have fewer parental rights than foster parents or legal guardians. As stated before, without legal authorization, stepparents can't even sign a field trip permission slip.

However, state law does make accommodation for the basic functions that stepparents fulfill. *De facto parent* status, simply obtained by willingly taking on the role of parent by sharing residence and providing caretaking responsibilities, affords stepparents the ability to discipline stepchildren. It also makes you accountable to parental laws, such as physical and sexual abuse prohibitions. Essentially, this allows you to function as parent in day-to-day terms (but still not having legal authority over the children). But this, too, has clear limits. Legally, de facto parent status and any financial support offered to a stepchild ends with the ending of the marriage, whether by death or divorce. After divorce, for example, a stepparent who wishes to continue a relationship with stepchildren will have to receive permission from the biological parent. A strong relationship does not afford any parental rights to the child. In the case of the death of a biological parent, stepchildren are no longer eligible for benefits and the stepparent is not legally obligated to share any inheritance money. Therefore, provision for children and the spouse after death necessitates estate planning (see chapter 10) or legal adoption (see above) that clearly grants the stepparent rights and responsibilities even after the marriage has ended.

So, what do you do in light of these realities? There are many in the U.S. who have proposed family law and policy changes that would legally recognize stepparents and provide uniform direction to current legal ambiguities. Examples include allowing, as does England, children to have three legal parents (two biological and one residential stepparent) or formalizing the de facto parent role. You could help petition for these changes, but barring these significant alterations in the law, here's what you can do:

- Be proactive in estate planning (see chapter 10). Don't leave your financial wishes to the state or attorneys to determine.

- Utilize the forms provided on my website (SmartStepfamilies.com/ view/permission-forms) to grant the stepparent functional permission to make medical decisions for stepchildren, travel with them away from home, obtain school information, etc. Signed and notarized by both biological parents, the forms make it clear to all interested parties that the stepparent is empowered to act in the children's best interests. In light of current law, these are a vital first step to empowering daily living.

- Focus on building a smart and strong stepfamily. At the end of the day, relational equity is worth more than legal governances because it fosters trust from children, motivates the child's heart to grant you influence, and invites grace from the other household.

## Final Thoughts

If you didn't find your unique parent or stepparent situation in this chapter, review the bonus material available at SmartStepfamilies.com/view/ learn. Chapter 11 addresses the important topic of faith development in stepfamilies and what parents can do when the other home's values are undermining your efforts to instill faith in your children.

Parenting is a lifelong challenge—and privilege. Be committed to being a good parent, for we are the ones who tell the next generation the praiseworthy deeds of the Lord so that they will know him, put their trust in him, and in turn will tell their children all that the Lord has done (Psalm 78:1–8).

### Questions for Discussion

There are no parent-child discussion questions in this chapter because the content was focused on parenting. However, if the material sparked questions you'd like to ask your child, feel free to do so.

■ FOR ALL COUPLES

1. Adult stepchildren: What insights did this section give you about the emotional responses of adult stepchildren? How might you have responded differently had you been aware of this early on? What difference will it make now?

2. Part-time parenting and stepparenting: In what ways is your perspective about the part-time schedule different and the same as your spouse's? To what degree do differences in perspective make you fearful of isolation in your relationship?

3. Birth order changes: What changes have your children experienced? What loss has it brought to them? What challenges have they responded well to?

4. Stepparenting adolescents: Because teens have many choices available to them that parents cannot control, parenting can be troubling and anxiety producing. Talk through this section. What emotions did it elicit in you and why?

5. Parenting the mutual child: What changed in you and in your family when you brought home your mutual child? What harmonies have you discovered and what hazards are you experiencing now?

6. Sibling relationships and parenting: Review the Parenting Siblings section and discuss any applications you think may be helpful in your home.

7. Adopting stepchildren: Discuss this statement and its implications for your family. "Both parent and stepparent should think of adoption of a stepchild as the capstone to the stepparent-stepchild relationship, not the path to one."

8. Legal matters in stepparenting: What steps have you already taken to provide the stepparent(s) permission to provide oversight of the

children? Which forms provided at SmartStepfamilies.com/view/permission-forms pertain to you?

## ▪ For Pre-Stepfamily Couples

1. Adult stepchildren: Discuss together how might you "lower the price tag of acceptance" for the adult children while you are dating or engaged.

2. Part-time parenting and stepparenting: During dating, both biological parent and future stepparent typically enjoy the part-time schedule because it allows them compartmentalized time to date each other or be with the kids. Marriage brings a new task: learning to balance couple time and family time. Discuss how you might handle this transition when the time comes and interview one stepcouple you know who has already walked down that road.

3. Birth order changes: How might the children's roles, expectations, and positions in the family change once you merge families? What can you do to mitigate the change?

4. Stepparenting adolescents: Teens need to feel heard. Engage your teens to hear their excitement and concerns about your relationship. Try to empower them to share their feelings and find a way to be influenced by something they say.

5. Parenting the mutual child: Express clearly your desire for or against having more children. Many couples skirt this issue as if it really isn't important—it is. Find agreement about your future together or consult a counselor to help you work through this matter.

6. Sibling relationships and parenting: What trends are you seeing currently in the kids regarding future stepsiblings? What has worked to help foster common interests and friendship between them? What has not worked so far?

7. Adopting stepchildren: Before reading this section, what hopes or expectations did you have about the stepparent ultimately adopting the children? How have those hopes been modified after reading this section?

8. Legal matters in stepparenting: Begin discussing estate planning and how you will combine your finances after the wedding. Most people underestimate the implications of these legal conversations for their family—start having your conversations in advance of marriage. (For more on financial matters, see chapter 10.)

# Smart Step Five: Side STEP (Part 1)

*The pitfalls common to stepfamilies*

Why did you bring us to the desert to die? Weren't there any graves in Egypt? What have you done to us by bringing us out of Egypt?

Exodus 14:11 NIRV

When they came to Marah, they couldn't drink its water. It was bitter. . . . The people told Moses they weren't happy with him. They said, "What are we supposed to drink?"

Exodus 15:23–24 NIRV

The journey from Egypt to the Promised Land was very long. Repeatedly throughout the trip the Israelites lost sight of God's faithfulness and protective hand. Grumbling and complaining, they voiced their lack of faith and fear of dying in the wilderness. From a human standpoint, even with God in control, the journey was challenging, filled with pitfalls and uncertainty. They had to cross the Red Sea, walk day after day through the wilderness without knowing where they would be when the day was done, and once they crossed the Jordan River, fight battles against fierce enemy nations.

From a spiritual standpoint, however, the journey was ultimately in God's hands. God did all the hard work; they just had to believe and act according to their confidence in God. That task proved to be one of the most difficult, and it continues to be one of the most difficult for us today.

A great many pitfalls threaten the stepfamily's journey to the Promised Land. We've already encountered some of the most strenuous:

- Adults who are disconnected from God and his church body due to personal shame and guilt or judgment from friends and church leaders.
- Unrealistic expectations that bring about unhealthy attempts to "blend" family members quickly instead of relaxing in a Crockpot-cooking style.
- A weak marital relationship eroded by preexisting loyalties to children, ghosts, and emotional baggage from previous relationships.
- Couples who don't function as a team because they have poor communication and conflict resolution skills.
- Battles with ex-spouses and poor co-parenting that cause stress for everyone.
- A poor parental team resulting from misguided parent and stepparent roles and ineffective parenting skills.

From a human perspective, stepfamily life is full of pitfalls and uncertainty. From a spiritual standpoint, however, God is still working on your behalf. You must continue to believe and act according to your confidence in him.

In addition to the pitfalls listed above, a number of other significant pitfalls must be sidestepped, including:

- Unrecognized loss and unexpressed grief
- Being driven by menacing emotions
- Combining holiday and family traditions
- Money matters (I'll devote the entire next chapter to this topic.)

Let's consider them one at a time, beginning with the one most hidden.

226

## Unrecognized Loss and Unexpressed Grief

Marriage is supposed to be a time when a new relationship and family is born. Hollywood tells us that marriage is just the beginning of "and they lived happily ever after." But for a stepfamily, a wedding is not the beginning, it is the middle. Stepfamilies are born out of the loss of previous family relationships; that is, they are created when a marriage follows death, divorce, or an out-of-wedlock birth. This loss creates a paradox of emotions for the new stepfamily: hand in hand with joy and hope linger sadness and grief.

For those of you currently married, think back to your wedding day. Do you recall any mixed feelings? Joy and anxiety? Optimism and fear? Happiness and sadness? Love and anger? Do you remember trying to decide whether to invite your ex-spouse's parents and how to break the news of the engagement to your children? If your spouse died, do you remember wondering if in the afterlife he or she somehow knew what you were doing? Did you feel your spouse's blessing to move on, or would your partner be troubled by your decision? What concerns did you have for your children and how did they voice their pleasure or apprehension about your remarriage?

Many adults readily acknowledge their conflicting emotions but are surprised to consider that their children probably felt a mixed bag as well. If you're courageous, spend some one-on-one time with each of your children and ask how they felt at the time of the wedding. Open the door to some honest conversation about mixed emotions, and be open to affirming the difficulties those created for you and your children. After all, everyone in a stepfamily has experienced loss. The trick is not allowing loss and sadness to remain hidden below the surface; it has more power there. Rather, expressing and sharing our loss diminishes its intensity and ability to divide.

> **Dating Couples**
>
> Have "What if?" conversations with your children to explore their feelings. For example, "What if I were to get engaged or married? How would you feel? What would your mom/dad feel? Your siblings?"

As you continue reading, note the typical losses experienced by others in your stepfamily (even those in the other home). Your losses are easy to identify. The challenge of understanding involves stepping into the shoes of others to experience what troubles them. Make a list of your realizations—it just might help you to relate better to someone in your home.

### The Enduring Nature of Loss

Loss is a journey, not a destination. You don't just get over it and move on. It is an ongoing journey with new layers added and persistent undercurrents just below the surface that are always present. Losing my son has most assuredly taught me this unfortunate lesson.

There are some losses that have a small to moderate impact on our lives; they hurt, they sting, they create inconvenience and stress, but they seem to resolve themselves and we move on. There are other losses that put us in the center of a massive earthquake and everything we know or possess is destroyed. We are shaken to our core and the pain is intense and enduring (a sorrow upon sorrow); frequently these losses cause us to question our faith and we discover that the framework of assumptions and surface theology we had based our lives upon is no longer adequate to make sense of life or find our way through it. Losing Connor has recalibrated my wife and me in such a way. And then there are the aftershocks.

> **If Loss Is Not Your Story**
>
> Sometimes stepparents who have never been married before and didn't bring children to the marriage find it difficult to understand the significance of loss. If this is you, ask questions and listen with empathy to the stories of the children and your spouse. Connect with their pain as best you can and minister to their hurt.

After the earthquake, there are continual aftershocks that originate near the epicenter but bring their own destruction. For example, it's been five years since my son died, and nearly every day I experience some ripple effect of his death that costs me something else or complicates life. Today just happens to be Sunday, and this morning my family went to worship the Lord. I still find the worship hour to be one of the most difficult of my week. I sing in celebration of Christ's victory over death (which happily means I'll see Connor again), but I cry through the singing of those songs because he's not here. At times during the past five years, trying to worship has isolated my wife and me and our other two boys from one another because some days one or two of us may have felt like participating and the others just wanted to yell at God.

And there's the aftershock of all the friends we've lost through the years. In the city we lived in when Connor died, we used to go to worship services to see and enjoy friends, but it soon became, except for a few, a sea of strangers who couldn't stand to be around sad people who couldn't smile or laugh or talk about surface, petty things anymore. That was such a lonely experience; first we lost Connor, then we lost our church.

We are now in a new city and looking for a new church, and I noticed yet another church aftershock. Just this morning I recognized that I was shrinking back from people at church. I told my wife and she asked in what way. I was holding back from getting to know people because introducing myself means telling them about Connor, which I am more than happy to do—I love talking about Connor—but I have learned that as soon as I bring up every parent's worst nightmare, most people get tongue-tied, end the pleasantries as quickly as possible, and head for the nearest exit. Or, even worse, some people continue talking to me, but never acknowledge the magnitude of what I just said. Instead, they keep talking like I just said I had pizza last night. (I estimate that only one in ten people can turn toward our grief story instead of away from it.) With much prayer I have learned to be compassionate toward those who freeze in the presence of a grieving parent, but I have become weary of the experience. Shrinking back is my natural self-protection; I am tired of having people look at me like I have leprosy. All in all, instead of being an uplifting and challenging opportunity, going to church still sometimes feels like swimming in shark-infested waters.

First comes the earthquake, then the aftershocks.

And so it is with you, your family, and your kids. First came the death, divorce, or breakup, and then come the aftershocks:

- Lost self-confidence and struggles with your worth.
- A lost sense of identity and place in the social world: Friends or family members who won't engage you as they did before or church members who treat you differently after the divorce.
- Watching your children experience repeated hurt from a disappearing dad or mom.
- Noticing how your children of all ages seem confused about their family as stepparents and stepsiblings come in and out of their lives.

229

- Trying to help kids cope with a non-specific depression that neither they nor you can explain, but you know is somehow related to how life is so incredibly different than it used to be.

- Wrestling with the all-important God questions: Why would God allow this? Doesn't God care about us like he does other families? When is God going to make our situation better?

- The helplessness you feel as you endeavor to bring your children to faith, but the other home or the hurt in their life, or both, are pulling them in another direction.

The list goes on and on. You can probably immediately list five to ten aftershocks in your life right now without much effort.

I find the enduring nature of aftershocks and their impact to be quite insidious and, sometimes, elusive. I've had more than one parent and stepparent say something like, "Thank goodness the kids were toddlers when the divorce happened. They don't have any memories of that time at all so it shouldn't be hard for them." Wrong! No, they don't remember life before the divorce, but every day after is an aftershock that brings its own complication and pain. With friends who live in biological homes, they may feel embarrassed as they try to explain why their parents can't sit together at the recital, or why they have to have two graduation parties, or why figuring out who is going to walk her down the aisle at her wedding is so stressful. Breaking up with their first teenage boy/girlfriend may shower them with emotions as they rewind life and imagine that's what you did to their other parent when they were two years old. Time with grandparents may be stressful because of the tension that remains between extended family members.

The point is this: Loss is not a one-time event. It starts with the original earthquake and is then followed by a series of ongoing aftershocks. Ask yourself, how can I reach into that pain, that complication, that place of instability and offer comfort?

To demonstrate what I call hugging the hurt, let me tell you about one more aftershock and how my wife reached into the pain of one of our other sons. Just recently Brennan, who was born two and a half years after Connor, but who is now two years older than Connor was when he died (that's still so weird for all of us), came into our bedroom late one night. Nighttime is when his grief comes out; lying in bed with nothing else on his mind, he thinks of Connor and gets sad. He can't be alone when he's sad, so he comes to our room. I was already asleep. This is the conversation that took place.

"Mom, can I sleep on the floor beside your bed tonight?"

Nan replied, "What's on your mind, sweetheart?"

"Mom, I just want to sleep by your bed."

"Tell me what is on your mind."

"You know, Mom."

"No, I need you to tell me what's going on."

"I'm sad."

"Sad about what?"

"I'm just sad."

"Sad about our moving to a new city, missing your friends?"

"No, I'm sad about Connor."

"Tell me more. Name the sadness and what triggered it tonight."

"I'm just sad."

"Go ahead, name it. You need to tell me what it's about."

"It's the end of the school year and I'm getting to finish another grade, but Connor isn't. I'm sad about that."

"I can see that. Thank you for sharing that with me. I love you and I miss Connor, too." She then gave him a big hug and he went to sleep.

Notice what is happening here. Brennan experiences an aftershock. Nan walks him through a simple process of naming the feeling and what's around it so he's not isolated in

> **Parenting Best Practices**
>
> Learn more about coaching children through grief at SmartStepfamilies.com/view/emotional-coaching.

his experience. Over the years, through a series of such conversations, we have attempted to coach our kids into understanding their own emotions and how to manage them (this cultivates emotional maturity). This not only breaks their isolation but also fosters open grieving, which prevents all of us from getting stuck emotionally; it keeps us moving *through* the grief *together*. As parents we can't fix the loss, but we can hug the hurt.

Consider as you read the following sections about loss for a variety of stepfamily members how you can hug the hurt of your spouse and children as *together* you move *through* the original earthquake and the ongoing aftershocks.

### Losses of Spouse/Partner

Whether by death or divorce, the loss of a marital relationship is very difficult. The grief cycle after divorce is often assumed to parallel the grief cycle most persons experience after the death of a loved one. There are, however, some distinct differences. When anticipating a death people tend to experience grief in stages; the most common tend to be denial, anger, bargaining, depression, and acceptance. After divorce, however, persons tend to experience a cycle of love, anger, and sadness.[1] Feelings of love, which include a fondness and longing to be with the person lost, the hope of reconciliation, and guilt over what has been lost, cycle periodically through a person's heart. Close behind this wave of emotion is anger, characterized by frustration over what was lost, resentment, rage, and hurt. The third wave of emotion to follow is sadness, which manifests itself in the form of loneliness, depression, despair, pain, and grief. Once the cycle is complete, it repeats. At first, feelings of love, anger, and sadness are experienced with great intensity. Over time the feelings become less intense and less problematic and the time spent in each phase of the cycle decreases.

It is out of this intense cycle of emotions that couples often begin new dating relationships. The new relationship rescues them from negative feelings, hurt, and depression, or so it seems. Forming relationships on the rebound is common and very dangerous. I have worked with numerous stepfamily couples who after ten or more years of marriage are suffering, believing themselves to be in a relationship that was never meant to be. "I was hurting when I met him, and he made me feel good again. On the wedding day, I had second thoughts but didn't want to disappoint everyone. I just thought I was scared. Looking back, I don't think I ever really loved him." Therefore, it is important for dating couples to be aware of this cycle of emotion, because depending on how quickly someone remarries, the cycle may continue at intense levels well into the new marriage. Not giving yourself or a dating partner sufficient time to grieve a loss may result in problems later. Persons who remarry in less than three years are likely to experience longing, anger, and sadness at substantial levels. New spouses may become insecure if they catch their mate, for example, fondly reminiscing over the lost relationship, yet this is normal to some degree and doesn't necessarily imply regret over a new marriage. Also, anger at a former spouse is to be expected and understandable, as should sadness and grief over what has been lost.

The task for new couples, then, is to set appropriate boundaries with former spouses that reflect the ending of a committed relationship, yet make space for sadness over what has been lost. Preferably couples would give each other plenty of time to resolve the ending of former relationships before beginning a new relationship. For many, however, the wisdom of waiting before another marriage is difficult to accept.

A second task is giving each other permission to struggle with grief even after recoupling. The story is told of a widow who married a widower and soon found herself challenged by a friend. "I suppose, like all men who have been married before, your husband sometimes talks about his first wife?" "Oh, not anymore, he doesn't," the newly married woman replied. "What stopped him?" the friend asked. "I started talking about my next husband." The underlying message of the wife's response could be said this way: "I feel insecure about us when you speak about her. Don't admit you ever enjoyed her, or I'll be angry with you." Obviously no one should ever idealize an ex-spouse in order to intimidate a current spouse. But neither should his past be completely off limits. This woman was withholding permission for her husband to feel sad over a relationship that at one time meant a great deal to him.

Michael's first wife, Sara, was killed in a tragic incident, leaving him behind with their seven-year-old son. After one year, Michael married Debbie, who brought her own child to the marriage. Debbie has continuously allowed her husband and his son to talk in her presence about Sara's death. Even when they express admiration for Sara, she is not threatened by their fond memories. For many people, allowing a spouse to express sadness over a previous spouse feels like moving themselves out of the family portrait. But Debbie's identity is not based on being the only focus of Michael's life; she acknowledges that everyone has special attachments in life. In addition, her identity is firm in her relationship with Christ and she trusts her husband's commitment to her. This empowers her not to be threatened by Michael's former bond to Sara. By the way, acknowledging her husband and stepson's grief is an incredible gift to her stepson. He is able to hold on to Mom in a meaningful way and isn't forced to move on without her.

Other losses for spouses after death or divorce include the loss of social status, financial stability (this is especially true for women and their children), friendships and family connections, and social shifts within a religious community. For example, many people find themselves socially out of place after the ending of a marriage—sometimes even cast off or mistreated by people who didn't agree with the divorce. As a result, many lose their church support system and connection with God.

One final significant loss worth mentioning is the loss of contact with children. Many noncustodial parents are hammered by the reality of seeing their children only a few days a month, sometimes less. The added emotional and mental strain can be quite debilitating. So much so, it leads some noncustodial parents to reduce contact even more because the process of saying good-bye is agonizing for them and for their children. "It is just easier not to put myself or them through the pain of leaving." This, however, is never recommended, as it inadvertently communicates a lack of care to the children.

In addition, after remarriage, a noncustodial parent may feel the loss of contact with his children when stepchildren enter the picture. I've heard many fathers, for instance, say they feel guilty spending time with a stepchild or sharing special moments when they can't experience the same things with their own children. To compensate, noncustodial parents may during visitation weekends minimize time with stepchildren and focus their energies on biological children. This mini-family activity is understandable, yet it may hurt their spouse's feelings when stepchildren are neglected.

Adults should strive to understand each other's losses and how they impact the decisions parents and noncustodial parents make. Giving each other space to take advantage of time with children as well as opportunities to voice sadness over time lost is important.

### Loss After Death

A common myth is that stepfamilies formed after a death adapt more readily than do stepfamilies formed after a divorce. While it does appear, statistically speaking, that remarriages following the death of a spouse have a better chance of lasting, they do have some unique struggles. John and Emily Visher have identified four major challenges.[2]

**Giving yourself and your children enough time to mourn the loss.** Time doesn't heal all wounds, but it allows for a decrease in the intensity of grief. Both adults and children need time, as do grandparents and extended family members. If a parent remarries too quickly, acceptance of the stepparent becomes more difficult. In addition, parents may find themselves holding on to material possessions and rituals (ways of doing things) because they haven't fully said their good-byes.

As stated earlier, most grief experts recommend waiting two to three years before beginning to date seriously or making a decision to remarry. Unexpressed grief clouds judgment about intimate relationships and leads people to step into relationships out of need, not choice. During a therapy session, James reflected on his now floundering remarriage after the death of his first wife to cancer. "I was lonely," he said. "I felt inadequate to provide for my daughter. I guess I needed a partner, and I wanted a mother for my daughter." This need and emptiness led him to look past his second wife's personality distortions and rush into a new marriage that was ending after just one year. Relationships that rescue people from grief are relationships of convenience. The problems come when the conveniences wear off. To explore this further, read *Dating and the Single Parent*.

**Making the dead person into a saint.** Memories of a deceased spouse or parent tend to be positive and interpreted through rose-colored glasses. It's easy to forget or minimize the frailties and failures of the person we love.

A second wife may find herself intimidated each Christmas, for example, when her adult stepchildren gather and share stories of "Mom's unbelievable blueberry pie." Even if the remark is not intended to offend their stepmother, she may find it difficult not to feel compared.

**Attempting to replace the spouse who died.** If a couple had a good relationship prior to death, it is natural for the remaining spouse to seek out someone with similar qualities and characteristics. This sets up the new spouse not to feel accepted for who he or she is and the bereaved spouse to be disappointed when the new partner doesn't match the other entirely.

The couple's "us-ness" will also be different, and if the surviving partner assumes it will be the same, disappointment will be the result. Taylor, for example, didn't realize just how much he and his first wife thought the same about vacations and the kind of fun they wanted to plan into family holidays until his second wife and he disagreed about them. It wasn't that they were exact opposites; it just didn't result in the same feeling. I reminded Taylor that, as was expressed earlier, yellow and blue make green, but yellow and red make orange. "Allow your marriage to be a different color or you'll be frustrated and your wife will never feel good enough."

**Money and inheritance.** Possessions and promised inheritances are particularly meaningful to children who have lost a parent to death. The presence of a stepparent may bring out the fear of losing those items if their other biological parent were to die before the stepparent. In addition, giving children (whether adults or minors) first choice over family possessions shows honor to the one who has died. One couple saw to it that each of their adult children took possession of whatever items they needed prior to their wedding. This made sure that Mom's dishes stayed in the family and that grandchildren grew up hearing stories of Grandpa when they used his golf clubs. Drawing up a new will that details the distribution of sentimental and monetary assets is also a good idea. For more, see the section on estate planning in chapter 10.

### Losses for New Spouses/Stepparents

No one grows up with the fantasy of someday getting married and having two or three stepchildren competing for the time, energy, and love of his or her spouse. The marriage fantasy Hollywood sells us is that of a man and woman riding off into the sunset together—perhaps on a horse or in a BMW—but never with children all around them. New spouses in stepfamilies experience the loss of privacy and exclusive access to their spouse they dreamed marriage would bring. In addition, the experience of being an outsider to the history and bond between their stepchildren and spouse is quite a shock for many.

Another significant loss for stepparents is the early bonding time that biological parents have had with their children. Stepparents are thrown into parenting with no owner's manual and very little working knowledge of the likes, preferences, personality quirks, and motivating attributes of their stepchildren. It is on-the-job training at best. If the stepparent has not had children as old as the stepchildren, it may be difficult to fit into the flow of parenting with a particular child. This leads to frustration and possible conflict with the child and/or spouse.

If stepparents have not had children of their own, pre-marriage fantasies may have led them to believe their need to nurture a child would be met by helping to raise a stepchild. When Randy married Judy, he was sure that living with her two children would satisfy his desire for children. Judy was relieved to hear his enthusiasm when she announced she didn't want any more children. But after a few years of marriage, Randy realized that the relationship he experienced with his stepdaughters would never fill the emptiness he felt. When he began asking about having a child together, she became angry. "He's going back on his promise," she complained. "I thought this was settled before we got married." Unfortunately, it was settled on a fantasy. Reality brought an unexpected loss to Randy and a complication to the marriage.

### Losses for Grandparents

The losses of grandparents are numerous but often unnoticed. When a son or daughter divorces or dies, contact with grandchildren usually diminishes. When the remaining parent marries again it may also reduce the amount of contact (especially if grandchildren live with an ex-daughter-in-law). After her daughter's divorce, Lana cherished holiday visits with her grandchildren. But when her daughter remarried and the children began to spend some holidays with their stepgrandparents, Lana's time with the kids was cut in half. Parents and stepparents should be sensitive to the loss of contact between children and grandparents (and extended family) and attempt, when possible, to bring the two together.

Two distinct patterns seem to emerge over time after a remarriage. Grandparents and stepgrandparents seem to either *replace* their former son/daughter-in-law and distance themselves from the previous son/daughter-in-law or *expand* their family connections and continue contact with everyone.[3] I believe that God would have Christian grandparents expand their connections, keeping alive supportive relationships with an ex-son/daughter-in-law and develop a relationship with a new son/daughter-in-law and stepgrandchildren. This is not to say that equal amounts of time and energy will be spent with all parties, but grandchildren should not suffer for the choices of their parents.

Keeping grandparents connected is, of course, a two-way street. Ex-sons/daughters-in-law have to cooperate with former in-laws in order for the children to remain freely connected. Sophia wrote to me sharing that after her husband left her and their three children, she was tempted to avoid his parents. But inspired by God's grace, she "built a bridge," as she called it, and continued to take the children to visit them and all his family. Her children were present for all of that side of the family's important moments (birthdays, funerals, weddings, etc.) and years later, when Sophia began seriously dating again, she introduced him to her former mother-in-law. "I wanted her to meet the man who was going to be raising her grandchildren," she wrote. "We visited, and she graciously accepted him and thanked him for the position he was stepping into." Sophia's gracious heart and efforts to keep grandparents and her children connected paid off for everyone.

### Losses for Children

*No one in stepfamilies experiences more loss than children.* This truth is difficult for most adults to recognize simply because they are consumed with their own losses. (It's human nature to notice our own wounds more than someone else's.) But if you will stop and think about it, they have lost a lot. Further, because children lack maturity and coping skills, they need more help processing their grief than adults.

The death of a parent or a parental divorce means children lose *control* of their lives, *contact* with parents, grandparents, and siblings, and *continuity* of living arrangements and routines.[4] Life in a single-parent family and stepfamily is full of transition and change. Here are just a few changes that bring loss to children (some changes have greater impact than others): their parents' divorce; changing residences or moving between two homes; a new stepparent they didn't ask for, and the death of the dream of parental reconciliation; new stepsiblings; having to share a room with a sibling or stepsibling; loss of a role in the family when marriage brings other people to the household; loss of familiarity with a school, teachers, neighborhood, friends, activities, and traditions; financial pressures; and changes in rules and expectations from their parent and stepparent. And this list just begins to capture the kinds of changes (losses) forced upon children when families end and begin.

For example, it's not uncommon for single parents and children to develop an extremely close bond during the fallout period after a death or divorce due to the "stick together and survive" mentality they share. Persons pull together and make life work the best they can. That's one reason why the announcement of a new marriage often brings more loss for children because it threatens the closeness they have with their custodial parent. I once worked with Jessey, a seven-year-old who was born out of wedlock; her mother had been single and, therefore, focused exclusively on Jessey her entire life. Mother and child had a very tight bond, and now her mother was planning to marry. I asked Jessey how she felt about her mom's decision to marry: "You know when you're playing with someone on the playground and they push you down and run off without you—that's what it feels like."

Wow! *Well said*, I thought. Another child, a four-year-old, told her mom why she was acting so angrily toward her mom's fiancé. "Me thinks it in my heart if you get married you'll have this much love for him [holding her hands apart] and only this much [holding her fingers close together] left for me."

> **How do you appropriately display pictures and memorabilia of a deceased parent?**
>
> Find the answer in the Smart Questions, Smart Answers bonus material, available at SmartStep families.com/view/learn.

I repeat this important truth—that marriage often disrupts the parent-child bond and produces insecurity in children—not to make you feel guilty. It's intended to help you parent wisely. If you are a parent, you need to understand the impact loss has on your children. If you are a stepparent, you need to empathize with—not resent—your stepchildren's grief. Remember the stepping-stone of *understanding* in chapter 2? I suggested that the experience of other members of your stepfamily is often dramatically different from yours and that you must strive to empathize with their perspective. That is nowhere more important than in regard to the losses children experience.

I believe that one of the hardest things children in stepfamilies must learn is to share a parent with a stepparent or stepsiblings. They've lost so much already, it's understandable why they would resist making space in their parental relationship for others to enter. To protect their relationships, children may push away the outsiders and block their involvement in the family. This brings about competition and insecurity, especially if a stepparent takes the threat personally. I wish I could count the number of stepparents who have described their stepchildren as "jealous" and "trying to be manipulative." I respond with, "I know that's what it looks like on the outside, but what they are on the inside is hurt. These children have experienced a great deal of loss in the past and that makes them scared of more hurt. One of the things they fear most is losing their parent to you. Don't get hooked into competing for time. You're the adult. Find your time with their parent, but balance it by backing away every once in a while to give them exclusive time with their parent so they don't fear you quite so much. Someday, when they relax toward your involvement, you can share time with their parent more equitably." Respecting the significance of the parent-child relationship is important for stepparents, just as is being aware of how previous losses create fear in children. But then again, it is not just children who become fearful after loss.

### Fear: The By-Product of Loss

How does loss impact your family's integration process? It slows it down. Imagine if someone walked up to you and firmly slapped your face. Do you suppose you might blink the next time he lifted his hand? Loss brings pain, and the experience of pain leads adults and children alike to "blink" when faced with the potential for more hurt. The fear of more pain powerfully leads people to build relational walls that protect them from further harm; this in turn can slow or stall the cooking process for a stepfamily. Walls can be built with many emotional bricks, but the most common are guardedness, distance, and anger.

Tim learned this the hard way. Shortly after his remarriage, he began to sense his second wife, Lisa, pulling away and his stepchildren's growing resentment. Prior to their mother's marriage, Lisa's children had a nightly ritual of lying in bed and waiting for Mom's good-night kiss. Lisa would lie with each child for a while and talk with her about the day's events. They shared stories, warm affections, and plans for the week ahead. It was a special and comforting time for the children and for Lisa.

Tim's fantasies of being with his new wife and building their marriage were quickly squashed by the realities of a busy stepfamily. Tim grew increasingly possessive of the time he and Lisa had together after the children went to bed. Because he felt cheated by her time with the children, Tim began to stand outside the children's bedrooms and monitor the amount of time she spent talking with them. If he felt it was too much, he would lean his head in and say, "Is she asleep yet? When are you going to come in here with me?" In effect, Tim was saying, "Hey, don't you think it's time you chose me over the kids?"

Little did Tim realize how he was sabotaging his marriage and his relationship with his stepchildren. Losses throughout the divorce process and her marriage to Tim had made the nighttime ritual even more important to Lisa and her children. Tim's whining led them to fear the loss of time together and the love it communicated. Lisa also grew resentful of Tim's jealousy and began to distance herself from any expectation that she would choose him over her children. This, of course, complicated Tim's fears, and he escalated his attempts to gain her loyalty. The children remained guarded with their new stepfather and angrily refused to grant him parental status over time. In the end, a vicious negative cycle of fear and resentment resulted.

But wait a minute, Ron, didn't you tell us in chapter 5 to prioritize the marriage? Shouldn't Lisa put him first? Yes, I did discuss the importance of the couple relationship, but in balance with the needs of the children. Keep reading.

### Anger: The By-Product of Fear

When we fear losing contact with someone we love, we naturally develop anger toward the person or persons we believe are responsible for that potential loss. The above example is a perfect illustration. Notice how each person makes sense of the other's behavior. Tim became increasingly angry toward his wife "because she babies her children." Anger toward his stepchildren took the form of a label—"they are spoiled rotten." His wife was angry with him for "forcing her to choose." His stepchildren were angry that he "was so selfish" he would invade their special time with Mom. (Notice that the stepparent is the recipient of more anger than anyone else. The insiders can hold on to one another, but stepparents are forced back to the outside when anger builds. I told you it is tough being a stepparent!) Each explained the other's behavior in very negative terms instead of acknowledging the losses and fears each was communicating through his or her insecurity.

Consider how this situation might be different if Tim was empathic with his stepchildren for all they had lost and was willing to sacrifice his couple time in order to ensure their bonding time with Mom. He would not have stood outside the bedroom door or watched the clock. He would have backed away from intruding on the nighttime ritual, yet still expressed his need for couple time with his wife. Couple time is very important—but not at the expense of valued parent-child touch points. How much better it would have been if Tim and his wife had compartmentalized their relationship and found some exclusive time together before bedtime or during weekends. Likewise, Tim's wife would be sensitive to his loss of a marital dream and may have tried to carve out some valuable time for their growing marriage—perhaps ten minutes of coffee-talk each night after dinner—even while unashamedly continuing to spend time with her children each night. Finding the balance takes teamwork and mutual trust, but it benefits everyone.

### Practical Strategies for Coping With Unrecognized Loss and Unexpressed Grief[5]

Coping with loss is not an easy task. Adults must set the example for how losses will be handled. Here are some tips to help.

**Identify painful losses for each family member.** Grief is an emotion that will not be denied. If it is not expressed, it will seep out in resentment, anger, bitterness, fear, depression, or blocked stepfamily relationships. Give permission to sadness and don't demand that others finish grieving on your timetable.

Make a list of each family member and the losses you believe he or she has experienced. Imagine what it has been like to be that person at each point along the way: pre-divorce or death, after the divorce/death, during the single-parent years, after the marriage was announced, since the wedding. You may be stunned by the number of losses you can identify.

**Look behind surface emotions to identify how loss is playing a role.** For example, children often display sad emotions with mad responses ("mad is really sad"). Also, spouses maintain a guarded distance from their mate through distrust in order to prevent further hurt from another loss. Be sympathetic to what's under the surface instead of reacting to what you see in front of you.

**Talk about your losses.** This helps children and teens know how to think about loss and gives permission to talk openly. Most children rarely have the privilege of hearing their parents talk openly about what concerns them, their vulnerabilities, how they think through decisions, and for that matter, their temptations. In no way am I encouraging you to make your children your confidants or support system—they should not be parentified in that way. However, it adds to their maturity when children hear you talk about a sadness, challenge, or something that makes you anxious in life and how you are coping with it.

This matures children in a number of ways. First, it teaches that vulnerability and "not knowing" is a part of life and does not signal weakness. Second, it helps them see that dilemmas are a normal part of life, and third, it shows them how to think through a situation from a faith-informed, value-centered perspective. This is the stuff wisdom is made of. Oh yeah, there's one other positive outcome: When adults talk about their losses and dilemmas, it helps children to talk about theirs.

**Help persons express sadness and grief.** One wise stepparent said, "I'm wondering if your refusal to go to the game with me is because you'd rather be with your dad than me right now. You miss him, huh?" He was right. Acknowledge loss when you see or hear it. "I can see you're hurting right now. Tell me what you're sad about." Then, as I discussed in the story about my son Brennan earlier, ask the child to name what they are feeling. In the beginning, you'll have to name the emotion for them (this teaches young children and kids without a vocabulary for loss how to describe what they feel), but eventually they'll be able to articulate it. Don't assume you know what they are feeling because emotions morph with time and circumstances; encourage them to verbally share it with you every time.

**Take advantage of the windows of opportunity life gives you.** One boy who had a brother living in the other household said, "I'm missing watching my brother grow up." That's a window into his grief. Peer through and become inquisitive. Respond with questions and statements like, "Tell me more. What else do you miss?"

Special days and moments in life also create windows of opportunity to help people grieve. Jerry Sittser wrote his seminal book on grief and grace, *A Grace Disguised,* in 1996, just a few years after his mother, wife, and daughter were tragically killed by a drunk driver in a head-on collision.

Jerry and his three other children survived the crash. Twenty years later he wrote the sequel, *A Grace Revealed,* which recounts the story of his family after the crash and how God redeems all of our stories into his (an absolute must-read book). After the tragedy, Jerry decided not to remarry, but to focus instead on raising his three remaining children. Nearly two decades later, as they graduated into adulthood, he found himself falling in love with Patricia. A wedding was planned. Jerry writes in his book of the wisdom Patricia displayed on the eve of their wedding. The couple had hosted a backyard barbecue the night before their wedding for around sixty people. After enjoying the food and fellowship, Jerry and Patricia spent a few moments honoring the important people in their lives, including Jerry's children and extended family. As Jerry asked everyone to join him in prayer, Patricia interrupted him to say she wanted to pay tribute to one more person. He had no clue who she was talking about. To everyone's surprise, she wanted to honor his deceased wife, Lynda.

Patricia had been a member of the church Jerry's family attended and she had watched their family from a distance, and Lynda in particular. She shared memories of Lynda's ministry within the church and her parenting. She spoke of the accident and how it impacted the church, and her observations through the years of the family grieving together. And then, she concluded by expressing to everyone attending, including Jerry's children, an indebtedness to Lynda. "I am marrying a man and inheriting three step-children who have been profoundly shaped by this good and godly woman."[6] In his book *A Grace Revealed,* Jerry reflects on that moment, noting how deeply Patricia honored the past of him and his children. I would add that she also entered the window of grief that the wedding undoubtedly created for them and honored their grief story. She wasn't intimidated by it nor saw it as something to avoid. Nor did she—and this is very important—create a sad moment for them when she brought up their mother. As a grieving parent, I can tell you most assuredly, at some level they were already sad. She could have left them there, alone and isolated in their sadness, but she didn't. She joined them there. That's one wise stepmom!

**Realize that grief cannot be "fixed."** You can't say something to make it go away, so don't try. Besides, that inadvertently stifles more conversation later. Saying, "I know you're sad that your dad won't call, but you'll feel better tomorrow" does far more harm than good. Instead, say, "I know you're sad that your dad won't call. Tell me about that." Then listen and acknowledge their feelings.

**If your child seems to be doing just fine, keep monitoring.** Children grieve in spurts, and the pain may resurface later, or they could be hiding it to relieve you of the burden of worrying about them. I've often said I worry most about a child who won't cry. Remain open to the possibility that future life circumstances will release emotions that have been hibernating and continue sharing your feelings so the child will know it's safe to talk when the day finally comes.

**Some young children will express their feelings with art or play.** Use whatever allows them to express their loss. Our work with rescued trafficked children in Ghana has reinforced to me the power of art and play therapy for children. They are able to tell us about their traumas without having to use words. You will need to find a qualified art or play therapist to pursue this strategy.

**Make changes in your stepfamily slowly.** Try to keep as much stability in the new home as possible. Remember, more change equals more loss.

**On occasion, biological parents should compartmentalize their life to spend exclusive time with children without the stepparent or stepsiblings.** Regular noncustodial parent access is also a must.

**Keep alive the "touch points" you have with your children.** Important rituals between parents and children, like a wink, holding hands in the park, or bedtime stories communicate love and commitment to children. Modern technology makes one-to-one "touches" very convenient. You can text a message or post something to their Facebook page during the day or weekend. When extended family transitions make you lose some of your touch points, try to reestablish this valuable form of communication.

**Help build connections between multiple generations.** Acknowledge the losses grandparents have experienced with grandchildren (and step-grandchildren). You as an adult child can talk to your parents—the grandparents—and make suggestions as to what their role might be in the new stepfamily.

## Being Driven by Menacing Emotions

But now you must put them all away: anger, wrath, malice, slander, and obscene talk from your mouth. Do not lie to one another, seeing that you have put off the old self with its practices and have put on the new self, which is being renewed in knowledge after the image of its creator. . . . Put on then, as God's chosen ones, holy and beloved, compassionate hearts, kindness, humility, meekness, and patience, bearing with one another and, if one has a complaint against another, forgiving each other; as the Lord has forgiven you, so you also must forgive. And above all these put on love, which binds everything together in perfect harmony.

Colossians 3:8–10, 12–14

In the above Scripture, God declares that his children cannot afford to be driven by negative emotions. We are the reflection of Christ, since we have been clothed with him. I shudder to consider how Jesus would have responded on the day he was to go to the cross had he given in to his emotions. He was fearful of being crucified, yet he "paid no attention to the shame of the cross. He suffered there [for our sake] because of the joy he was looking forward to" (Hebrews 12:2 NIRV). Everyone's emotions get the best of them at some point in time, but you can't afford to be dictated by them; if you are, you can be driven to destructive behavior toward yourself and your stepfamily.

Resentment led Larry to envy the material possessions his ex-wife gained upon her remarriage. She had left Larry and her children after having an affair with a wealthy businessman in their community. Larry was left to raise the children and manage on a moderate income; she was driving a new car, taking tennis lessons with a private instructor, and living without concern for the future. Bitterness, anger, and revenge are close cousins of resentment, so it was no surprise when Larry started using his custody rights to the children for leverage in his legal battles with his ex-spouse. Needless to say, Larry was a terrible co-parent and was responsible for generating a great deal of pain for himself and his children.

Guilt is another menacing emotion. Whether it relates to decisions you made or circumstances your children have been forced to endure through no fault of your own, guilt is debilitating if we allow it to be. For example, parents who think their children "have suffered enough" frequently loosen their discipline and lower their expectations for proper behavior (for more on paralyzed parenting, see *The Smart Stepdad* and *The Smart Stepmom*). This simply teaches children that acting mad, depressed, or hurt gives them license to get their way. While we must be sensitive to children's emotions, we should not fall victim to them. Boundaries need to be firm and expectations maintained.

The prescription for these difficult emotions is forgiveness and releasing the burdens to God. For a full discussion of the forgiveness process, go back to chapter 6, but let this section remind you of the need for managing your pain. Turning over to God what you cannot control relieves your burden and brings back the choice of holiness, compassion, kindness, humility, gentleness, and patience. Be in the Word each and every day so you can more closely imitate your Savior in daily life. Our humanness will never allow us to completely escape our emotions. But with the Spirit's help, we do not have to be subject to them either.

## Combining Holiday and Family Traditions

The stepping-stone that applies most to the area of traditions is flexibility. Traditions—sometimes called rituals—refer to the activities and patterns of interaction that we repeat on a daily, weekly, or even annual basis. How you greet one another at the end of the day is a valuable ritual and just as important over time as your twenty-year tradition of eating Thanksgiving dinner at Grandma's house. Traditions are important because they communicate our identity as a family, and their predictability provides security to our lives. When traditions are broken or changed—even if the change is preferred—something dies inside us. Most people have no idea how important traditions are to them until they can't do them anymore. Oh, how we'll fight to keep our traditions alive.

The issue of belonging and family identity is very much tied to traditions. During the integration years, stepfamilies discover a good bit of positioning taking place between the insiders and outsiders as individuals try to keep their traditions alive. Persons who don't share in a given tradition feel like outsiders and a divided family identity is obvious. But that's to be expected, since the Crockpot has not had time to bring people together. Finding common ground for traditions over time requires a great deal of flexibility, particularly from adults. When parents and stepparents refuse to be flexible, battle lines are drawn, pitting insiders against outsiders.

Holiday traditions in particular put co-parent relationships to the test. If you find yourself in a Fiery Foe or Angry Associate relationship with an ex-spouse, don't expect the holidays to work out just as you had hoped. Yet even the best co-parent relationship, characterized by considerate negotiation regarding time with the children, still can't erase sadness over traditions lost and memories from previous family holidays. Getting used to new traditions, different food, and being with strangers in unfamiliar homes is awkward at best.

Holiday experiences open the underlying hidden dynamics of stepfamily life. Ongoing silent battles between co-parents, for example, often become open battles as parents pressure children regarding how much time they will have together and how travel plans will be made. Loyalty conflicts and issues of loss can easily spoil the joy of the season for children if parents are not careful.

David, an eleven-year-old whom I was counseling, decided it was just easier not to visit his dad at Christmas one year for a number of reasons. First, his parents maintained a low-grade battle for control that demonstrated itself in proposals and counter-proposals of how David would get to his father's house and for how long. A second reason related to his stepmother, who "wants me to be part of her family. I don't want to be with her or my stepbrother when I visit Dad. I just want to be with my dad. Why can't she just leave us alone?" As usual, my conversations with the adults in each household revealed their belief that the other parent was responsible for David's not wanting to visit his dad. Mom blamed Dad; Dad and Stepmom blamed Mom. In truth, it was David who thought it best to keep the peace, not make his parents negotiate (which he knew they couldn't do), and avoid feeling intruded upon by his stepmother when he was with his dad. He just stayed home.

### Practical Strategies for Combining Holiday and Family Traditions

**Be flexible and make sacrifices.** You cannot make everyone happy all the time. Accepting this truth immediately takes away the pressure to give everyone what they want. Being flexible means realizing you can combine, modify, or sacrifice old traditions during a given year in order to give your stepfamily an opportunity to develop new ones. Set the tone for negotiation by showing a willingness to sacrifice. If you won't, why should your children or stepchildren?

**Plan, plan, plan.** As a couple, be proactive in discussing upcoming holiday plans. Determine your preferences and wishes and what sacrifices you will make on behalf of the other home. Then contact the adults in the other home and start negotiating. If you have three or four homes involved in the equation, start planning very early. But, even when plans are set, remain flexible should circumstances change.

**Complex stepfamilies may have to be really creative.** Maintaining a Crockpot mentality may help you find solutions to seemingly impossible situations. Stepfamilies who have children from both adults often find themselves pulled in multiple directions during the holidays. One creative approach is to let each parent and children spend the holidays with the extended family members of their choosing. This may lead them to be in different homes for Easter dinner, yet acknowledges their differing family connections and honors family traditions. This may be particularly useful to new stepfamilies. As the stepfamily integrates over time, the decision to combine holiday activities may be met with less resistance.

**Do what you can do and accept what you cannot change.** Work on your co-parental relationship throughout the year so as to improve your chances of respectful negotiation during the holidays. But realize that ultimately you cannot control the other household and you may have to grin and bear it. When stuck in awkward or tough situations, appeal to difficult family members with "For your dad's sake, let's try to put our differences aside."[7] Hopefully this will be motivation enough. In the end, lay at God's feet what you cannot change and go on.

**Maintain the stepping-stone of patience.** Not all family members will adapt quickly to new traditions or changes to old. Try to give everyone a little "grace-space" to get used to things.

**Parent 364.** It's easy to get so caught up in the uniqueness of the holidays that we obsess in making them perfect. Don't forget that what really matters most to children is what happens the other 364 days a year.

**Give permission.** Give kids your permission to enjoy the other household and all their family members while away from you during the holidays. When a mother says, "I'm thrilled that you will be spending time with your dad and stepmom over Christmas; have lots of fun!" you are releasing them from guilt and worry over how you will fare during their departure.

**Live and learn.** One stepfather found himself disappointed year after year because his stepson had to be rushed off to his father's house in the middle of Christmas Day. He was never able to fully enjoy the day with his wife and stepson because everyone was watching the clock. Eventually he and his wife proposed a change to her ex. As it turned out, her ex-husband was also discouraged each Christmas and was open to changing the visitation agreement. They settled on an alternating arrangement that gave each home an undisturbed Christmas holiday while the other home had an undisturbed Thanksgiving holiday. The loss of togetherness experienced during a given holiday was moderated by the joy they received during the other.

**Be compassionate regarding your child's preferences during the holidays.** At the same time, teach children that sacrifices sometimes have to be made to make the new stepfamily a priority.

**Daily rituals of connection are important to the integration process.** The small, simple behaviors that families repeat on a regular basis communicate care and commitment. Hugs before leaving for school, a special note in a lunch box, Friday night pizza and a family DVD, and Sunday dinner with Grandma are rituals that keep people connected. Biological parents should strive to keep alive pre-stepfamily rituals of connection, while stepparents work to create new comfortable ones. For example, a parent will hug children before leaving for work, and the stepparent may touch them briefly on the arm. A parent may write an "I love you" note and hide it in a backpack while the stepparent's text message notifies the child of a raise in allowance. Take advantage of repeated behaviors to communicate care and develop trust in steprelationships.

### Summary:

Stepfamilies have a number of pitfalls that can be avoided, if not entirely, at least partially. The pitfalls discussed in this chapter, if not addressed, can easily add stress and conflict to your marriage and home. Be proactive as you work to address these and other issues, and seek God's wisdom as you look for solutions.

### Questions for Discussion

■ FOR PARENT-CHILD DISCUSSION (Discretion based on the age of the child and the quality of adult-child relationships is advised.)

1. Kids in stepfamilies often experience what I call the Big Five emotions: loss, sadness, fear, guilt, and confusion. Which of those have you experienced and when?

2. I tried to write down some of the losses I think you may have experienced in life so far. Would you mind looking at the list? How did I do?

3. Would you mind if I shared with you one of the losses I've experienced in life? [After sharing] Now would you mind telling me about one of yours?

4. What new traditions has our family developed that you really enjoy? Which ones could you live without? Which old ones do you miss?

### ■ FOR ALL COUPLES

1. For each person in your home, make a list of the losses he or she has likely experienced. How does this list help you to understand each person's behavior?

2. What losses has this chapter made you aware of that you hadn't considered before?

3. Do a case study in stepfamily loss, fear, and anger. Review the comments made by the Thomas family at the beginning of chapter 1.

   • How are their losses evident in their current fears?

   • List the fears for each person. Discuss the possible similarities in your home.

   • Notice how fear and anger are expressed, especially by John, Susan, and Frank.

4. Review the Practical Strategies for Coping With Unrecognized Loss and Unexpressed Grief in this chapter. Which strategies are you already doing, and which could be improved?

5. Identify and list some of your menacing emotions. What are you doing to lay them at God's feet?

6. What traditions have you yet to sort out? What successes have you had? Share some of your creative solutions.

7. Stepparents: What rituals of connection have you developed thus far with your stepchildren?

### ■ FOR PRE-STEPFAMILY COUPLES

1. Has this current relationship grown during a time of intense grief? Did you wait two to three years before deepening this relationship? If

not, slow down your dating and give yourself time to grieve former losses.

2. Share how you would feel if your dating partner were to admit to feelings of fondness for his or her previous mate.

3. What are your desires for more children?

# Smart Step Five: Side STEP (Part 2)

*Financial pitfalls: managing your money*

> The best food and olive oil are stored up in the houses of wise people. But a foolish man eats up everything he has.
>
> Proverbs 21:20 NIRV

> Well done, good and faithful servant. You have been faithful over a little; I will set you over much. Enter into the joy of your master.
>
> Matthew 25:21

A good writer knows when to ask for help. The finances of stepfamilies are incredibly confusing and diverse, so I asked for help. I have turned to trusted friends and experts on stepfamily finances, Margorie Engel, PhD, and Greg S. Pettys, to contribute significantly to this section. Dr. Engel is past-president of the Stepfamily Association of America, an author and media consultant, and a writer on stepfamily finances. She will discuss the daily management of money and how couples choose to pool their income and pay expenses. Greg Pettys is a certified financial planner and president of Aspire Group, Inc. He

253

will consider long-term perspectives about money, including inheritance, retirement, and estate planning.

In all marriages (first or subsequent) money issues are reported to be a top source of conflict. The popular response to that fact is to blame divorce on money issues. Yes, it is true that differences around the management of money can cause harmonious couples to argue and grow frustrated with each other. But more often than not, in my opinion, the reason money matters divide couples has little to do with the numbers and much to do with their values and issues of power and control.

### Leftovers From the Past

Two-thirds of all remarried couples have financial issues that are tied to their past relationships. Debts, bills, and settlements are among the top relationship issues for remarried couples.[1]

A few years after divorcing his first wife of twenty-seven years, Carter, a financially successful businessman with three adult children, met and fell in love with a younger woman. LaShonda had one child, born to a cohabiting relationship, and had been on her own for many years after the father left her without financial provision. Carter had acquired significant financial assets over the years, while LaShonda barely made it day to day. If it weren't for her parents' support, life would have been very difficult for LaShonda and her child.

Coming together with significantly different experiences and attitudes about money presented some difficulties for Carter and LaShonda, but trust was an even deeper issue. LaShonda needed to know she was valued and prized by Carter and that she had some control over her financial future (something she had not been able to achieve previously), while Carter needed to know that LaShonda's "live for today" attitude about spending would not squander his wealth and children's inheritance. He insisted on a prenuptial agreement. LaShonda accused him of being a control monger. Carter defended his decision as necessary in order to provide long-term for his children. Both struggled to trust the other to be fair and a permanent fixture in their life—again, something neither of their previous partners had done.

When the daily matters of money management and long-term decisions regarding financial planning are not comfortable to both parties, fear increases in marriage. When fear increases, trust decreases, which decreases emotional safety. And not feeling safe taints every aspect of the relationship.

Fear, as I've discussed throughout this book, can exist separately and apart from the specifics of finances. Leftover pain from the past and the fear of more pain can color how one perceives the issues of power, autonomy, separateness, and long-term provision. Matters of fear and trust are a common fuel to the fires of financial disagreement; they must always be considered an integral part of what divides couples (look again at chapter 5 for more on managing fear in marriage). In addition, you must follow sound financial principles if you are going to manage your home and future well. For advice on that we turn to Dr. Engel and Greg Pettys.

*The following section is written by Dr. Margorie Engel.*

## Managing Money: Daily Considerations

Money does not have a neutral connotation in stepfamilies. Money may be a major issue for remarried couples because trust, commitment, and the guarantee of permanence are underlying issues. As a result, it is hard to put together the perfect money management package. However, because of previous life experiences, these couples are typically ready to search for creative solutions to new challenges. Stepfamilies often have a combination of three money pots: yours, mine, and ours.

Some remarried couples cannot fathom pooling all of their financial resources, while other couples can't imagine not doing it. Each side is convinced their philosophy is the secret stepfamily strategy to a happy financial relationship.[2]

### Separate Accounts: "Yours" and "Mine"

Husbands and wives may be embarrassed to initiate a discussion about ways to keep stepfamily finances separate. Feeling the need for separate money seems to evolve from circumstance as much as temperament. When couples desire separate finances, they are acknowledging that they have separate or different interests and that they want to make certain financial choices without needing to ask permission.

Even though they love each other deeply, the desire to avoid potential hassles prompts many couples to keep their money as separate as possible. Avoiding dependency is another reason for choosing to keep separate stepfamily money. Divorce laws have sent a clear message to married women that financial dependency is not, and will not be, rewarded. Stepfamily couples may deliberately arrange their finances to preserve individual autonomy in routine money matters, even though most of them have not negotiated a formal financial contract.

> **To Spend or Not to Spend: How Should the Spending of the Other Home Affect Ours?**
>
> Find the answer in the Smart Questions, Smart Answers bonus material, available at SmartStep families.com/view/learn.

Two separate families living under the same roof tend to be created when each parent pays for herself or himself and her or his children's expenses. These "separate pot" couples strongly believe that each partner must contribute an equal share toward stepfamily household expenses, which is seldom fair. Most wives do not earn as much as their husbands, and incoming child-support payments don't often make up the difference. Therefore, her 50 percent of the family's expenses will be a much larger percentage of her income than her husband's 50 percent share of the expenses. When this equal concept doesn't work out, the wife winds up feeling dependent and the husband feels he is paying too much. The old model of men providing all financial support for the family doesn't fit for stepfamilies; neither does the newer idea of a fifty/fifty split.

A completely separate system also tends to fall apart in a stepfamily financial crisis. Two particularly decisive moments illustrate this well: A can't-turn-down career opportunity in another city (which usually forces the other partner out of their job and, therefore, provision for their children) or a corporate downsizing causing job loss. By necessity, these situations awkwardly force separate pot couples into merging their finances—at least until the crisis is resolved.

### Mixed Accounts: "Yours," "Mine," and "Ours"

Even when remarried couples begin a relationship with the intention of keeping money separate, they tend to drift into at least some pooling of funds. Because they are married, couples cannot legally escape responsibility for each other's economic decisions. From a practical standpoint, individual preferences for separate stepfamily accounts often begin to take a backseat to convenience.

It appears that the best of all worlds for many remarried couples may be one of two variations on the "three pots—yours, mine, and ours" system:

- Small separate accounts and a large joint account
- Large separate accounts and a minimal joint account

Joint accounts are funded equally or, more often, in proportion to each spouse's income. Stepfamily couples will compromise on issues that are joint financial responsibilities and handle their own accounts independently.

For most stepfamily couples, each spouse comes to the remarriage with a credit history, credit cards, and individual bank accounts. They may also have brokerage accounts and/or retirement accounts. Couples typically continue to maintain their own accounts. Remarried couples often agree that each will pay for ordinary expenses related to their own biological children (residential and child-support payments), insurance premiums, repairs and maintenance of property individually owned (cars, rental property), and personal expenses for clothing, business costs, medical expenses, hobbies, and gifts. Joint expenses such as rent/mortgage, groceries, entertainment, and family/couple vacations are paid for in a flexible manner according to ability to pay. Most remarried couples also struggle valiantly to accumulate savings for emergency funds and investments.

Financial advisors suggest keeping cash flow separate from investments. It is preferable to fund joint accounts for children and household with the income stream from employment and/or child support. This avoids the typical situation wherein wives spend most of their money for consumables (family food, clothing, vacations, treats for the children) and husbands put most of their money into appreciable assets (mortgage, stocks, retirement funds).

### One Big "Ours" Account

Stepfamilies often find themselves easing into pooling their finances. This pool drift frequently starts by establishing a joint vacation fund, purchasing a replacement household appliance, or having an "ours" child. Sometimes there's a purely psychological transition.

Stepfamily experts Gordon and Carri Taylor suggest you create a "Gripe Agreement." Here are the rules: When making a significant financial decision, if one of you is clearly uncomfortable with proceeding, the answer is "no." If one is not necessarily uncomfortable, but less enthusiastic than the other and you decide to proceed, the less enthusiastic partner gives up "Gripe Rights" and you are in this together. If for some reason the decision doesn't work out as expected, there will be no "I told you so. . . . I really didn't want to do this anyway" talk. This will help you take personal responsibility for your actions, be accountable to one another, and build trust.[3]

When all of the money is put into a common pot, couple decision-making is critical to successful money management. Confrontation may arise regarding one spouse dominating financial decisions or non-recognition of the pooling—and that is usually what the remarried couple is trying to avoid.

It is important to make basic decisions about management of stepfamily money in the common pot. These include:

- A record-keeping system (running totals or monthly tallies)
- Who will be responsible for bill-paying from the account
- What will be paid for out of the joint account
- How much each spouse can withdraw without discussing it with the other

The joint bank account needs to be set up where it is convenient for each spouse to deposit, withdraw money, and manage the account with online or smart phone access. As with most team efforts, husbands and wives typically handle different financial activities according to their ability to get the job done. Sometimes, especially after a bad financial experience in a prior marriage, couples need to earn each other's trust.

### However Money Is Handled . . .

Separate accounts, pooled accounts, or a his-hers-ours accounts system—there's no absolute right or wrong way to handle the finances in a remarriage. The comfortable balance will change with the amount of money available, the length of the marriage, and changing needs. The initial stepfamily money management system needs to be flexible, not carved in stone.

Talk about each of the options. During this discussion, consider how you will treat each other if the initial choice doesn't work well after a trial period. Once the foundation of your new financial system has been laid, schedule regular review periods. Ask yourself, "Is it broken? Should we fix it?" Something is always working and something is always failing. Keep the choices that are working well and replace the duds with new options. It's an ongoing process that requires compromise and renegotiation.[4]

### Keys to Financial Harmony

- For couples to share the relationship spirit, each partner should have a reasonable amount of discretionary money to meet personal needs.

- Each spouse must have credit in their own name. It is too important a commodity in our society not to be protected (in case of spousal death).

- It's very important for each spouse to keep some readily available money for emergencies.

- Marriages need nurturing. All couples need financial plans that provide money for private time and enjoyment together. One of the essential elements of any healthy financial plan is periodic celebration of its achievements.

### Good Reasons to Share Financial Management:

- It's fair.

- A lifestyle is determined by spending decisions, so both partners deserve a voice in making decisions.

---

**What do You Value About Money?**

"Highly satisfied couples have common values about the spending and saving of their money. Happy couples showed at least 80 percent agreement on what they would spend their money on, but unhappy couples had less than half that rate of agreement. Likewise, the percentage of happy couples who agree on how much money they should save is nearly three times that of unhappy couples. Value similarities or differences prove once again to be a strong factor in what unites or divides a couple."[5]

---

- It's effective.
- Sharing makes for better decisions, actions, and further reason to trust your spouse.
- It's successful.
- People who share in decisions have a reason for making them work.

*Decisions, Decisions:*

1. When money is separate:

   - What money is to be separate (checking/savings/investment accounts)?
   - How much will each partner contribute to the household?

2. When money is pooled:

   - What money, if any, is to be personal?
   - What money is to be shared?
   - What expense categories are most important?
   - Will yearly expense plans be created? By whom? How closely will they be followed?

3. Who will manage the books?

   - How will they be kept?
   - How often: weekly or monthly?
   - How accurately?

4. How much discussion is appropriate (and whose opinion prevails) when purchases are made?

5. Whether money is kept separate or shared:

   - How will financial emergencies and unexpected expenses be handled?
   - When will credit be used?[6]

> ## Common Mistakes in Stepfamily Estate Planning[7]
>
> - Leaving everything to the surviving spouse with the assumption that the individual will take care of the children. Even with good intentions, sometimes the money or assets are swallowed up by the surviving spouse's creditors, new spouse, or children.
> - Failing to update beneficiary designations on non-probate assets (life insurance, retirement plans, and payable-on-death accounts).
> - Leaving significant property outright to minor children. If the ex-spouse is the guardian of the children, the ex will likely have significant control over the assets.
> - Not taking into account the surviving spouse's right to make a claim against the deceased spouse's estate for a statutory or elective share.
> - Failing to communicate plans during life to their spouse and loved ones.

## Estate Planning

I (Ron) was returning calls one day, and was elated to find myself talking with an eighty-year-old man who was proactively trying to get some answers to his financial questions. "I'm getting married again," he said, "and I want to make sure both my wife and my kids are well cared for—and I don't want them fighting over what is left after I die." The more we talked, the more I recognized his voice. The name left on the recorded message sounded familiar, but I couldn't place it before the call. But after listening to him for a few minutes, I connected the dots. The gentleman was a famous former NFL football player turned TV personality. Yet, here he was, like everyone else facing the unique financial issues of remarriage, trying to figure out how to be responsible to his loved ones and prevent unnecessary conflict between stepfamily members. "Can you get a prenuptial agreement and still have a covenant marriage?" he asked.

I shared with him what I'm about to share with you. "I can tell, sir, that you are looking for the win-win arrangement between your new wife and your kids." He affirmed that I was on target. "A prenup makes people feel like they are planning for failure of the marriage—that doesn't engender trust or confidence in the couple. I've got something better. My friend Greg Pettys recommends a Shared Covenant Agreement instead. A Shared Covenant Agreement is designed to actually clarify many emotionally charged issues and to reaffirm commitment to the permanency of the marriage. Shared Covenant Agreements are not for every remarrying couple, but if done in the right spirit, will allow a Christian couple to focus on a detailed vision of an optimistic future together."

I then recommended that he find a qualified trust and estate lawyer who shared his Christian values in order to ask if the Shared Covenant Agreement was appropriate in his case. As Greg points out, a Shared Covenant Agreement should always be a part of an overall financial and estate plan, which incorporates other financial tools and legal advice.

Before turning to Greg's advice, I do want to explain why many Christian financial planners insist that couples consider the possibility of divorce. On the surface this consideration is offensive to Christian couples, who obviously believe that marriage is for life. In my experience, however, when someone has already experienced a divorce, they can't help but be exceedingly aware that it can happen again. Life has already taught them that it takes two to tango, but the dance is over when only one leaves the dance floor. They can't help but worry about it on some level.

And then there's the related question of how children will be provided for in the event of a breakup. Or what if the biological parent dies? How will assets be divided between a new spouse and biological heirs? This is an extremely important question given that laws around the world are biased toward blood relatives and marriage partners, but may not represent the wishes of the parent/spouse. Even further, estate laws make it possible, should you die, for your assets to be passed along not only to your kids, but to a new spouse of your widow. Ultimately, all of these questions and estate issues need to be considered and settled.

Again, let me repeat: Financial planning that gives voice to these possibilities is, ironically enough, calming for many couples. They feel as though they have gone the extra mile to provide for their spouse and children should the unthinkable happen. That can actually bring a sense of peace to the relationship and reduce resentment. Not everyone will agree

> **Money Talk**
>
> "Simply put, there is no one-size-fits-all estate plan for the blended family. Every estate plan for a blended family is different, and the concerns and goals of the families are undoubtedly different also."[8]

with this thinking, but it is a unique aspect of remarriage finances worth considering.

*The following section is written by Greg S. Pettys, president of Aspire Group, Inc.*

### Shared Covenant Agreement[9]

A Shared Covenant Agreement or SCA is a written agreement drafted by a qualified trust and estate lawyer, preferably one who shares your Christian values and understands domestic relations law. It is not merely a legal document, though it can and should be entered into with legally binding authority. An SCA is a detailed declaration of loving financial intentions between dating or married partners in the event of death, divorce, disability, or the need for long-term care. Based upon Christian values, an SCA is more than just legally binding—it is morally binding. The specific stipulations can vary but will always center around the loved ones within the blended family network (including the homes of former spouses/parents). It can include specific commitments about financial support, details concerning the distribution of certain assets, as well as the rights, roles, responsibilities, and overall total well-being of spouses, children, stepchildren, grandchildren, stepgrandchildren, parents, stepparents, grandparents, stepgrandparents, and other significant relationships.

> **A Word of Advice**
> - Pay the money to get your estate planning done right.
> - Provide your financial planner all the legal and financial documents necessary so he or she can adequately advise you and give you confidence that your intentions are being carried out.

Consider Greg and Jenny Smith, a Christian couple contemplating remarriage. If things keep moving in the right direction, their big day is only six months away. Greg has two young boys from a previous marriage and Jenny has a teenage girl named Melissa; they both would like to have at least two more children together. Greg is a successful land developer and has recently received a modest inheritance from his deceased aunt. He has had difficulty keeping debt out of his life. Being a CPA who dots her I's and crosses her T's, Jenny, on the other hand, is very good at managing money. She currently has been caring for her elderly mother, Eunice. Her mother is generally healthy, but recently has begun to forget some important things. Jenny is concerned that soon she may need to make good on her promise to move her mom in with her. Greg's ex-spouse has made it clear that she will not allow him to take the boys out of the state, and furthermore that they will one day attend in-state colleges. Jenny never hears from or sees her ex-husband, who has had legal problems and a lien on their still jointly owned home. Greg has not yet had the nerve to tell Jenny that he definitely wants his business and some of his recent inheritance to go to his boys instead of Jenny or Melissa. He is willing to make provision for them and any future children they may have together, but wants his sons to maintain control of his business and the inheritance from his aunt.

What did the creation of a Shared Covenant Agreement do for this couple? First, it required them to sit down and share all their financial facts, strengths, and weaknesses. Jenny found out about Greg's debt problem. Greg discovered that his future mother-in-law may live with Jenny. Together they agreed to purchase long-term care insurance for her mother and to work toward assisted living support instead of carrying all of the responsibility themselves.

Greg communicated his interest in a Qualified Terminable Interest Trust or QTIP, which was drafted by his attorney. In the event of his death it assures Jenny income from the inheritance he received from his aunt, and also includes provision for his sons. In addition, the SCA motivated Greg to finally have a buy-sell agreement written for his business. That document, which gives his sons first rights of refusal to buy his company funded with a life insurance policy on Greg, is now reflected in the SCA along with references to the QTIP. Plus, the SCA clearly spells out that Greg is going to take out an additional one million dollars of permanent life insurance on himself, and name Jenny, her children, and any future children they may have together as beneficiaries. The policy will be owned by a trust so that the value of the benefit will not be included in Greg's estate and will provide for their needs.

Finally, the Shared Covenant Agreement addressed how they would manage money on a daily basis: Jenny would take oversight of their joint budget and they would share a joint savings account (but each would maintain 40 percent of all liquid assets in separate accounts for the first five years of the remarriage). They also agreed that Greg would seek counseling and become accountable for his debt so they could eliminate it.

In the end, the SCA provided this couple peace of mind regarding their finances and their relationship, which deepened their confidence and trust in each other. In the unlikely event of a divorce, every asset is accounted for, and Greg and Jenny's prior commitments can all be maintained without much disruption of either of their lifestyles. Greg has the peace of mind that his sons will have the choice and liquid funds to buy their father's business. Jenny, her daughter, and any future children they may have together get the benefit of the one million dollar life insurance policy, and Jenny's mother has the long-term care insurance to fund her care. The financial promises are all made in an attitude of Christian care regardless of what happens to the marriage.

### What Are the Advantages of a Shared Covenant Agreement?

Shared Covenant Agreements allow for a time of full and complete discovery of all your financial matters. There must be integrity and complete transparency. This full and fair disclosure is a legal requirement with a prenuptial agreement, but a moral one in the Shared Covenant Agreement. You must share the intimate details of both of your balance sheets and income statements. You may discover important facts about each other that have been hidden or previously unshared. You will find out each other's income, assets, and liabilities, and any impending inheritances or big business deals around the corner. If the possibility of highly personal information being publicly disclosed is a deterrent, you can also ask the attorney for a confidentiality agreement to ensure that the information is held confidential. Creating a Shared Covenant Agreement without complete financial disclosure could later undermine trust in the marriage.

You will also gain from the process of creating a Shared Covenant Agreement by communicating openly about the topic of money. This, of course, can occur when already married, but before marriage is the most ideal time to work through money matters. You may discover, for example, that merging all of your separate financial assets and debts may be a recipe for a disaster given tax, inheritance, and domestic relations laws.

The Agreement is essentially allowing you to write the rules for your marriage. It takes your marital vows and brings much needed detail to what are often complex stepfamily issues. Many remarrying couples have considerable wealth to protect and certain hard-to-value assets that need clarity for proper estate planning. On the other hand, a Shared Covenant Agreement also protects you from a debt-laden second spouse. It helps you determine, before tying the knot, just how much of their credit card bills you will be personally liable for in the event the marriage does not make it for some unforeseen reason. Keeping some assets in only one of the spouse's names might be necessary to protect them from any future creditors.

> **Money Talk**
>
> Only 45 percent of adult Americans have a will. Without a will, intestacy takes over under current law. Intestacy favors the surviving spouse as the recipient of the property and usually puts the surviving spouse in control of the estate even if there are children from a prior union. Learn more at mystatewill.com.[10]

More important to many of us in remarried situations, the Shared Covenant Agreement alleviates worries about whether your children from a previous marriage will be provided for. It ensures that your estate is distributed as you wish and gives peace of mind to the business owner for the transferal of this large portion of wealth to the right people in the most efficient manner.

If you have or foresee having a business or professional practice, having a Shared Covenant Agreement is a must in order to have it equitably valued and disposed of if the surviving spouse cannot or will not run it upon the owner's death.

For those who expect to one day receive sizable inheritances during marriage, having a Shared Covenant Agreement could alleviate any concerns that the person delegating your inheritance has regarding your second marriage. This layer of planning will give confidence to the executor of an estate to distribute assets without delay due to any confusion or relational friction.

Older couples entering into second marriages may have retirement issues or long-term care issues to grapple with. This is another reason for having an SCA.

### What Are the Disadvantages of a Shared Covenant Agreement?

Some are opposed to the Shared Covenant Agreement on moral or philosophical grounds because it seems to plan for divorce. Is this written Agreement an example of mistrust or a lack of faith in God? Could even raising the subject have a negative effect on your relationship? It is important not to force your partner to enter into this discussion; doing so could bring harm to the relationship. When first bringing up the subject, test the water carefully to see how open your partner is to the topic. Do not pressure or coerce the other to sign anything or you will completely ruin the foundation of trust. If bringing up the topic results in significant negativity, speak directly to your financial planner to see if there may be any other way to achieve the same desired outcomes and financial goals without using the Shared Covenant Agreement (see "Alternative Options" below).

### Special Categories of Marital Property That Create the Need to Consider a Shared Covenant Agreement

Shared Covenant Agreements can be especially helpful with these five types of marital properties:

1. Pensions and other retirement benefits
2. Stock options
3. Professional licenses and degrees
4. Closely held corporations and other businesses
5. Professional goodwill

**Pensions and other retirement benefits.** Entering into a Shared Covenant Agreement will save you a lot of time, hassle, and costs if you have the largest amount of your assets in qualified retirement plans and pensions.

In most states, pensions and other retirement benefits are considered marital property if any part of them is earned or accrued during your marriage. This is true even if you cannot access your retirement funds or you do not actually receive your pension benefits until many years after your marriage has ended. Further, this is true even if your pension is not vested at the time of your divorce and you still must work additional years in order to guarantee your payout.

Your ex-spouse will almost always be entitled to their portion of benefits. For example, let's say that you were married only ten years and your pension required you to work for twenty in order to be vested. That does not mean the ex-spouse is out of the picture. He or she can still claim half of the pension.

Two methods of dividing pension and retirement plans are being used in these cases. Since the pension holder's ex-spouse often has claim to half of the pension holder's assets, one option is to buy out the non-pension-holding spouse's share by offering lump sum cash payment or making up the difference with other marital assets.

**Money Talk**

U.S. law requires that a non-working spouse be the beneficiary of a qualified retirement plan. Your children cannot be named unless your spouse waives in writing any interest in the plan.[11]

The second method is for the pension holder to pay the other spouse when they are actually paid by using a Qualified Domestic Relations Order or QDRO. This saves the pension holder from having to pay before the pension is actually paying out.

The QDRO may also allow the pension holder to avoid all the taxes on paying a lifetime of pension income out to the ex-spouse at once and instead will require the spouse that gets the QDRO to pay the taxes as money is received.

Social Security benefits are a sub-topic under pensions and retirement benefits. Unlike other types of retirement benefits, Social Security benefits do not count as marital property in divorces. However, you may be able to receive spousal Social Security benefits based on your spouse's Social Security contributions even after you have divorced. This is true as long as the spouse was eligible for Social Security benefits. See the website of the Social Security Administration at www.ssa.gov for more details.

**Stock options.** Stock options are another area where spelling out your commitments in a loving way within the Shared Covenant Agreement is a stabilizing factor to the finances and the remarriage. Options like these often provide employees the opportunity to buy or sell the company's stock at a predetermined price, called a "strike price," after a certain period of time. They are typically nontransferable and non-assignable.

If you are awarded stock options during your marriage, most courts will consider those options marital property, even if you do not actually exercise those options during your marriage.

This is still the case even if the stock options are not yet vested at the time of the divorce and you must hold them for more time before exercising.

In the event of an unforeseen divorce, courts usually must first determine what portion of the stock options was actually earned during the marriage. This could be somewhat complex because there are two forms of stock options: One is given as an incentive to work hard in the future and another as thanks for hard work done in the past. So it may be difficult at first to determine which type the option is and therefore how much of the stock option is considered marital property. The courts may award completely opposite rulings based on their view of forward- or backward-looking options.

Regardless of the type, timing, vesting, or other complex options, the Shared Covenant Agreement will simplify things and provide a clear directive to the court, which can alleviate many potential problems.

**Professional licenses and degrees.** There is a small possibility—yet a real possibility—that a divorce court could consider your professional license or degree as "marital property." If so, then it would be subject to division. Though a license or degree cannot be sold for profit or handed over to anyone else, each state has its own variation of how professional licenses and degrees are considered at the time of a divorce.

According to attorneys that specialize in this area, this issue has morphed somewhat over the last fifty years and requires each couple to check with legal counsel as to how to draft the SCA within the framework of their state's laws. New York is one of the few states that does look at the professional license or degree itself as a divisible asset, whereas most other states also consider the future earning power that a license or degree provides. States have been known to award a non-licensed or degreed spouse in order to compensate for their sacrifices and contributions toward their spouse's license or degree.[12]

When you think about it, a license or degree could be the most valuable asset acquired during the marriage! Let's say that your spouse put you through medical school and then into your advanced surgical training. Now that you are a successful surgeon with $775,000 per year of earnings in your early thirties, your present value might be several million dollars to the divorce courts of New York.

Especially if you will be the supporting spouse, my recommendation is that you consider looking into the value of having a Shared Covenant Agreement before entering into your relationship. Doing so can save a ton of headache and heartache down the road.

**Closely held corporations and other businesses.** Businesses of any kind that are built during a marriage are generally considered marital property in the event of the unplanned for and unforeseen divorce. Even businesses or closely held corporations that are invested into before marriage have often increased in value, and that increase will also usually be deemed marital property.

Businesses and shares of closely held corporations are challenging to value and to divide in a divorce. Often a couple jointly owns a family business, and if it is not equally owned in joint tenancy, then typically the spouse most involved in the business (and who holds shares of closely held corporations) buys out the other spouse's interest in it. However, this often involves the costly and long drawn-out process of having the business valued, using expert analysis of appraisers and financial professionals. Several valuation methods are employed, which may end in a wide range of valuation figures by the professionals employed by both spouses. One such method is the capitalization of earnings method, where the businesses and shares of closely held corporations are given a multiple of earnings somewhere between one and four times net earnings to arrive at a dollar value.

The end result is that either you or your ex-spouse now owns or expects to invest in a business or closely held corporation. Was this a desired financial outcome discussed prior to marriage? Having a Shared Covenant Agreement that carefully outlines both the business owner's and non-owner spouse's wishes could bring clarity to this reality.

**Professional goodwill.** Be aware that the goodwill or reputation value of your professional private practice could be subject to division in the event the marriage does not last as expected.

In these situations, the only asset of any real value is the practice's reputation and prestige. Though the practice might have a very low business valuation, using traditional methods, there are other ways to value in these cases. No, you can't deposit in a bank your reputation, but the goodwill value of the business ensures that the business will be profitable in the future.

Depending on the unique facts in each case and the state in which you live, the goodwill value of your professional practice may or may not be considered marital property. One method commonly used is the capitalization of excess earnings method. The earnings of your practice are compared to the earnings of an average professional in your field and geographical area, with experience, expertise, and education similar to your own. The difference in your earnings and the average earnings of a comparable professional is called your "excess earnings," and is then multiplied by a capitalization factor to arrive at a value for your professional goodwill. Therefore, it might be in your best interest to consider an SCA, which outlines exactly how your professional goodwill is to be handled in the event of a divorce.

It is a mistake to think that a common buy-sell agreement that sets forth the value for your practice's professional goodwill will be enough. The courts do not automatically accept the goodwill values set forth in partnership agreements when making decisions in a divorce. Your partnership agreement might provide that your practice's goodwill is worth zero, for example, so the partnership will have to pay as little as possible if one partner decided to leave the practice. A divorce court, however, might still decide that your practice's goodwill is worth several hundred thousand dollars, despite the provisions of your partnership agreement.

Spouses have certain automatic rights to each other's estates. Thus your business assets might end up distributed completely different from your intentions without a Shared Covenant Agreement in place.

**Money Talk**

Property titled as joint tenants with rights of survivorship will pass to the surviving spouse no matter what your will says. Have an estate planner review real estate deeds to determine how that property will pass at death and whether changes need to be made to preexisting deeds.[13]

**Alternative options.** One alternative is to have an attorney draft a trust and use it as a financial tool that may get some of the desired results. Keep in mind that this trust will not address all of the nonfinancial aspects of remarried life that the Shared Covenant Agreement addresses.

Often individuals have two goals when planning for a remarriage with children. One goal is to provide for your new spouse, and the other is to make sure that your children from the first marriage receive the inheritance intended. This ensures that your assets do not pass along to any future spouse of your husband or wife.

A Qualified Terminable Interest Property Trust (QTIP) is an increasingly popular choice in these cases. Here's why: It allows you to leave your assets to your surviving spouse for the duration of his or her lifetime. When your surviving spouse dies, the assets in the QTIP are passed on to your children, grandchildren, or charity. It allows you to control your assets from your grave! Your current spouse can have access to all of the income from the QTIP and your children are provided for. Moreover, the QTIP allows your spouse the "unlimited marital deduction" so that the inheritance is exempt from estate taxes.

Make sure that you find and work with a qualified trust and estate lawyer who understands domestic law to determine whether the QTIP is appropriate in your case. There may be yet other ways to gift now and restructure your estate to achieve all of your estate goals.

### When to Start Planning

Before marriage, do not wait for engagement to begin planning whether to utilize a trust or Shared Covenant Agreement. Waiting too long to bring up emotionally laden issues like inheritances or estate legacies may open the door for tension and problems later. Consider these discussions part of your decision whether to marry; once both of you are satisfied with your financial plans, you will feel a greater confidence in your decision to marry. If already married, we suggest you talk through these matters as soon as possible.

Together with your partner and a Christian trust and estate lawyer you will want to discuss:

- How the Agreement affects all of your current and future property rights as well as those of your children and grandchildren from all marriages.

- Whether the Agreement takes into consideration career sacrifices you may make during the marriage.

- College funding for his, hers, and "ours" children. Who will be paying what amounts or percentages of the college bill? Is your philosophy the same for all of the children? What about advanced degrees? Keep in mind that all spouses, including ex-spouses, have assets and income that will be looked at for the FAFSA when college aid applications are made.

- How to handle the support of elderly parents and other family issues involving long-term care.

- Specific guidelines on roles in the budgeting, asset management, and debt management for each spouse. Should accounts be joint or separate, and if separate, what amounts or percentages will each contribute to expenses?

- All current estate planning documents, their purpose, and who to contact (phone numbers, addresses of all key financial advisor team members, etc.) regarding each.

- All business planning documents like the buy-sell agreement. Include in simple terms the intentions of the owner-spouse.

- Issues such as living wills, final illnesses, burial arrangements, and memorial services.[14]

### Action Steps

So there you have it—Estate Planning 101. Of course, working through the actual details is the fun part, right? So where do you start? In their excellent guide *Estate Planning for the Blended Family,* L. Paul Hood Jr. and Emily Bouchard outline five action steps to get you going. With their permission, I (Ron) share them with you.

> **Money Talk**
>
> Name contingent beneficiaries for your non-probate property so that if your original beneficiary doesn't survive you, your non-probate property won't pass to your estate.[15]

1. Review any estate-planning documents you have that are signed and legally binding. Do they reflect your current wishes and current family structure? Note any changes you see that need to be made and write down any questions that may have occurred to you while reading this section. You may be considering one or more of the following questions:

   - Is our real estate in joint tenancy and is this taking care of both of our most important values and concerns?

   - Who are the written beneficiaries of our individual and shared non-probate property? This includes life insurance, annuities, retirement plans, and Registered Retirement Savings Plans (in Canada), IRA's (in the USA), and pay-on-death (POD) accounts.

273

Are these the beneficiaries I want now? Do we have backup beneficiaries named?

2. Determine the status of your power of attorney and durable power of attorney or advanced health-care directives. Are they in place and with the people you want to be in those roles at this time? Are those people aware of their roles and what is required of them in those roles? Are they aware of your expressed wishes?

3. Put all of these relevant documents in a locked, protected file and make copies for both you and your partner. Make sure the relevant parties in your estate plan know where these documents are located.

4. Create a binder with tabs for each section so that as you go about your estate planning, all the information you are gathering is easily accessible in one place for yourself, and for your family members, should something happen to you or your partner unexpectedly.

5. Schedule specific appointments in your calendar where the two of you can tackle your estate-planning questions and concerns. If it's scheduled, you'll take action and it will get done![16]

Finally, you might consider hiring a consultant to help you wade through the details. If nothing else, review my list of recommended resources to guide you.

## Recommended Reading

*For more on stepfamily finances review these resources.*

1. *Estate Planning for Blended Families: Providing for Your Spouse and Children in a Second Marriage* by Richard E. Barnes (2009). Berkley, CA: Nolo. The Sample Estate Planning Questionnaire and Sample Estate Plans (found as appendix A and B in that book) are especially helpful.

2. *Estate Planning for the Blended Family* by L. Paul Hood Jr. and Emily Bouchard (2012). Bellingham, WA: Self-Counsel Press, Inc.

3. *The Smart Stepfamily Marriage* by Ron L. Deal and David H. Olson (2015). Bloomington, MN: Bethany House. See the chapter on Remarriage Finances.

4. *Money Advice for Your Successful Remarriage* by Patricia Schiff Estess (2001). Lincoln, NE: ASJA Press.

5. View the series of Step-Money articles at SmartStepfamilies.com/view/step-money.

## Questions for Discussion

■ FOR PARENT-CHILD DISCUSSION (Discretion based on the age of the child and the quality of adult-child relationships is advised.)

1. With teens or young adults: From your perspective, what seems to have changed over time regarding how money is managed in our family?

2. With teens or young adults: Do you feel that things are fair in our home regarding how money is spent? What could be different from your standpoint?

3. With teens or young adults: What would you like to learn about money management? Can we share with you our values and why we make the decisions we do?

4. With adult children: What items would you like to keep in the family line (e.g., deceased mother's dishes or keepsakes)? What questions do you have about inheritance, assets, etc.? (This is also an opportunity to inform the children of your financial arrangements should you die.)

■ FOR ALL COUPLES

1. The topic of money often stirs deep feelings within persons who have experienced unwanted loss and family transition. What emotions were stirred within you as you read this chapter?

2. Share any fears (money ghosts) you have identified related to money and one story that illustrates where the fear came from.

3. Which, if any, of your preferences or assumptions about money management were challenged by this chapter? What do you need more time to consider?

4. What has been your system of money management so far? Share whatever changes you believe necessary at this point in time.

5. Unity in your system of money management is vital. What elements of money management do you already agree on? What's your plan to

address the ones you don't agree on (e.g., take a Christian stewardship course or hire a financial consultant)?

6. Share your thoughts about the Shared Covenant Agreement strategy.

7. If you do not have an estate plan, what is your first step to creating one?

### ■ FOR PRE-STEPFAMILY COUPLES

1. Schedule a time to discuss your ideas about money management in the new family. Start by trying to develop a tentative plan as you work through the Decisions, Decisions questions.

2. It is strongly advised that couples work with a financial planner to create their estate plan before the wedding. What steps need to be taken for you to do so?

3. In the meantime, start by working through a series of questions on money management for dating couples. Find them here: SmartStep families.com/view/money-questions.

# Smart Step Six: STEP Through

*The wilderness: Overcoming special challenges*

Every craftsman makes excellent use of his tools. The craft of building a strong family requires a variety of tools—and the skill to use them.

The journey for stepfamilies to the Promised Land can be long or relatively short, but one thing is certain: the journey will bring challenges. This chapter discusses special challenges in the Christian stepfamily home and gives strategies for managing their impact. Special challenges include managing sexuality and spiritual formation in stepfamily children.

## Sexuality

A mother once asked me, "We really don't have to talk about this, do we?" Unfortunately, yes, we do. The matter of sexuality in the stepfamily is important (it's important in any home), whether you want it to be or not. Educating children about healthy sexuality is an important part of all Christian parenting. Protecting children from the sexual abuses and myths of the world is another. Stepfamily couples, like biological parents, must keep both of these objectives in mind as they raise their children and stepchildren. But the stepfamily has an added challenge that must be addressed.

While the research on stepfamily sexual exchanges is still coming in, it does seem that children not living with both of their biological parents run higher risks of child sexual abuse from both family members and others.[1] This finding is not limited to stepfamilies but pertains to children living in single-parent and cohabiting homes as well. Don't assume, however, that this is due to the "less than ideal" structure of a stepfamily. Family structure itself, that is, the composition of a home (single parent, biological, or stepfamily), is not as responsible for this increased risk of sexual abuse as is the process of interactions within the home. In other words, sexual boundaries are not going to be crossed just because you live in a stepfamily, but there is increased risk, and you need to protect your home from the potential devastating impact of sexual abuse. When you have poor adult psychological functioning, new relationships with unclear roles and boundaries, poorly defined values, and stress that leads to a lack of proper parental monitoring, there is vulnerability that can lead to sexual abuse.[2] In addition, when families are not proactive in managing sexual boundaries between stepsiblings, temptation can become opportunity. Biologically related family members have a natural taboo against sexual attraction; siblings do not look on their siblings with sexual desire. But stepsiblings don't have the DNA taboo, making attraction one step more likely.

Karen and Frank learned something that would shake the foundations of their stepfamily. For a period of two years, Karen's fifteen-year-old son had been entering his fourteen-year-old stepsister's room to fondle her genitals. "How could this happen?" asked Karen. "Frank and I have been married for ten years. The kids have known each other since they were five and four. They've grown up together. How could something like this happen now?" Her shock and pain were quite evident.

The discovery of sexually violating behavior is both traumatic and baffling. How *could* something like this happen?

### The Command for Closeness

When two families come together, there is an assumption that people will form affections for one another. Displays of affection, warmth, and hugs of endearment are non-sexual ways of communicating this coming together. However, these non-sexual touches can take on sexual implications for confused teenagers or people whose psychological boundaries are not strong.

For example, biological fathers sometimes report a growing discomfort with their daughters' physical changes during adolescence. A sweet little girl begins to look like a beautiful woman within a short period of time. Fathers, who don't want their daughters to feel in any way that their dad is thinking of them in a sexual way, sometimes pull away from any physical contact. Unfortunately, this may be interpreted by an adolescent girl as a rejection instead of an acknowledgment of her increasing femininity.

Stepfathers, as well, often find themselves confused about the physical relationship they have with their stepdaughter. Hugs from a little girl take on a strange new meaning from a blossoming stepdaughter. A conscientious stepfather may, too, pull away from physical contact. However, even that can be seen as a comment on her developing sexuality. Biological fathers must remember to keep hugging and physically connecting with their daughters during adolescence (it helps to affirm an insecure girl of her worth and value as a woman). Stepfathers should seek to present clear non-sexual intentions to their touch and restrain the temptation to view a stepdaughter's touch as having any sexual connotation.

In addition, a stepfather who works to create a happy marriage with an adolescent girl's mother helps to reduce sexual anxiety. "As they mature, girls begin to view a good marriage in a stepfamily as a kind of sexual insurance policy. The girl thinks that the closer the stepfather is to her mother, the less likely will be his real or imagined advances toward her. Once the sexual threat is tabled, often a girl becomes more accepting and open."[3]

### A Sexually Charged Environment

In addition to an expectation of closeness, stepfamilies have a sexually charged environment. This occurs for a number of reasons. First, children watch their parent go through a period of dating and developing romance. Children may even coach their parent on how to act or talk, or what perfume to wear on a date. In addition, a child is often witness to the increasing physical affection and touches that couples share as romance deepens. One father shared how this impacted his children. "While dating, I kissed my future bride in front of the house before saying good-night. My youngest son poked his head around the corner and yelled, 'Goooooo, Daddy!'" Children can't help but witness these romantic gestures and hear discussions of where the couple will go on their honeymoon. And then there's Uncle Roger's "1,001 Erotic Nights" gag gift at the wedding reception.

But romance doesn't stop there. A second reason for a sexually charged environment is what happens after the wedding. The first year of marriage is frequently speckled with romantic gestures and snuggling on the couch before bedtime. All of which communicates the message that "sexuality is alive and well in this household."

Bob recalled, "When my wife and I were first married, my stepdaughter came into our room in the morning and said, 'What's he doing in here? And where are your pajamas, Mom?'" Connie said her five children and stepchildren saw her and her husband kiss a lot during their first year of marriage. One of her daughters was uncomfortable with it and always tried to pull them apart. His daughter, on the other hand, would say "Ooo-la-la," while the boys teased them about "tongue twisting." While these examples are embarrassing, to say the least, some observations by children, if not handled well, can be debilitating to the family.

Shortly after Nicole's remarriage to Tony, her nine-year-old daughter, Lisa, started walking into her mother's bedroom at night to see if they were having sex. At times, Lisa would sit outside their bedroom door to see if she could hear them making love. Lisa's curiosity about the sexual aspects of her mother's marriage was brought on when Nicole started closing the bedroom door. Prior to remarriage, Nicole had an open-door policy with her children. As a single parent, she felt it important to be available to her children, especially at night. She slept with her door open so her children could reach her if they had any need. It was her way of reassuring her children after her husband's death.

Upon remarriage, Nicole began to close her door so as to have some private time with her husband. Making love was just a part of that time, but closing the bedroom door was, for Lisa, an unmistakable nonverbal comment on the couple's sexuality. This fed Lisa's curiosity. "Why didn't Nicole and Tony just lock their door?" someone might wonder. Because they didn't have a lock on the door. Pay attention, everyone, here comes Ron's big tip for improving your sex life: Get a lock on your bedroom door!

On one occasion, Lisa was successful. She burst through the door at two in the morning to discover her mother and stepfather having intercourse. She went running through the house, screaming, "They're having sex! They're having sex!" Tony and Nicole were embarrassed beyond belief. And because their embarrassment paralyzed them, they did nothing. They simply couldn't talk about it with Lisa. After that night, whenever the couple closed their door, even for nonsexual reasons, Lisa would later accuse them of going in their room "just because you want to have sex." The couple's shame deepened, and they began accommodating their marriage to avoid any accusation from nine-year-old Lisa. Quickly Lisa had more power over their sexual and marital intimacy than did Tony or Nicole.

A natural result of good sex education is curiosity. We cannot fault Lisa for that. However, the first time she burst into her mother's bedroom and accused them of "just wanting to have sex," two things should have happened. First, the couple should have put a lock on their bedroom door and begun educating all the children on respecting one another's privacy. Second, Nicole could have used the situation as a springboard into discussions of sexuality. Whether Nicole and Lisa had talked about sex before or not, this was a perfect opportunity to teach about God's gift of sex to married couples. The content and frequency of Nicole and Tony's sexuality is off limits, but the acknowledgment of God's gift is not. Tony's participation in this conversation is up to the couple and should be based on his level of connection with Lisa. Beyond this initial response, Nicole would need to assign a behavioral consequence to further misbehavior, accusations, or inappropriate questions about their sexual practices. "It's none of your business whether we went into our bedroom to have sex. If you want to talk about sexuality, we can do that tomorrow evening, but I don't want to hear questions about our intimacy. The next time you ask, you will be grounded for three days. And that includes gymnastics practice. Your choice."

A third reason for a sexually charged environment in stepfamilies is developing teenage sexuality. Our society is obsessed with sex. It pervades the movies, music, and conversation of the average adolescent. Sex is every-where—even inside the bodies of teens. Changes in hormones and physical appearance also lead to many confusing thoughts and feelings for teenagers. It is imperative that parents present a godly view of sexuality—its purpose and prom-ise—throughout the life of a child. But the guidance parents give during adolescence is the most critical. If parents begin early to discuss God's design for our bodies and sexuality, important conversations with confused adolescents will be easier. Easy or difficult, they must take place.

> **When Children Engage Each Other Romantically**
>
> What should you do if step-siblings are mutually attracted to each other or have already engaged in a romantic connec-tion? Visit SmartStepfamilies.com/view/stepsibling-romance for answers.

In summary, children in stepfamilies, and adolescents in particular, are surrounded by a number of dynamics that call attention to sexuality. Biologically related relationships contain a natural taboo against sexual exchanges that step-relationships do not have. To make up for this natural genetic protection, stepfamilies need to set behavioral boundaries that discourage intentional and unconscious sexual attractions.

### Boundaries That Honor

The goal is to set boundaries (rules governing behavior) that teach fam-ily members to honor one another. Respecting privacy and valuing the specialness of each family member is an important message for everyone to learn. Here are some suggestions to help you get there.

**Set rules that honor privacy.** It may feel totally unnecessary, but con-sider having a dress code. Teenagers, in particular, can overlook how their dress invites others to see them in sexual ways or consider them a symbol of sexuality. Girls, for example, who sleep in their underwear and a long T-shirt may be comfortable walking around the house dressed for bed. Little do some girls realize how that arouses a natural curiosity within boys about their body shape.[4] Boys can easily entertain thoughts that cross from non-sexual curiosities to sexual ones. To counter this possibility, set a dress code and explain why it is necessary. The dress code teens would naturally assume if on a church youth retreat would work well. Make sure you discuss as a couple what the standard should be. Get on the same page and stick together. Then call a family meeting and invite your elementary-age and teenage children to give their input and determine the rule.

Other rules you might implement include knocking before entering bedrooms and how persons will share the bathroom. It always amazed me how the children on *The Brady Bunch,* who were similar in age but unrelated, never showed any embarrassment or sexual tension while sharing a bathroom. Again, Hollywood's version of family life doesn't even come close to reality. Help your children work out a respectful system for shower schedules and sharing bathrooms.

These boundaries are particularly important when a stepsibling from another home moves into your home. Children and teens who have known each other for years, but never lived together full time, need clear rules of conduct. Finally, be sure not to turn a blind eye to any signs that someone is uncomfortable. If you perceive a child withdrawing or showing signs of stress, calmly approach the child to investigate the situation. Err on the side of caution.

**Have frank discussions with teens and pre-teens (separately) about sexual boundaries and healthy sexual attitudes.** Setting rules that honor sexuality and privacy is sure to create opportunities for adults to speak with children and teens about sexuality. Take advantage of such opportunities to teach God's purpose for sexuality and the protection his statutes provide. The message parents give children in stepfamilies is the same fundamental message any parent would give—it just applies to people both inside and outside the home. The message is this: Your sexuality and the sexuality of others is a gift from God that is to be honored and protected. Healthy sexuality between two married people helps build their relationship to each other and to God. Sexuality outside

> **Online Pornography**
>
> Access to pornography increases the likelihood of sexual exploration and distorted attitudes toward the opposite sex. For example, porn objectifies a woman's body and fosters a "girls are here for my pleasure" attitude in boys. Porn teaches girls to be excessively sensual outside of marriage. Exposure to porn distorts healthy sexuality and can create an unsafe environment in the home.

God's boundaries erodes relationships and creates a sin barrier between God and us.

Unfortunately, some parents rely on scare tactics to encourage sexual purity before marriage. In an effort to keep their children from having sexual thoughts or urges, they scare them with the consequences of premarital sex. I believe we should be honest with children and teens about the potential emotional and physical consequences of premarital sex. However, the scare method doesn't present sex as a gift from God to be honored. It turns it into a curse to be avoided. When children grow to be married adults, switching the messages in their brain to see sex as something to be embraced and pursued is often difficult. It is much better for parents to teach sex as a gift to be protected and honored. God's law that sex be saved for marriage is meant to protect us from harm and provide for our sexual pleasure in marriage. We can teach our children to protect one another's honor and their own so that the gift of sexuality can be enjoyed later in its proper marital context.

**Talk about sexual attractions in a matter-of-fact manner.** Having healthy and honest conversations about the sexual truths of life normalizes them for children. For example, explaining menstruation to a preadolescent girl or wet dreams to a boy before they occur prepares the child for the onset of such experiences. Preparing and normalizing such experiences is important because, in addition to teaching children proper hygiene, it gives the child a God-perspective on the event. ("You're becoming a woman!" or "There is no reason to be ashamed of having a sexual dream that results in ejaculation or to think that you've sinned.")

In the same way, acknowledging that sexual attractions between stepsiblings can occur normalizes them for the child. This is not to give permission to them but to teach a proper perspective. The alternative is to say nothing and leave the child to determine the meaning of such an attraction (not a good idea), or to give negative messages that needlessly shame children (e.g., "How could you think something like that about her? That's disgusting").

Instead, a parent might say something like this to his son: "You know, son, as we talk about sharing the bathroom with your stepsisters, it occurs to me that some kids in a stepfamily like ours have passing sexual thoughts about their stepsiblings. If that ever happens to you, it doesn't mean you are bad or a disappointment to God. There will be lots of times in life that you have passing or unwanted sexual thoughts or feelings toward other people, but it would be inappropriate for you to act on them or keep thinking about the person in that way. So if it happens, ask God to help you to stop thinking about your stepsibling in that way. And make sure you don't dishonor the other person by acting on the attraction or thoughts. If the thoughts keep happening, and you get concerned about it, feel free to talk to me. I won't be angry. We'll find a way to handle it. Any questions?"

### Final Thoughts

While the occurrence of sexual abuse or stepsibling attraction within stepfamilies is more common than it is in biological families, the odds of it happening are still very low (except in some cultures that turn a blind eye to stepfather abuse). There is no cause for excessive alarm or fear. However, wise parents will recognize the risks and be proactive to ensure that inappropriate behavior does not become a problem.

## Spiritual Formation in Stepfamily Children

It was a heartfelt question that I didn't know how to answer. "My kids have been through a lot," Kara began. "They have witnessed anger and manipulation, fights between their dad and me, six rough years living with a poor single mom, and now they have lived through a difficult stepfamily transition with three stepsiblings. How is all this going to impact their faith development?" I don't really know. I don't think anyone does.

Without question, the loss of an intact family due to a parent's death or divorce will have a significant impact on a child's faith formation. There has been some research into what the positive or negative impact will be (more later), but we simply cannot say for sure. Some stepfamily children will demonstrate an increase in spiritual growth due to the trials they experience, as did many people in the Bible who experienced spiritual growth due to hardship. (In 2 Corinthians 1:8–11, the apostle Paul points out that a time of great stress led him to a deeper reliance on God.) But parents need to face the fact that, while some positive outcome is possible, the impact on the faith of some children will be negative.

### Family and Faith

God's plan for making himself known to children has always been centered on the family. Psalm 78:1–8 (NIRV) captures the essence of that plan:

> My people, listen to my teaching.
>> Pay attention to what I say.
> I will open my mouth and tell stories.
>> I will speak about things that were hidden.
>> They happened a long time ago.
> We have heard about them and we know them.
>> Our people who lived before us have told us about them.
> We won't hide them from our children.
>> We will tell them to those who live after us.
> We will tell them about what the Lord has done that is worthy of praise.
>> We will talk about his power and the wonderful things he has done.
> He gave laws to the people of Jacob.
>> He gave Israel their law.
> He commanded our people who lived before us
>> to teach his laws to their children.
> Then those born later would know his laws.
>> Even their children yet to come would know them.
>> And they in turn would tell their children.
> Then they would put their trust in God.
>> They would not forget what he had done.
>> They would obey his commands.
> They would not be like their people who lived before them.
>> Those people were stubborn. They refused to obey God.
> Their hearts were not true to him.
>> Their spirits were not faithful to him.

Children come to know God when the stories around them point to God's mighty works and love. And it is parents who are handed the responsibility to tell their children the stories of God. Parents tell these stories in three ways.[5]

**Share the biblical story of God's work in the world and the sacrifice of Jesus Christ.** Parents and stepparents must be diligent in impressing upon children the commandments of God. In Deuteronomy 6:7–9, Moses instructs the people to share the commands of God throughout the natural rhythms of everyday living. When you're driving to school, coaching a soccer team, or making decisions about money, share with your children how your relationship to God is influencing your thinking and behavior. You can also reference a Scripture and how it pertains to what's happening in your life. The goal is to train your children to quite naturally think of God in the big and little moments of life.

**Share your personal faith stories.** Telling children the stories of God also occurs when parents and stepparents share their personal stories, including their peaks and valleys and times of plenty and drought. Most adults have never told their children how they came to know the Lord or about the key people throughout their lives that have deepened their conviction and knowledge of God. This is one of the most significant stories parents can share, because it extends beyond the biblical stories of God's work in the world to modern times—and to the child's own heritage. Even sharing the valleys or dark days of your spiritual walk is helpful. Instead of showing your children or stepchildren that you were weak (as many people fear), it shows how God can be counted on to extend mercy. It also reveals the imperfections of our faith and conveys the value of "coming home to the Lord." Simply put, sharing your faith story adds an array of color to the black and white of the Bible.

Recently some friends of ours had a difficult time being open to God's direction when a military commitment would take them far from extended family to an unfamiliar part of the country. They struggled about what they hoped to see happen, but when the answer to their prayers was "no," Greg and Elisa eventually found peace in submission and blind trust. Because their two daughters were too young to comprehend the significance of the trial, I suggested they write their girls a letter about the experience—a letter the girls would read in adolescence when the testimony of Mom and Dad's faith would mean something. Through this letter, a current natural rhythm of life could still be a teachable moment later in life.

**Live your faith.** Telling the stories of God includes parents living out an unmistakable faith story in front of their children. Modeling a dedicated walk is far and above the most important story parents "tell" their children. Years ago someone shared with me part of a poem that captures the importance of example.

> I'd rather see a sermon than hear one any day.
> I'd rather one should walk with me than merely show the way.
> The eye's a better pupil and more willing than the ear,
> Fine counsel is confusing, but example's always clear.
>
> Edgar A. Guest (1881–1959)

Life is a story. If your life story isn't oriented around a relationship with Christ, your children will view Sunday school and family devotions as interesting experiences, but nothing of true lasting significance. In order for truth to come alive, it must be lived out in front of our children. Otherwise, truth is just one concept in a world full of alternative philosophies.

Fathers tell a specific story about God. It occurred to me years ago that as a father I had a tremendous task: to be the first positive impression my children would have of God. Children generally formulate their first picture and impression of their heavenly Father based on their experience with their earthly father. Just as God created man in his image, men (we dads) "create" God in our image.[6] If you are distant and unavailable, your children may have difficulty sensing God's presence or trusting his work in their life. If you explode in anger when your children make mistakes, guess from whom they will run after giving in to sin? If you are rigid and punitive, God easily becomes someone to fear rather than draw near to. Consider Martin Luther's statement: "I have difficulty praying the Lord's Prayer because whenever I say 'Our Father,' I think of my own father, who was hard, unyielding, and relentless. I cannot help but think of God in that way." Your influence and behavior as a father are critical to your child's spiritual development. Some stepfathers will also have this kind of influence on their stepchildren, especially stepfathers of young children who become their second concrete image of God. Since your stepchildren have a biological father who is also creating an image of God, you can never be sure to what extent your stepchildren are "listening" to your behavior. The task, then, is to live as if your example is all they will ever hear.

Will we ever be perfect fathers? I know I'm not. (Having to ask my children for forgiveness happens much more often than I'd like.) But the challenge is to give our children a taste of who God is—a taste that arouses their thirst for more. We are God's ambassadors, not just of his message but of his image. We have the opportunity to model for our children a heavenly Father who is thrilled with the presence of his children and who longs to be with them. That kind of introduction to God comes primarily through our life story. Dad, Stepdad, what kind of story is your child reading from your life?

Families also have a life story. It can be one of faithfulness or selfishness, sacrifice or self-preservation, warmth or coldness, safety or insecurity, unconditional love or conditional rejection. All of these aspects of family combine to create a culture that either encourages or discourages spiritual relationship with God. If a child's experience of family is one of chaos, where parents are not in charge and children, having few boundaries, learn self-indulgence, why would the difficult and narrow road of discipleship be attractive? If the family is abusive or neglectful, anger is easily shifted toward God, who—from the child's perspective—seems to have abandoned the child. On the other hand, wouldn't children who experience love, boundaries, and stability in their home be more likely to find a relationship with Christ? What if a child witnesses love between marital partners? Wouldn't that improve the chances of a growing faith? One body of research discovered that adolescents whose parents were happily married were many times more likely to take God seriously than teens whose parents were unhappily married.[7] So what about children whose parents divorce and remarry?

### Divorce, Remarriage, and Faith Formation

Early in this new millennium, a friendly debate has developed among researchers over the long-term impact of divorce on children. Many of the conclusions are based on the well-being, short-term and long-term, of children. Unfortunately, well-being is generally limited to aspects like academic performance, juvenile delinquency, vocational aptitude, and the presence of mood disturbances or drug problems. But what about moral behavior?

One well-respected researcher, Mavis Hetherington, who concluded that only 20 percent of children from divorced homes have long-term emotional, psychological, and behavioral difficulties following parental divorce, also recognized what I call a significant impact on moral behavior.[8] When compared to their parents—who were mostly raised in the '60s, no less—children of divorce emerged more self-serving and materialistic. Hetherington cites a number of specific examples related to sex, cohabitation, and childbearing: While 10 percent of their parents were sexually active by age fifteen, half of the children of divorce were; less than 5 percent of their parents cohabited before marriage, but half of the children did; 20 percent of their parents said cohabitation was a good trial marriage compared to 80 percent of the children. Finally, she noted that almost 20 percent of children of divorce gave birth out of wedlock and 58 percent had had an abortion.[9]

Without question, the challenges of parental divorce and stepfamily adjustment impact child and young adult spiritual decision making and behavior, which in turn brings complicating consequences to adult spirituality. In addition to an impact on moral behavior, there also seems to be an impact on understanding the biblical narrative and matters of faith.

Elizabeth Marquardt has conducted numerous interviews with children of divorce and discovered that many of them cannot relate to key characters in Bible stories.[10] For example, to a child with one parent who has remained distant, the father in the parable of the Prodigal Son is unrecognizable. Even worse, when a parent abandons the faith, children experience a role reversal in which their parent is the prodigal and they are the ones left waiting for the parent's return. Other children of divorce find it difficult to keep the fourth commandment—to honor their father and mother. It's almost as if kids say, "If they didn't honor each other in marriage, why should I have to honor them?"

In her seminal study of the moral strivings of children from divorced homes, Elizabeth Marquardt reported in her book *Between Two Worlds: The Inner Lives of Children of Divorce* that kids are forced into becoming what she called "early moral forgers." They must confront their parents' differing values and beliefs and determine, alone and at a younger age than other children, what their own beliefs and values will be. Answering the fundamental questions of life, such as "What do I believe?" and "How do I know what is right or wrong?" is a confusing process because children are sometimes influenced by two different standards from their parents. I believe it is even more complicated for stepfamily children. Imagine a child with divorced parents who each remarry. When the stepparents enter the picture, they add two more value opinions to the equation for a total of four. If one of the parents divorces again (re-divorce) and forms a significant relationship with yet another adult, that's five. As children seek to fold into the value set of each home (so as not to choose sides or anger adults), they become proficient throughout childhood at embracing multiple value sets. This fosters a postmodern view of the world (no one belief system is better than another), which dramatically dilutes not only their value system, but when added to the millions of children growing up in this situation, the values of a nation (what many argue is happening in America and across the world right now). Clearly, children whose parents have divorced bring a host of complicated emotions and formational belief practices to their understanding of God, his Word, and matters of faith.

> ### Culture Watch
>
> Just to be clear, I am not blaming divorce and remarriage as being responsible for postmodernism in our culture, but I am suggesting that when children follow their parents in and out of a series of marriages or cohabiting relationships, it does foster postmodern thinking. Serial divorce and remarriage is a vehicle through which postmodern thinking flourishes.

Even as I write these words, I am well aware of how depressing this must be to you who desperately want to raise faithful children. It is also likely resurrecting your anger and guilt over a past you cannot change (don't look now, it's pursuing you again). But all hope is not lost. I remind you again of chapter 1 and the discussion of Jehovah-Rophe—the God who heals. The Creator of the universe can turn the bitter waters of life sweet once again. Part of that healing is made easier when your current stepfamily is strengthened and you model the lifestyle you want your children to adopt. While the transitions through divorce and remarriage undoubtedly derail normative faith formation stages within children, a strong, stable stepfamily, I believe, can set children back on track much of the time. By intentionally creating a culture of faith within your home, you make the story of God come alive for your children and stepchildren.

### What If the Values Being Taught in the Other Home Conflict With the Christian Faith?

"I really want my two children to love the Lord and have a relationship with their father. But when they spend time with their dad and stepmom, they are exposed to a lifestyle that goes against what the Bible teaches. What can we do? I'm tempted to discourage them from going to see their dad." Michelle's question is one I hear repeated around the country. Christian parents want their children to grow in faith. But what can you do when the other household is leading the sheep away from the Shepherd?

Before offering specific suggestions, let me address Michelle's temptation to limit the contact between her children and their father. While her desire to protect the faith of her children is understandable, becoming a barrier between the other biological parent and your children is not recommended. When this happens, children often grow to resent the parent who blocks access to the other parent. In the end, you weaken your spiritual influence. In addition, the other parent may feel cheated and retaliate, exposing your children to more conflict.

Guarding your children from every negative influence is simply not within your power. You must find other ways of influencing your children. Here are some suggestions.

**First, admit that you cannot control what is taught or demonstrated in the other home.** I realize this is a tough reality, especially when you know there are ungodly influences in the other home. Wanting the behavior to stop is understandable, but trying to take control of their lives doesn't work. (If you couldn't change your spouse during your marriage, what makes you think you can change this person after your divorce?) If anything, it bolsters them against you and gives them an excuse to blame you for being a self-righteous Christian. Letting go of controlling them forces you to let God be in control of what you can't change; instead, channel your time and effort into influencing your children.

**Influence your children toward the Lord while they are in your home.** All parents need to *model* the Christian walk and *impress* on their children the decrees of God (Deuteronomy 6:4–9). But you will also have to *inoculate* them. Inoculations are controlled injections of a virus; they allow the body to develop antibodies that can combat a live virus, if ever encountered. Spiritual inoculations present viewpoints that oppose the Word of God and then teach biblical concepts that help children combat them. For example, you might view and discuss a TV program that glorifies greed, and then show children a spiritual view of money and stewardship.

Children who have one parent who is not living a Christian life will need inoculation to help them deal with an environment that is hostile to their growing faith. It is critical, however, that you remain neutral about the other parent; the inoculation cannot be a personal attack. A comment like "Your father shouldn't be lying to his boss—he's so self-centered" pulls on children's loyalties and burdens them with your hostility. Ironically, it also diminishes your influence as they react defensively against your negativity. A more appropriate response would be, "Some people believe lying is fine when it serves a purpose. But God is truth and wants us to be honest as well. Telling the truth like God does helps us build and keep our relationship with him. Let's talk about that. . . ."

**You may have to endure years of prodigal living as your children try out the values of the other home.** This is a truth that many parents fear. Children may experiment with the "easier" lifestyle of the other home, especially during the teen years when they are deciding whether the faith they've been handed (inherited faith) will become their own (owned faith).[11] Lovingly admonish them toward the Lord (not away from the other parent), and be close enough to reach when they turn around.

Having a prodigal is an emotionally gut-wrenching journey for any parent. You will need support from friends, a pastor, and perhaps other parents who have struggled down the same road.

**Pray daily for the strength to walk in the light, and introduce your children to Jesus at each and every opportunity.** Your model is a powerful bridge to their personal commitment to Christ. Do all that you can to take your kids "by the hand and lead them in the way of the Master" (Ephesians 6:4, THE MESSAGE paraphrase).

### Questions for Discussion

■ FOR PARENT-CHILD DISCUSSION (Discretion based on the age of the child and the quality of adult-child relationships is advised.)

1. For biological parent and child: Has there ever been a situation in our stepfamily that made you feel embarrassed or physically uncomfortable?
2. What privacy rules would you like for us to establish?
3. If you haven't previously, have a frank, matter-of-fact conversation with your kids about sexuality within your home (and sexual temptations in general). Review the script in the "Talk About Sexual Attractions in a Matter-of-Fact Manner" section and modify it to fit your family situation.

4. Spiritual formation: Has there ever been a time that you were confused about the differences in values between us as parents and stepparents? Between homes? I realize that puts you in an awkward spot—trying to figure out what you believe and trying to be respectful of us as well. What is that like for you?

### ■ For All Couples

1. What boundaries do you have in place to deter unhealthy sexual attractions? Which ones might you need to add?

2. What aspects of healthy sexuality have you discussed with your children?

3. How much time have you dedicated to reading the Bible and learning its wisdom for your home? Pray together now and ask God to make his love come alive in your lives.

4. What fears do you have regarding your children's faith formation?

5. What strategies for faith training did this chapter suggest that you are not doing well?

6. How well does your walk match your talk?

7. How are the spiritual values of your child's two homes different? What are you doing to inoculate them against non-Christian messages?

### ■ For Pre-Stepfamily Couples

1. Discuss the potential impact of sexuality on your family and boundaries you will adopt.

2. Prior to remarriage, I believe it is very important for couples to seriously consider scriptural guidelines for remarriage. I strongly encourage you to arrange a meeting with your minister to discuss this matter.

3. Discuss your expectations for the stepparent regarding spiritual training.

4. Begin now to make prayer and informal, spontaneous discussions about God's role in your life a regular family practice. Develop your game plan for spiritual formation for yourselves and your children.

# Smart Step Seven: STEP Over

## *Into the Promised Land*

> Moses, the servant of the LORD, died. . . . the LORD spoke to Joshua . . . "I want you and all of these people to get ready to go across the Jordan River. I want all of you to go into the land I am about to give to the people of Israel. . . . as I promised Moses. . . . Be strong and brave. You will lead these people, and they will take the land as their very own. It is the land I promised with an oath to give their people long ago. Be strong and very brave. Make sure you obey the whole law my servant Moses gave you. Do not turn away from it to the right or the left. Then you will have success everywhere you go."
>
> Joshua 1:1–3, 6–7 NIRV

Is there hope for the weary? Yes, there is.

Because of their lack of faithfulness, God prohibited the Israelites from entering the Promised Land for forty years; the journey could have taken only about two weeks. At the end of their long wilderness wandering, I'm certain they were weary. But as they finally stood on the brink of their destination, the reward for completing the journey lay just ahead. All they had to do was cross the Jordan and lay claim to the land God had promised.

But God could see that they needed some final encouragement. Moses, their steadfast leader, was dead, and Joshua had been granted leadership. Once they crossed the Jordan into the Promised Land, a fury of battles awaited them as they claimed the land. Joshua and the people needed a boost to their courage, and the Lord gave it to them: "Be strong and brave. . . . I will be with you everywhere you go" (Joshua 1:9 NIRV).

The trip to the Promised Land for most stepfamilies is sprinkled with uncertainty and frustrating dilemmas. But perhaps you are standing on the brink of your Promised Land and don't even know it. Just one more river to cross and a few more battles to face, and significant rewards await you. You just need some final encouragement.

Let me share with you one such Promised Land stepfamily story. Many others are available to you in the bonus material found at SmartStepfamilies.com/view/learn.

## Painfully Beautiful: The Spangler Family Hybrid

Ever wonder what others would write on your grave marker if they had to sum up your life in one sentence? What would they say about you at your funeral?

I didn't know Cheryl Spangler, but I know something about her from what her stepson, Mathew, said about her at her memorial service on April 4, 2013. Cheryl died after a long battle with cancer. Her stepson—or should I say *son*—shared the following thoughts at her funeral. He wasn't intending to write a Promised Land story for this book, he was just bearing witness to Cheryl's legacy as his stepmom. Nevertheless, it is a Promised Land story worth shouting from the rooftops. With Mathew's permission, as well as Cheryl's husband, Sandy's, permission, I'm shouting.

*For all of my adult life my parents have been talking about leaving a legacy. But I can honestly tell you that when I began to write this, my very first thought was recalling the times when Mom would repeatedly teach me the value of a crisp hospital corner when I make my bed. My mom had a great deal of wisdom. And if you knew her, you knew she was rarely shy about sharing that wisdom. . . . Most of it, I have utilized. And some, I have ignored to my detriment. . . . I don't believe I have made my bed with a hospital corner since I left for college.*

*Here are some of the other lasting memories I will treasure about my mom—a taste of some of the idiosyncrasies that made her . . . my mom. I hope some of these sound familiar to you and make you smile like they do me.*

- *Soft-serve ice cream is the only type of ice cream worthy of being on a cone.*
- *A sundae without hot fudge is just ice cream with fruit sauce.*
- *A curled potato chip, the kind with that fold in the center, is worth fighting for.*
- *A properly vacuumed room will always have straight symmetrical lines in the carpet . . . AND you haven't really vacuumed unless you've moved the furniture.*
- *I can't fully explain the satisfaction I get from ironing a sharp crease in the sleeve on my dress shirts. That comes from her.*
- *She taught me the proper viscosity of homemade gravy.*
- *She taught me how to drive a stick shift either because Dad didn't have the patience or maybe the guts. I grew up out in the country, and I remember getting pulled over by a park ranger as she was teaching me . . . because I kept stalling out. He told us to find some place safer. She leaned her head over me toward the driver's side window and told the ranger, "This is Leroy County. We're in the middle of nowhere. Where are we going to find some place more secluded than this?" He drove off and let us keep stalling our way down the road. (My mother was not easily intimidated.)*
- *I remember her teaching me how to slow dance before my first middle school dance.*
- *She told me to observe Anita, my then-future mother-in-law, before I proposed because chances are, that will be Stacy in twenty years. That was some of the quality advice I made good use of.*

- *She explained to me the importance of giving my wife flowers for no good reason.*

*While this may sound pretty normal, our relationship was not cookie cutter. I believe Mom's lasting legacy to me is the experience of grafting a hybrid plant. You may recall what a hybrid plant is from seventh grade science class. It's where you cut two separate plants in such a way as to match the stems. A new stem is grafted into the stem of a rooted plant. You attach them together and you let it grow. I remember this being a really cool experiment in seventh grade science class. The experiment is not quite so cool when your life is one of those metaphorical plant stems; the cutting and grafting is painful.*

*My mom spent a good portion of her life grafting severed families together, starting with her own. Up until about fifteen years ago, I called my mom Cheryl. As you may have guessed, Cheryl is not my birth mother. But I hope you can tell from what I mentioned earlier, she is most definitely my mom. I recognize this sounds a little peculiar as I say it out loud, but I know she realized I was her son long before I realized she was my mom. I know this because I can remember the precise conversation when this began to dawn on me. I was twenty-one, and the two of us were discussing the planning of my wedding.*

*Let me give a little context. My dad and my birth mom, Nancy, were separated before I was even in school. Cheryl and my dad got married when I was six. By the spring of fifth grade, my life was pretty complicated for an eleven-year-old. I ended up moving in with my dad, and thus began the grafting of our new family. Nancy remained an inconsistent and unhealthy part of my life as I grew up. By the time I was twenty-one, she had essentially dropped out of my life. As we were discussing the planning of my wedding, Mom asked me about Nancy and whether she was going to be at the wedding, and if so,*

> **Looking Back**
>
> Mathew Spangler reflecting on the early days forging a relationship with his stepmom, said, "From my memory, most of our early struggles boiled down to fighting over Dad's attention. I don't know if I ever verbalized this to Mom, but I distinctly remember thinking, *He was my dad before he was your husband.* It took a long time to understand that I needed to be a half-notch below her in his hierarchy of responsibilities."

*who was going to light the unity candle. I remember this catching me off guard, because never for one moment had it even crossed my mind that Nancy would do this. The unity candle is reserved for the mothers of the two getting married.*

*That conversation forced me to later consciously realize what she had long before understood—somewhere between my age eleven and age twenty-one—we became the Spangler Family Hybrid. We had been grafted together. I remember arguments where I would spitefully tell her that she was not my mother. At some point, she knew differently and had willingly assumed that role. While we have no common blood and no matching physical characteristics, we have been grafted together by God as mother and son. I think sociologists would define us as a blended family. I prefer to think of us as a hybrid family, grafted together by God.*

*Paul uses a similar illustration in Romans where he discusses the adoption of the Gentiles as children of God by grafting them into the roots of the nation of Israel into one family. My family is a painfully beautiful illustration of this.*

*What beautiful symmetry God has woven into my life through my mom. I'm an adopted son. I'm an adoptive father of two little girls. And I am an adopted child of God. When this day passes, and today becomes next week, or next month, or next year, my understanding of my mom's legacy will be this: Someone who leveraged everything she had to graft severed people and severed families into the hybrid family of Christ.*

## Final Thoughts

I think it very fitting that the final story of this book is about a stepson giving testimony to the love of his stepmother. The Spangler family story is *painfully beautiful.* The agony of loss gave birth to a new family, one dominated by insiders making space for outsiders (the choice to love), grace, and a redemptive spirit. And in the end, loss again entered the story, but was overshadowed by gratitude and a legacy of persistent love. *Painfully beautiful.*

No matter what cooking phase of the Crockpot your family is in (early, middle, or late), I can imagine that some of life has been painful. And I can imagine that you have experienced some beautiful moments as well, though maybe not as many as you'd like. Either way, if you are allowing God to wrap your imperfect story into his perfect redemptive story, you are experiencing the redemption of your home and the next generation.

Are you in process? *Yes.*

Are you perfectly blended? *No.*

Can you trust God to provide a path through the Sea of Opposition? *Yes.*

Will he move through your faith in him to redeem your family story? *Yes.*

Will that produce a beauty from your ashes? *Yes.*

Will it remove the ashes? *No.*

But might his grace change the story you tell about your ashes? *Yes.* Just ask the Spanglers.

Recently at a conference a couple approached me. "Nine years ago we read your book *The Smart Stepfamily* and that book saved our marriage. We went into our first year of marriage with so much information that we would have never known—and it saved us. We had our ups and downs, but we made it through because of the things we learned in your book. Thank you very much." As much as I loved hearing their gratitude, what moved my heart most was knowing that this couple—by the sweat of their brow—were redeeming the futures of their children from the past. A pivotal moment in history was occurring before my eyes.

There are more chapters to your family story yet to be written; some in this generation and some in the generations to come. But when you walk with the Author, you are redeeming the future one step—or should I say *one stepfamily*—at a time.

## Questions for Discussion

■ FOR PARENT-CHILD DISCUSSION (Discretion based on the age of the child and the quality of adult-child relationships is advised.)

1. *For younger children:* Invite your child to select from their dolls, play characters, or Lego characters a piece that represents each person in your family. Ask them to make up a story about the characters and place them close or far from one another based on how things really are in your family. Have fun with the made-up story, but make some observations about where they place the characters. Feel free to say things like, "I noticed you and Daddy are pretty far from each other.

What does that mean?" You might learn a lot about your child's perspective of the family.

2. If you were writing a story about the life of our family, who would the main characters be and what would be their challenges?

3. What chapters in our family story are yet to be written? What do you think comes next—and what title would you give to the chapter?

### ■ FOR ALL COUPLES

1. Which aspect of the Spangler story do you most identify with? Why?

2. In what ways is your life not exactly what you planned? In what ways is your life blessed, in spite of your plan?

3. What has God taught you about surrendering to his will through your family experiences?

4. Cheryl Spangler had to wait a very long time before she saw and heard her stepson acknowledge her true place in his life. If you haven't reached that point yet, what reminders do you need to keep going toward the Promised Land? How can you help each other keep this perspective on tough days?

5. *Painfully beautiful* is a poetic way of pointing out that beauty and ashes often exist side by side. Further, we must learn to live in the tension between them and trust God with it. Talk about this aspect of your journey.

6. What are your attitudes and feelings about those who seek counseling? How would you know if seeking outside help was a good idea?

For further encouragement, read the bonus Promised Land stories at SmartStepfamilies.com/view/learn.

# Resources

## *for Stepfamilies and Churches*

### Organizations and Websites

FamilyLife Blended™. www.familylife.com/blended. Part of the international ministry of FamilyLife®. Founding director, Ron Deal.

Family Medallion. www.familymedallion.com. Planning to get remarried? This site provides medallions that parents can give their children during the wedding ceremony.

Smart Stepfamilies™ (Ron Deal). www.SmartStepfamilies.com

The Smart Stepmom (Laura Petherbridge). www.TheSmartStepmom.com

Find updated links to other helpful organizations at www.SmartStepfamilies .com/links.php.

### Books and Study Resources

View an updated list of recommended resources online at SmartStep families.com/view/recommended-resources.

Adler-Baeder, Francesca. *Smart Steps for Parents and Children*. National Stepfamily Resource Center, *stepfamilies.info,* 2002. Ideal for those in a secular, nonreligious environment, this six-week curriculum includes training for both stepfamily adults and their children. Includes two videos and a CD with PowerPoint and handout masters. A Christian supplement entitled "Growing in Wisdom" by Ron L. Deal is also available.

Becnel, Moe and Paige. *God Breathes on Blended Families (second edition).* Vision Communications Creative and Publishing, 2009. Workbook also available.

Daughtry, Tammy. *Co-Parenting Works! Helping Your Children Thrive After Divorce.* Grand Rapids, MI: Zondervan, 2011.

Deal, Ron L. *Dating and the Single Parent.* Bloomington, MN: Bethany House, 2012. Includes discussion questions and an online profile.

———. *Life in a Blender: Living in a Stepfamily (booklet for children ages 10+).* Little Rock, AR: FamilyLife Publishing, 2012. Includes parent discussion guide. Available only at familylife.com.

———. *The Marriage Mentor's Guide to The Smart Stepfamily (Revised and Expanded edition),* 2014. A 13-session guide available through Marriage Mentoring.com.

———. *Ministering to Stepfamilies DVD.* Little Rock, AR: Smart Stepfamilies, 2011. Available at familylife.com.

———. *The Smart Stepfamily Marriage Small-Group Study Guide.* Little Rock, AR: FamilyLife Publishing, 2015. 13-week study guide to accompany the book. Available at familylife.com.

———. *Remarriage Success DVD.* Little Rock, AR: Smart Stepfamilies, 2011. Available at familylife.com.

———. *The Smart Stepdad: Steps to Help You Succeed.* Bloomington, MN: Bethany House, 2011. Includes discussion questions.

———. *The Smart Stepfamily Participant's Guide.* Bloomington, MN: Bethany House, and *Smart Stepfamilies,* 2014. Study guide to accompany the DVD.

———. *The Smart Stepfamily Small Group Resource DVD.* Bloomington, MN: Bethany House, and *Smart Stepfamilies,* 2014. Eight sessions for group or individual use.

———. *Tus Hijos, Los Mios, y Nosotros (Spanish version of The Smart Stepfamily, first edition).* El Paso, TX: Casa Bautista of Pubns, 2008.

Deal, Ron L., and David H. Olson. *The Smart Stepfamily Marriage: Keys to Success in the Blended Family.* Bloomington, MN: Bethany House, 2015. Includes discussion questions and an online profile.

Deal, Ron L., and Laura Petherbridge. *The Smart Stepmom: Practical Steps to Help You Thrive!* Bloomington, MN: Bethany House, 2009. Includes discussion questions.

Mathis, Dale and Susan. *The Remarriage Adventure: Preparing for a Lifetime of Love and Happiness.* Carol Stream, IL: Tyndale House, 2012.

Stuart, Gil and Brenda. *Restored and Remarried: Encouragement for Remarried Couples in a Stepfamily.* Vancouver, WA: Seven Trees Media, 2009.

Taylor, Gordon and Carri. *Designing Dynamic Christian Stepfamilies: Bringing the Pieces to Peace* (DVD and Study Guide). Oklahoma City: Opportunities Unlimited, 2003.

## Become Stepfamily Smart

If you are looking for a live conference event, or more in-depth resources for stepfamilies, please visit www.SmartStepfamilies.com.

# Notes

**Preface to the Revised Edition**

1. B. R. Karney, C. W. Garvan, and M. S. Thomas, published report by the University of Florida: *Family Formation in Florida: 2003 Baseline Survey of Attitudes, Beliefs, and Demographics Relating to Marriage and Family Formation.* These findings were replicated in two other state representative samples.

2. Ibid.

**Chapter 1: Through Wilderness Wanderings**

1. Ron L. Deal, *Dating and the Single Parent* (Bloomington, MN: Bethany House, 2012), 29.

2. E. M. Hetherington and J. Kelly, *For Better or For Worse: Divorce Reconsidered* (New York: W. W. Norton & Company, 2002), 197.

3. James Bray, *Stepfamilies: Love, Marriage, and Parenting in the First Decade* (New York: Broadway Books, 1998), 12.

4. Ibid., 3.

5. R. M. Ryan and A. Claessens, "Associations Between Family Structure Changes and Children's Behavior Problems: The Moderating Effects of Timing and Marital Birth," *Developmental Psychology*: August 6, 2012. Advance online publication. doi: 10.1037/a0029397.

6. Tianyi Yu and Francesca Adler-Baeder, "The Intergenerational Transmission of Relationship Quality," *Journal of Divorce & Remarriage*, 47: 2007, 3, 87–102.

7. Listen to the series "Stepfamilies and the Holidays" that originally aired on *FamilyLife Today,* December 17–18, 2012, www.familylife.com/audio/series/series-featured-in-2012/stepfamilies-and-holidays.

**Chapter 2: Key Stepping-Stones**

1. H. T. Blackaby and C. V. King, *Experiencing God: Knowing and Doing the Will of God* (Nashville: LifeWay Press, 1990), 108–125.

2. I am well aware that some marriages are extremely dangerous due to physical or sexual abuse toward a spouse or children. The matter of perseverance in the face of evil and dangerous circumstances changes dramatically. I would not encourage anyone in physical jeopardy to stay in a situation where the marriage covenant has been broken and there is little hope of reconciliation of the marriage. If you find yourself in such a circumstance, please seek professional help immediately.

3. Bray, *Stepfamilies: Love, Marriage, and Parenting in the First Decade*.

4. Patricia Papernow, *Becoming a Stepfamily: Patterns of Development in Remarried Families* (New York: Gardner Press, 1993), 387.

5. Lawrence H. Ganong and Marilyn Coleman, *Stepfamily Relationships: Development, Dynamics, and Interventions* (New York: Kluwer Academic/Plenum Publishers, 2004), 134–138.

6. Papernow, *Becoming a Stepfamily*, 387.

7. Ibid., 330–331.

### Chapter 3: Smart Step One: STEP Up!

1. Ron L. Deal, *Life in a Blender: Living in a Stepfamily,* with parent discussion guide (Little Rock, AR: FamilyLife Publishing, 2012). ©2012 by FamilyLife. All Rights Reserved. Used by Permission.

### Chapter 4: Smart Step Two: STEP Down

1. Wendy Swallow, *The Triumph of Love Over Experience: A Memoir of Remarriage* (New York: Hyperion, 2004), 1–2.

2. Emily B. and John S. Visher, *Stepfamilies: Myths and Realities* (Secaucus, NJ: Citadel Press, 1979).

3. All the credit for this one goes to John and Emily Visher (personal communication, April 1999).

4. Ron L. Deal, *The Smart Stepdad: Steps to Help You Thrive* (Bloomington, MN: Bethany House, 2011), 161.

### Chapter 5: Smart Step Three: Two-STEP

1. Gil and Brenda Stuart, *Restored and Remarried: Encouragement for Remarried Couples in a Stepfamily* (Vancouver, WA: Seven Trees Media, 2009), 39.

2. Shaunti Feldhahn with Tally Whitehead, *The Good News About Marriage: Debunking Discouraging Myths About Marriage and Divorce* (Colorado Springs, CO: Multnomah, 2014), 2–41, 98. Based on data from Krista K. Payne, "First divorces in the U.S., 2008" Family Profiles Series FP-10-06, National Center for Family and Marriage Research, Bowling Green State University, Bowling Green, Ohio, 2011, www.bgsu.edu/content/dam/BGSU/college-of-arts-and-sciences/NCFMR /documents/FP/FP-10-06.pdf. NOTE: The remarriage divorce rate is about remarriages, not specifically stepcouples.

3. Find this and other stepfamily statistics at smartstepfamilies.com/view/ statistics.

4. The stepcouple divorce rate is tough to nail down. Much of our data is about remarriage; not all remarriages are stepcouples and not all stepcouples are remarried. Therefore, projecting the stepcouple divorce rate is difficult. Shaunti Feldhahn (*The Good News About Marriage*, 99) points out that only one-third of remarried couples *has divorced* (this does not, however, predict how many will, i.e., the expected divorce rate). Hetherington and Kelly found that stepcouples, specifically, had a divorce rate 50 percent higher than remarried couples without children (see Hetherington and Kelly, *For Better or For Worse*, 178). If, then, the current rate of remarriage divorce is 34 percent, I estimate the current stepcouple divorce rate (those that have actually divorced) to be 40–45 percent. The *projected* rate of divorce (an estimate of how many will divorce over their lifetime) could be considerably higher, but it is very difficult to calculate given the limitations of current research.

5. Papernow, *Becoming a Stepfamily*, 54.

6. Adapted from Ron L. Deal, "Ghost Whispers," published on SmartStep families.com, May 2007.

7. Ron L. Deal, *Shared Ghost Busting: When Your Spouse Has a Ghost* (2008). Available at smartstepfamilies.com/view/spouse-ghost, accessed April 2013. Used with permission.

8. Ron L. Deal, *Dating and the Single Parent* (Bloomington, MN: Bethany House, 2012), 83.

9. Nathan Heller, "The Disconnect: Why Are So Many Americans Living by Themselves?" *The New Yorker*: April 16, 2013, Accessed online at www.newyorker.com/arts/critics/books/2012/04/16/120416crbo_books_heller.

### Chapter 6: Smart Step Four: STEP in Line (Part 1)

1. Dr. Margorie Engel (personal communication, 1998).

2. Carol R. Lowery, "Psychotherapy With Children of Divorced Families" in M. Textor, ed., *The Divorce and Divorce Therapy Handbook* (Northvale, NJ: Jason Aronson, Inc., 1989), 225–241.

3. W. F. Horn, "A Misconception About Divorce," *Fatherly Advice* column in *Washington Times* (August 29, 2000). See also, P. F. Fagan and R. Rector, "The Effects of Divorce on America," The Heritage Foundation Backgrounder Executive Summary (June 5, 2000), The Heritage Foundation, Washington, DC.

4. J. Wallerstein, *The Unexpected Legacy of Divorce: A Twenty-Five-Year Landmark Study* (New York: Hyperion Books, 2000).

5. Hetherington and Kelly, *For Better or For Worse*, 228.

6. J. H. Bray, "Children in Stepfamilies: Assessment and Treatment Issues" in D. K. Huntely, ed., *Understanding Stepfamilies: Implications for Assessment and Treatment* (Alexandria, VA: American Counseling Association, 1995), 59–72.

7. J. H. Bray, "Children's Development During Early Remarriage" in E. M. Hetherington and J. Arasteh, eds., *Impact of Divorce, Single Parenting, and Stepparenting on Children* (Hillsdale, NJ: Erlbaum, 1988), 279–298.

8. R. J. Haurin, "Patterns of Childhood Residence and the Relationship to Young Adult Outcomes," *Journal of Marriage and the Family*, 54 (1992), 846–860.

9. G. D. Sandefur, S. S. McLanahan, and R. A. Wojtkiewicz, "The Effects of Parental Marital Status During Adolescence on High School Graduation," *Social Forces,* 7 (1992), 103–121.

10. W. S. Aquilino, "Family Structure and Home-Leaving: A Further Specification of the Relationship," *Journal of Marriage and the Family,* 53 (1991), 999–1010.

11. A. Thornton, "Influence of the Marital History of Parents on the Marital and Cohabitational Experiences of Children," *American Journal of Sociology,* 96 (1991), 868–894.

12. E. M. Hetherington, "Families, Lies, and Videotapes," *Journal of Research on Adolescence,* 1 (1991), 323–348.

13. By Tammy Daughtry, MMFT. Available as a free download at *CoParenting International.com.* Taken from *Co-Parenting Works!* by Tammy Daughtry, 213–214. Copyright © 2011 by Tammy G. Daughtry. Used by permission of Zondervan. www.zondervan.com.

14. Papernow, *Becoming a Stepfamily.*

15. Bray, *Stepfamilies: Love, Marriage, and Parenting in the First Decade,* 83.

16. Emily Visher and John Visher, *How to Win As a Stepfamily* (New York: Brunner/Mazel, 1996), 110–112.

17. Adapted from Everett & Volgy, *Healthy Divorce* (San Francisco: Jossey-Bass, Inc., 1994), and Visher and Visher, *How to Win As a Stepfamily.*

18. List for item #12 developed from Margorie Engel, "President's Message," *Stepfamilies,* Vol. 18, No. 2, 1998.

19. Compiled by Tammy Daughtry. Used with permission. Available for download at coparentinginternational.com/downloads/Co-ParentingIntl_Top10Things KidsCouldSay.pdf.

20. Adapted from Constance R. Ahrons, *The Good Divorce,* ©1994 by Constance R. Ahrons, 52–58. Reprinted by permission of HarperCollins.

21. Visher and Visher, *How to Win As a Stepfamily,* 93.

22. V. Rackley, "Forgiveness in Relationships" (personal communication airing on *Life-Talk* with Ron L. Deal, KBTM 1230 AM radio, Jonesboro, AR, 1997).

23. Patricia Papernow, "Dealing Across Households: Scripts to Get by On," cassette recording (Williamsburg, VA: Stepfamily Association of America, 1995). Used with permission.

24. Richard A. Warshak, *Divorce Poison: How to Protect Your Family from Bad-Mouthing and Brainwashing* (New York: Harper, 2010), 55–56.

25. Ibid, xxvii, 9.

26. Warshak, *Divorce Poison,* xxii.

### Chapter 7: Smart Step Four: STEP in Line (Part 2)

1. Todd M. Jensen and Kevin Shafer, "Stepfamily Functioning and Closeness: Children's Views on Second Marriages and Stepfather Relationships." Social Work advance access, published March 24, 2013, doi:10.1093/sw/swt007.

2. R. M. Hoffman, "Why Is Stepmothering More Difficult Than Stepfathering?" *Stepfamilies,* Summer 1995.

3. Jean McBride, *Encouraging Words for New Stepmothers* (Fort Collins, CO: CDR Press, 2001), xv.

4. R. H. Lauer and J. C. Lauer, *Becoming Family: How to Build a Stepfamily That Really Works* (Minneapolis, MN: Augsburg Fortress, 1999), 147.

5. Adapted from Ron L. Deal, *The Smart Stepdad: Steps to Help You Succeed* (Bloomington, MN: Bethany House, 2011). Used with permission.

6. Margorie Engel, Stepfamily Association of America Training Institute (Kansas City, MO: April 1999).

7. M. Fine, "The Role of the Stepparent: How Similar Are the Views of Stepparents, Parents, and Stepchildren?" *Stepfamilies,* Fall 1997.

8. Bray, *Stepfamilies: Love, Marriage, and Parenting in the First Decade.*

9. Ibid.

10. K. Pasley, D. Dollahite, and M. Ihinger-Tallman, "What We Know About the Role of the Stepparent," *Stepfamilies,* 2000.

11. Bray, *Stepfamilies: Love, Marriage, and Parenting in the First Decade.*

12. K. Pasley, "What Is Effective Stepparenting?" *Stepfamilies,* Summer 1994.

13. Pasley, Dollahite, and Ihinger-Tallman, "What We Know About the Role of the Stepparent."

14. Dr. Susan Gamache, *Building Your Stepfamily: A Blueprint for Success* (Vancouver, BC: Council for Families, 1997).

15. E. B. Visher and J. S. Visher, *Old Loyalties, New Ties: Therapeutic Strategies With Stepfamilies* (New York: Bruner Mazel, 1998), 212–216.

16. While a stepparent is building emotional bonds with stepchildren, he or she still has practical matters to attend to. For example, a lack of legal bonds with stepchildren makes handling medical emergencies difficult. Obtaining permission to make medical decisions is important; see the permission forms available with the bonus material at SmartStepfamilies.com/view/learn.

17. Bray, *Stepfamilies: Love, Marriage, and Parenting in the First Decade,* 57–58.

18. Dr. Susan Gamache, "Parental Status: A New Construct Describing Adolescent Perceptions of Stepfathers" (PhD dissertation, University of British Columbia, 2000).

19. Based on the work of Dr. Susan Gamache in *Building Your Stepfamily: A Blueprint for Success.* Used with permission.

20. M. A. Fine, "The Stepfather and Stepchild Relationship," presented at the Stepfamily Association of America Training Institute, Kansas City, MO (April 1999).

21. Hetherington and Kelly, *For Better or For Worse,* 201–202.

22. Bray, *Stepfamilies: Love, Marriage, and Parenting in the First Decade,* 195.

23. Based on Ron L. Deal, "Breaking Through Barriers," an article that first appeared in *HomeLife* magazine: July 2013. Used with permission.

### Chapter 8: Smart Step Four: STEP in Line (Part 3)

1. Wikipedia: Heinz 57, available here: http://en.wikipedia.org/wiki/Heinz_57. Accessed 2/4/13.

2. Terri P. Smith, *When Your Parent Remarries Late in Life: Making Peace With Your Adult Stepfamily* (Avon, MA: Adams Media, 2007).

3. Adapted from Ron Deal, "Part-Time Parenting," an article that first appeared in *HomeLife* magazine: March 2011. Used with permission.

4. K. Leman, *Living in a Stepfamily Without Getting Stepped On: Helping Your Children Survive the Birth Order Blender* (Nashville: Thomas Nelson, 1994).

5. K. Pasley and C. Garneau, "Remarriage and Stepfamily Life," 2011, 149–171 in Froma Walsh, ed., *Normal Family Processes: Growing Diversity and Complexity*, 4th ed. (New York: The Guilford Press), 161.

6. James D. Bray and John Kelly, *Stepfamilies: Love, Marriage, and Parenting in the First Decade* (New York: Broadway Books, 1998), 256.

7. Learned through personal communication, 1998.

8. Susan D. Stewart, *Brave New Stepfamilies: Diverse Paths Toward Stepfamily Living.* (Thousand Oaks, CA: Sage Publications, 2007), 62–64.

9. A. C. Bernstein, "Stepfamilies from siblings' perspective," *Marriage & Family Review*, 26 (1997), 1563–1575.

10. W. R. Beer, *Strangers in the House: The World of Stepsiblings and Half-Siblings* (New Brunswick, NJ: Transaction, 1989).

11. The research summaries in this section are taken from K. Pasley and C. Garneau, "Stepsibling Relationships" in R. E. Emery, ed., *Cultural Sociology of Divorce: An Encyclopedia* (Thousand Oaks, CA: Sage, 2013).

12. Susan D. Stewart, "Brave New Stepfamilies: Diverse Paths Toward Stepfamily Living" (Thousand Oaks, CA: Sage Publications, 2007), 85–89. *Note:* Based on data from the 1987–1988 National Survey of Families and Households, Dr. Stewart estimates that between 5 and 10 percent of stepparents have adopted at least one stepchild.

13. Susan D. Stewart, "The Characteristics and Well-Being of Adopted Stepchildren," *Family Relations*, 59, 2010, 558–571. Said another way, this same research suggests that nonadopted stepchildren can fair just as well as adopted ones. There is not a clear "adoption advantage." The one exception to this finding centers around stepchildren adopted at a young age. This study indicates that children adopted under the age of twelve were more similar to children with two biological parents than stepchildren adopted over the age of twelve. Keep in mind, however, that this difference is likely more related to the clear absence of the biological parent and the child's length of time in the stepfamily Crockpot than the adoption itself.

14. This section is not intended to be viewed as legal counsel, but a summary of general family law issues for stepfamilies. With any legal concern, seek out legal counsel from a qualified attorney in your state.

15. Sarah E. C. Malia, "How Relevant Are U.S. Family and Probate Laws to Stepfamilies?" (548) in Jan Pryor, ed., *The International Handbook of Stepfamilies: Policy and Practice in Legal, Research, and Clinical Environments* (Hoboken, NJ: John Wiley & Sons, Inc., 2008), 545–572.

16. Malia, "How Relevant Are U.S. Family and Probate Laws to Stepfamilies?" 548, 551.

17. M. M. Mahoney, "Reformulating the Legal Definition of the Stepparent-Stepchild Relationship" (192) in A. Booth and J. Dunn, eds., *Stepfamilies: Who Benefits? Who Does Not?* (Hillsdale, NJ: Lawrence Erlbaum, 1994), 191–196.

### Chapter 9: Smart Step Five: Side STEP (Part 1)

1. R. Emery, *Renegotiating Family Relationships: Divorce, Child Custody, and Mediation* (New York: Guilford Press, 1994), 26–28.

2. Visher and Visher, *How to Win As a Stepfamily*, 97–100.

3. K. Pasley, "Relations Across the Generations: The Complications of Divorce and Remarriage," *Stepfamilies*, Spring 1995.

4. Visher and Visher, *Old Loyalties, New Ties: Therapeutic Strategies With Stepfamilies*.

5. Adapted from Visher and Visher, *Old Loyalties, New Ties: Therapeutic Strategies with Stepfamilies*.

6. Jerry Sittser, *A Grace Revealed: How God Redeems the Story of Your Life* (Grand Rapids, MI: Zondervan, 2012), 162–163.

7. Patricia Papernow, *Dealing Across Households: Scripts to Get by On*, cassette recording.

### Chapter 10: Smart Step Five: Side STEP (Part 2)

1. Ron L. Deal and David H. Olson, *The Smart Stepfamily Marriage: Keys to Success in the Blended Family*. (Bloomington, MN: Bethany House, 2015), chapter 13, "Remarriage Finances."

2. It seems that both sides may be right. Informal studies show that couples who favor pooling their money into an "ours pot" are no more or less satisfied with their money management than those who keep money separate. In either case, the legal realities of marriage are binding enough that pooling is not necessary to make the couple financially linked and interdependent.

3. Carri Taylor, *Stepfamily Finances: Money & Stuff, Part 4* (2005). Available at smartstepfamilies.com/view/268.

4. Margorie Engel, *Managing Stepfamily Money: Yours, Mine, and Ours* (Lincoln, NE: Stepfamily Association of America Press, 2000). Used with permission.

5. Deal and Olson, *The Smart Stepfamily Marriage*, chapter 13, "Remarriage Finances."

6. Margorie Engel, *Managing Stepfamily Money: Yours, Mine, and Ours* (Lincoln, NE: Stepfamily Association of America Press, 2000). Used with permission.

7. Richard E. Barnes, *Estate Planning for Blended Families: Providing for Your Spouse and Children in a Second Marriage* (Berkeley, CA: Nolo, 2009), 23–24.

8. L. Paul Hood Jr. and Emily Bouchard, *Estate Planning for the Blended Family* (Bellingham, WA: Self-Counsel Press, 2012), xvi. Used with permission.

9. Based on the article "When and How to Use a Shared Covenant Agreement in a Christian Remarriage" by Greg S. Pettys (2009). Used with permission. Available at smartstepfamilies.com/view/shared-covenant-agreement. Greg S. Pettys is a

Christian author and speaker with ASPIRE GROUP, INC based out of Springfield, IL. Learn more by visiting the ASPIRE GROUP website at http://gp.impression.me.uk.

10. Hood and Bouchard, *Estate Planning for the Blended Family*, xvi-xvii. Used with permission.

11. Ibid., 61. Used with permission.

12. Online blog by Goldberg-Jones, "She Gets What? Dividing a Professional Degree in Divorce," Jan, 30, 2013. Accessed Dec. 26, 2013, at http://www.goldbergjones-sandiego.com/blog/?s=degree.

13. Hood and Bouchard, *Estate Planning for the Blended Family*, xviii. Used with permission.

14. Special thanks to my friend Greg Pettys for this financial wisdom.

15. Hood and Bouchard, *Estate Planning for the Blended Family*, xix. Used with permission.

16. Hood and Bouchard, *Estate Planning for the Blended Family*, xx-xxi. Used with permission.

### Chapter 11: Smart Step Six: STEP Through

1. J. Giles-Sims, "Current Knowledge About Child Abuse in Stepfamilies" in *Stepfamilies: History, Research, and Policy*, M. Sussman and I. Levin, eds. (New York: The Haworth Press, 1997).

2. Dr. Francesca Adler-Baeder (personal communication, June 2001).

3. Hetherington and Kelly, *For Better or For Worse: Divorce Reconsidered*, 198.

4. This is not to imply in any way that victims make their offenders abuse them. Offenders are solely to blame for their actions.

5. I'm grateful to Ron Rose for these three points (personal communication, July 1995).

6. Ron L. Deal, "Fathers: Our First Impression of God," *Today's Father 5*, No.1 (1997): A1 (Shawnee Mission, KS: National Center for Fathering).

7. D. K. Lewis, C. H. Dodd, and D. L. Tippens, *The Gospel According to Generation X: The Culture of Adolescent Belief* (Abilene, TX: ACU Press, 1995).

8. Hetherington and Kelly, *For Better or For Worse: Divorce Reconsidered*.

9. Ibid., 271–272.

10. Elizabeth Marquardt, "Children of Divorce: Stories of Exile," *The Christian Century* (February 2001).

11. J. H. Westerhoff III, *Will Our Children Have Faith?* (San Francisco: Harper and Row, 1976).

**Ron L. Deal** is founder and president of As For Me and My House Ministries and Smart Stepfamilies™ (www.RonDeal.org) and director of FamilyLife Blended™, a division of FamilyLife®. He is a family therapist and conference speaker specializing in marriage enrichment and stepfamily education.

Ron is author of *The Smart Stepfamily Small Group Resource DVD, The Smart Stepfamily Participant's Guide, The Smart Stepdad, Dating and the Single Parent, The Smart Stepmom* (with Laura Petherbridge), and *The Smart Stepfamily Marriage* (with Dr. David Olson), which is based on the largest survey of remarriage strengths ever conducted. He is a member of the Stepfamily Expert Council for the National Stepfamily Resource Center and is a licensed marriage and family therapist and licensed professional counselor.

Ron has extensive experience with the media. He has appeared on dozens of national radio and TV broadcasts in the UK, Canada, Australia, and the U.S., including *The 700 Club,* Fox News, ABC *Nightline,* WGN-TV News, *FamilyLife Today®, Family Talk,* and *Focus on the Family.* His work with stepfamilies has been referenced by ABCNews.com, *New York Daily News, USA Today, Chicago Tribune, Ladies Home Journal,* and newspapers/blogs throughout the world.

He and his wife, Nan, have been married since 1986 and have three boys. Find resources and conference information at www.RonDeal.org.

# Get the Most out of
## *The Smart Stepfamily*!

For more resources and insight from Ron Deal, visit smartstepfamilies.com.

These eight sessions support *The Smart Stepfamily* book and are ideal for small groups, seminars, or individual couples. Ron Deal's personable presentation combines instruction and encouragement, offering useable solutions and tips for everyday living.

*The Smart Stepfamily DVD*

This interactive workbook is guaranteed to help you get the most out of *The Smart Stepfamily*. It includes discussion questions for before and after each DVD session, space to take notes, bonus reading material, leader instructions, and guidelines for facilitating effective groups.

*The Smart Stepfamily Participant's Guide*

**More Resources From Ron Deal**
When children are involved, dating gets complicated. In this book, Ron Deal guides single parents—and those who date them—through the emotional ups and downs of dating with kids, including how to navigate relationships, avoid potential pitfalls, and strengthen their families.

*Dating and the Single Parent*

# More Resources for the Smart Stepfamily

Because the role of stepmom can be confusing and lonely, Ron Deal teams up with experienced stepmom Laura Petherbridge to offer the hope, encouragement, and practical advice women need to survive *and thrive* as a stepmom.

*The Smart Stepmom* by Ron L. Deal and Laura Petherbridge

Here is the survival guide every stepfather needs to succeed. Ron Deal equips stepdads everywhere with advice on everything—from how to connect with your stepchildren to handling tricky issues such as discipline and dealing with your wife's ex.

*The Smart Stepdad* by Ron L. Deal

In this handy resource, divorce recovery expert and experienced stepmom Laura Petherbridge shares proven advice that will help you better understand your blended family and navigate the drama. These topically arranged, bite-sized tips are perfect for the busy stepmom, offering solutions she can immediately implement.

*101 Tips for the Smart Stepmom* by Laura Petherbridge

## BETHANYHOUSE

 Stay up-to-date on your favorite books and authors with our free e-newsletters. Sign up today at bethanyhouse.com.

 Find us on Facebook. facebook.com/BHPnonfiction

 Follow us on Twitter. @bethany_house